PARTY SYSTEMS AND COUNTRY GOVERNANCE

Schuldkraut
2011

Tufts
University

PARTY SYSTEMS AND COUNTRY GOVERNANCE

Kenneth Janda,
Northwestern University, USA
with
Jin-Young Kwak,
Konkuk University, Korea

Paradigm Publishers
Boulder • London

Thanks to the Russian journal Political Science for permission to reprint portions of Kenneth Janda's article, "'Governance,' Rule of Law and Party Systems," which appeared as К. Джанда. "Governance", верховенство закона и партийные системы, 113–142, in Политическая наука 4 (2010).

Published in the United States by Paradigm Publishers, 2845 Wilderness Place, Boulder, Colorado 80301 USA.
Paradigm Publishers is the trade name of Birkenkamp & Company, LLC, Dean Birkenkamp, President and Publisher.

Library of Congress Cataloging-in-Publication Data
Janda, Kenneth.
    Party systems and country governance / Kenneth Janda, with Jin-Young Kwak.
        p. cm.
    Includes bibliographical references and index.
    ISBN 978-1-59451-932-1 (hardcover : alk. paper) — ISBN 978-1-59451-933-8 (pbk. : alk. paper)
    1. Political parties.   2. Political indicators.   3. Comparative government.   I. Kwak, Jin-Young.   II. Title.

    JF2051.J36 2011
    324.2–dc22

                            2011008023

Printed and bound in the United States of America on acid-free paper that meets the standards of the American National Standard for Permanence of Paper for Printed Library Materials.

Designed by Staight Creek Bookmakers.
Typeset by Chris Davis, Mulberry Tree Enterprises.

15 14 13 12 11   5 4 3 2 1

To my wife, Ann Janda,
who has put up with my computer usage and
political parties research for fifty years

Contents

List of Boxes, Figures, and Tables

Chapter 3

Chapter 4

Chapter 5

Chapter 10

Chapter 11

Appendix C

Preface

This book targets three audiences: students, teachers, and researchers. It informs students how political party systems vary across the world and how these variations affect the performance of political systems in terms of country governance—a problematic concept that the book clarifies. It provides teachers with instructional material for courses on political parties, comparative politics, and research methods. (Appendix C suggests how students can undertake research projects explaining why certain countries perform much better—or much worse—than predicted by our analysis.) It invites researchers to consider more innovative approaches to cross-national analysis of party systems, studying a greater range of countries, considering new measures of party system competition, and suggesting that new measures be not merely proposed and mathematically adjusted through scholastic exchanges in professional journals but actually applied in testing party theory with empirical research. Accordingly, this study tests party system theory using original data on political party systems in 212 countries. These countries correspond to those scored on six Worldwide Governance Indicators, a monumental effort undertaken by researchers at the World Bank.

Writing for three audiences presents the problem of hitting the right level for different readers. Not unlike Goldilocks, some readers will find the text "too complicated," others "too simple," and perhaps too few "just right." Students may find it too complicated because the study, by its very nature, requires elementary statistical analysis. That cannot be avoided in a worldwide study that assesses the effects on country governance of party system traits such as competitiveness, aggregation, and stability.

Having taught elementary statistics to undergraduate students for nearly four decades, I believe that almost all students can learn the statistical concepts and analytical tools in this book. That includes standard deviation, z-scores, correlation analysis, and multiple regression. Each is clearly introduced in the context of research and explained in text boxes that those who already understand the content can skip. At every opportunity, I cater to students by explaining analytical concepts, often using everyday illustrations—for instance, using logarithms to compare Bill Gates's wealth with that of average wage earners. At one point, in Chapter 4, I warn that the following few pages require close attention, but the going should be smooth afterward. I pray that more readers will find the discussion too simple rather than too complicated.

The idea for this book originated in 2007 with Jin-Young Kwak, then chairperson of the Department of Political Science at Korea's Konkuk University, who proposed spending her 2007–2008 sabbatical year at Northwestern University. Her statement of proposed research exposed me seriously, for the first time, to the role of political parties in the (to me) confusing concept of governance. While working together during her sabbatical, Professor Kwak and I hammered out the idea of studying party systems, instead of individual parties, and using the Worldwide Governance Indicators as measures of country governance. We divided the 212 countries into two halves and began recording the percentages of seats won by the top three parties in two elections in every country. We then reported the results of our data collection in a paper at the 2009 Meeting of the Midwest Political Science Association.[1] After Professor Kwak returned to Konkuk University, we continued discussing the research via e-mail. Although she provided comments on the manuscript from abroad and deserves recognition for her substantial contributions early in the project, she should not be held responsible for the direction and shape of the analysis or its interpretation. This book was written with her invaluable assistance but not coauthored by her. I am accountable for any errors in fact or interpretation.

Julieta Suarez-Cao, while a PhD candidate at Northwestern University, offered her help on the project as reader and critic. At several points, she raised questions about theory and research that resulted in significant revisions in convention papers and the book manuscript. Along with Jin-Young Kwak, Suarez-Cao contributed to papers delivered at the 2010 meetings of the Midwest Political Science Association and the American Political Science Association.[2] Julius Parod, a sophomore political science major at Knox College, volunteered to read the entire manuscript during the summer of 2010. Having never taken a course in statistics, he was well-qualified to flag points at which the discussion was unclear or he had trouble understanding the methodology or theory. His helpful comments improved the presentation in several places.

My wife, Ann Janda, also read each chapter of the manuscript very carefully. She was professionally suited to this task as a former full-time Russian-language instructor at Loyola University; former bibliographer (unpaid) on my National Science Foundation–funded International Comparative Political Parties Project; former editor of the *SIGCHI Bulletin*, a quarterly publication of the Special Interest Group on Computer & Human Interaction; and for two decades Northwestern University's official representative to the Interuniversity Consortium for Political and Social Research. She found writing errors of omission and commission, caught gaps in logic and argument, and generally improved the presentation of material. I am very grateful for her scholarly help.

Many years ago I promised to write a textbook on elementary statistics and dedicate it to Ann. I never got around to doing that, so this book will have to serve instead.

We are grateful to the Russian journal *Political Science* for permission to reprint portions of Kenneth Janda's article titled "'Governance,' Rule of Law and Party Systems," which appeared as К. Джанда. "«Governance», верховенство закона и партийные системы," in *Политическая наука* 4 (2010): 113–142.

Notes

1. Kenneth Janda and Jin-Young Kwak, "Competition and Volatility in Parliamentary Party Systems for 212 Polities" (paper presented at the annual meeting of the Midwest Political Science Association, Chicago, Illinois, April 2–4, 2009).

2. Kenneth Janda, Jin-Young Kwak, and Julieta Suarez-Cao, "Party System Effects on Country Governance, I" (paper presented at the annual meeting of the Midwest Political Science Association, Chicago, Illinois, April 22–25, 2010); Kenneth Janda, Jin-Young Kwak, and Julieta Suarez-Cao, "Party System Effects on Country Governance, II" (paper presented at the annual meeting of the American Political Science Association, Washington, DC, September 2–5, 2010).

Introduction

Our book is titled *Party Systems and Country Governance*. Readers will have some idea of "party systems," but they may be unclear about the meaning of "country governance." Chapter 1 defines country governance as the extent to which a state delivers to its citizens the desired benefits of government at acceptable costs. Does the nature of a country's political party system (detailed in Chapter 6) affect the quality of its governance? Thomas Carothers, a leading authority on democratization and governance, thinks it does. The governmental role that parties perform, however, is far from clear. Carothers describes "the standard lament" about political parties as follows: They are corrupt and self-interested, do not stand for anything except winning elections, squabble with one another, and are ill prepared for governing.[1] In fact, he calls political parties the "weakest link" in establishing popular control of government in new or struggling democracies.[2] Nevertheless, Carothers says, "problematic, aggravating, and disappointing though they are, political parties are necessary, even inevitable. No workable form of democratic pluralism has been invented that operates without political parties."[3] Contemporary theorists agree that a modern state cannot practice democracy without competitive political parties.[4] A United Nations publication says, "In many countries today, political parties are an essential part of the apparatus of governance":

> Parties in a democratic system serve several purposes. They aggregate interests by persuading voters to support various issues, and they lend coherence to voter choices. They may mobilize the masses outside of elections. In conflict situations, they can be crucial in determining whether there is a move forward into recovery or a relapse back into hostilities. Once elected, parties play a major role in shaping public policy, securing resources and orienting the government around certain platforms. Parties also foster future political leaders and monitor elected representatives. An institutionalized party system can hold elected politicians accountable.[5]

Endorsing the importance of political parties in democratic governance, international and nongovernmental organizations have poured millions of dollars into party development under the rubric of democratic assistance.[6] These expensive party-aid efforts have generated mixed results. According to one scholar, African leaders have "only grudgingly permitted multiparty politics under donor pressure" against "a current of underlying skepticism," arguing that parties breed conflict, represent urban elites not the grass roots, and are themselves corrupt.[7] Another scholar sees the same skepticism in Asia: "Ironically, in the eyes of many people, political parties, the hallmark of modern democratic government, have become the biggest obstacles to democratic consolidation and good governance in much of democratic Southeast Asia."[8]

In truth, people across the world have a love-hate relationship with political parties. Most scholars value them highly for enabling popular control of government, but many leaders and citizens mistrust them.[9] As two experts write, "The widespread perception that parties are procedurally necessary for the effective functioning of democracy does not translate into their being widely supported or respected."[10] Ambivalent judgments about the role of parties in government appear in these conflicting statements by other party scholars. One praises their contributions to democratic theory—

> In representative democracies, political parties perform a variety of functions that maintain and foster democratic governance. Perhaps the most important role they play is that of a linkage between the governed and the governors.[11]

—but another thinks that parties have not delivered on their promised contributions:

> Some contemporary models of political parties reinforce the fears of early theorists that political parties would intervene between elected governments and the achievement of the public good.[12]

Does any body of research specify how parties affect the popular control of government? Not according to these comparative scholars: "But whilst there is a striking consensus on the importance of the actual or potential contribution parties can make to the democratization process and specifically to democratic consolidation, within the relevant literature there is not in fact any extensive body of writing that explicitly seeks to pin this contribution down."[13]

This book proposes and tests a theory of party system effects on country governance explicitly designed to "pin down" the contributions of political parties.

Normative or Empirical Theory?

Theories can be described as informed understandings created to explain events or outcomes. Some theories can be shown to be false, but no theory can ever be proven to be true. Throughout history, theories regarded as true have been replaced by others providing more satisfactory explanations of relevant events or outcomes. Political theories, attempting to explain politics, are commonly divided into two categories: normative (dealing with values) and empirical (dealing with facts). Normative political theory attempts to explain (in the sense of justifying values) how people and political institutions should behave. Empirical theory attempts to explain (in the sense of linking facts) how people and political institutions actually do behave.

Most Western comparative scholars, UN officials, and others engaged in promoting democratic government in developing countries are guided by a normative theory: It is good to have political parties competing to control government in open elections. That theory, or value judgment, reflects a modern democratic ideal for nation-states: Political parties that alternate in power should guide governments. In an often-quoted statement published decades ago, E. E. Schattschneider says, "The political parties created democracy and modern democracy is unthinkable save in terms of the parties."[14]

Normative theory asserts what is good—what we should value. Accordingly, it cannot be tested by observation and thus proven right or wrong. A normative theory that values political parties, however, also assumes the existence of an empirical relationship: Countries with competitive party systems perform better than those without them. In practice, this assumption has been accepted as true in the absence of testing to determine whether it is false. That is not too surprising. Theories often rely on empirical assumptions that are not completely true. In making road maps, for example, cartographers assume that the world is flat. The equation for the law of falling bodies assumes that they fall in a vacuum. Economists assume that individuals "act rationally"; they also assume that financial markets are informationally efficient—meaning that securities are priced and traded at their fair value.[15]

Sometimes—as in making maps and calculating how swiftly bodies fall—incorrect assumptions pose no real obstacle to producing correct results. At other times—as with the assumption of a rational market—serious consequences can flow from flawed assumptions. By and large, international efforts to promote party politics in developing countries have been guided by normative judgments relying on assumptions that have not been adequately tested through empirical research, if they are tested at all. They often go untested for three major reasons.

One stems from the value commitment to political parties in normative theory. Those who value political parties may think it obvious that countries are governed better when a reasonable number of stable political parties compete for votes in free elections—compared with countries that hold no elections, that have elections but no parties, or that have only one party. Why document the obvious?

Another reason flows from the difficulty of settling on research rules for acceptable answers. For example, how could one demonstrate that financial markets are informationally efficient? What evidence might show that democratic party systems perform better than nondemocratic systems? What do you mean by performance? How can performance be measured? One might even ask, What do you mean by a competitive party system? How can one identify and measure the characteristics of political party systems?

Yet a third reason has prevented determining whether countries with competitive party systems perform better than those without such systems. Even if scholars could settle on an acceptable research design, difficulties in collecting the necessary data might block the research. One might find adequate party system data on about thirty established democracies and on a like number of developing countries, but what about the more than one hundred remaining countries whose party systems are rarely studied systematically? And where would one find the matching country data on government performance?

The Theory to Be Tested

This study converts the underlying empirical assumption about the performance of political parties into an empirical political theory of party system effects on country governance. Chapter 6 formally presents the full theory, which consists of conditions assumed to be true and propositions to be tested. Here is an informal summary: A popularly elected government is more responsive to public opinion than one not popularly elected. Some governments, even elected governments, do not have political parties. A party government (even a one-party government) is more responsive to public opinion than a nonparty government. Political parties are formed to articulate social and economic interests in government. Political parties that control parliament seek to retain control. To the extent that elections decide control of parliament, governing parties respond to public opinion. Public opinion favors government policies that serve general interests more than policies serving special interests. General interests are served when governments deliver benefits that serve public values. Political parties contest elections to attract votes needed to win government offices. Competing to gain control of government, parties propose government actions designed to appeal to the electorate. The more regularly parties participate in elections, the more the electorate learns about the parties and their records of achievement. To the extent that stable political parties aggregate social and economic interests in competing for votes in popular elections, government becomes responsive to public opinion, and citizens enjoy the benefits of government.

From a set of seven assumptions in Chapter 6, we deduce four broad empirical propositions about party system effects on country governance:

1. Countries with popularly elected nonpartisan parliaments score higher on governance than those with unelected nonparty parliaments, which score lower on governance than those with parties in parliament.
2. The more competitive the party system, the better the country governance.
3. The more aggregative the party system, the better the country governance.
4. The more stable the party system, the better the country governance

That is the theory. It is an empirical theory with origins in normative theory. Whether the observable facts conform to the theory remains to be determined. That is the task of this book.

The Challenge of Country Governance

People generally recognize that country governments differ in their ability to deliver ordinary goods and services to their citizens. They see that some governments fare much better than others. Most people suspect that public rule is notoriously bad under dictators. For several years, *PARADE* magazine (a popular Sunday supplement to hundreds of U.S. newspapers)[16] has published an annual unscientific list of the world's ten "worst dictators." With brief comments on their countries' political problems, here is *PARADE*'s list of the worst dictators for 2009:

1. *Robert Mugabe, Zimbabwe:* Unemployment and inflation are high.
2. *Omar al-Bashir, Sudan:* Darfur remains a hotbed of violence.
3. *Kim Jong-Il, North Korea:* He runs the world's most repressive regime.
4. *Than Shwe, Myanmar:* He delayed access to aid after devastation.
5. *King Abdullah, Saudi Arabia:* This country has the most oppressed women in the world.
6. *Hu Jintao, China:* He controls all media and represses religion.
7. *Sayyid Ali Khamenei, Iran:* He permits the execution of juveniles.
8. *Isayas Afewerki, Eritrea:* There are no national elections, and he controls the media.

9. *Gurbanguly Berdymuhammedov, Turkmenistan:* He restricts religion and represses the media.
10. *Muammar al-Qaddafi, Libya:* Reports of torture are common.[17]

Regardless of whether these really were the world's ten worst dictators, most observers would place them at or near the top of any list of hard leaders.[18] Regardless of how nasty their autocratic regimes might be, however, all these dictators headed governments that kept some degree of order and control over civil life. Some countries, like Somalia, had no dictator but little or no government either.

According to the journal *Foreign Policy,* Somalia in 2009 was "a state governed only by anarchy."[19] For years, Somalia's lack of government allowed Somali pirates to seize with impunity ships sailing off its coast. In 2009, pirates attacked the *Maersk Alabama,* a container ship flying a U.S. flag, and kept its captain hostage for days before U.S. Navy SEAL marksmen shot his three captors and rescued him.[20] Somalia qualified as a failed state—one whose central government had little practical control over much of its territory. Scores of states with a billion or more inhabitants have either collapsed, are near collapse, or "are unable to provide even the most basic services for their citizens."[21] Some observers contended that Pakistan in 2009 also qualified as a failed state for submitting to Taliban insurgents in its Swat district and allowing them to impose their extreme version of religious sharia law instead of secular Pakistani law.[22]

In contrast to these examples of dictatorship and failed states, consider the Latin American country of Costa Rica, which abandoned its standing army in 1948 and entered a sustained period of democratic elections. Writing in 2009, *New York Times* columnist Thomas Friedman said, "More than any nation I've ever visited, Costa Rica is insisting that economic growth and environmentalism work together."[23] With more than 25 percent of the country's land in national parks or otherwise protected, Costa Rica's government policies have led to it generating more than 95 percent of its energy from renewable sources—hydroelectric power, wind, and geothermal.

Or consider the tiny land-locked nation of Bhutan, tucked between India and China in the Himalayas. Bhutan had been an absolute monarchy, where kings functioned as dictators, but in 2005 Bhutan's king announced that he would transform his country into a democracy.[24] He stimulated the creation of a party system, instructed citizens in voting and elections, and abdicated his throne in favor of his son, who headed a constitutional monarchy after Bhutan's first elections in 2008.[25] Bhutan also stood apart from other nations by proclaiming gross national happiness (GNH[26]) as a governmental goal, whereas other nations pursue gains in gross national product (GNP[27]).

On the other side of the world lies the island nation of Iceland, which, like Bhutan, is small. With about 300,000 people living on only 100,000 square kilometers, Iceland is actually twice Bhutan's physical size but has only half the population. Whereas Bhutan had been an absolute monarchy, Iceland claims the world's oldest continuous parliament, a history of multiparty politics, and competent democratic government. Until 2008, Icelanders enjoyed one of the highest incomes per capita in the world (more than twenty-five times that of Bhutan) as well as one of the most egalitarian distributions of wealth. Although priding itself on its "New Viking" aggressive economic policies in the early 2000s, Iceland suffered heavily in the 2008 global financial meltdown. Its currency plunged by about 50 percent in value, and the small country suffered losses estimated at $30,000 for every man, woman, and child.[28] In 2009, Iceland's voters ousted the free market Independence Party that had governed the country for two decades and replaced it with a governing coalition of the Social Democratic Alliance and the Left-Green Movement.[29]

Finally, consider the enormous country of China, which *PARADE* included in its list of dictatorships. Under one-party dictatorial rule by the Communist Party (led by Hu Jintao, *PARADE*'s number-six dictator), the Chinese government depended on substantial annual growth in GNP to satisfy the material needs of over 1 billion citizens. Confronted with the 2008 collapse in the world economy, its government launched a huge stimulus program in early 2009. China, with its centralized command economy, could coordinate spending and investment to a far higher degree than could the United States, which in February 2009 undertook its own controversial stimulus program. A World Bank economist quoted in the *Wall Street Journal* said, "China is unusual in that it has this incredible capacity to mobilize all its institutions."[30]

In contrast to China, the U.S. government, which operates under capitalism and a vigorous two-party system, faced more constraints in devising its stimulus plan. Most House Democrats supported President Barack Obama's plan, but Senate Republicans demanded and got spending reductions and forced more tax cuts.[31] China's Communist leaders encountered no serious opposition from Communist deputies in its one-party national assembly and swiftly launched its more coherent plan of monetary expansion and infrastructure spending. The chief executive officer of the U.S. company Caterpillar, which sells excavator equipment worldwide, said that China could launch construction projects more quickly: "It's something like nine months [in the United States] versus nine weeks in China."[32] In fact, the Chinese economy responded much more quickly than did the U.S. economy to their respective stimulus programs. In the summer of 2009, after both programs had operated for six months, the U.S. economy remained flat with rising unemployment, while the Chinese economy grew by nearly 8 percent. That July, a World Bank official said, "China will be among the first countries to lead the global economy out of this recession."[33]

Clearly, *PARADE*'s governmental dictatorships differ from the failed governments of Somalia and Pakistan—and both sets of countries differ from the democratic governments of Costa Rica (which practices conservation) and from the monarchical government of Bhutan (which promotes cultural values). Although Iceland, China, and the United States all pursued economic growth, they did so under very different party systems. Iceland operated under a multiparty system that decisively punished economic failure. China's one-party government could concentrate its resources on economic recovery without fear of losing power. The United States' two-party system forced the government to balance competing interests while trying to craft its economic policy.

Is it possible to meaningfully compare such diverse nations concerning how well they deliver the benefits of government? We think so. In recent years, social scientists have refined the concept of governance to allow such comparisons. This book uses country governance as a criterion for determining the effects of country party systems. Although we identify and explain the effects of two other major factors (country size and country wealth) on selected measures of governance, we do not claim to represent the complex relationships among all the variables that account for all the cross-country variance in governance. Instead, we focus on the independent effects of party systems (after controlling for country size and wealth) on country governance. In the language of research, the traits of party systems are our independent variables, and country governance is our dependent variable.

In effect, country governance serves as an indicator of government performance, a broad concept studied by others. Decades ago, Harry Eckstein identified four dimensions of performance: durability, civil order, legitimacy, and decisional efficacy.[34] Later, G. Bingham Powell Jr. used as aspects of political performance "citizen participation, government stability and mass violence."[35] More recently, Edeltraud Roller analyzed performance as effectiveness in major domestic policy areas—domestic security policy, economic policy, social policy, and environmental policy.[36] Although Powell's study of twenty-eight party systems in twenty-eight democracies uses very different indicators of governance, his comes closest to this study of parliamentary parties in 212 countries.

Overview of Research Design

Studies that compare politics in different countries typically employ either the most-similar- or most-different-systems design. The most-similar-systems design selects countries that are "as similar as possible with respect to as many features as possible."[37] By selecting a few countries that share many economic, cultural, and political characteristics, but that differ on one or more key variables, this design attempts to control for many important variables while observing the effects of the variable of interest. For example, research might focus on (1) Latin American (2) democracies (3) with a presidential form of government and (4) multiparty systems and then compare their citizens' satisfaction with government, depending on whether they have a federal or unitary form, perhaps theorizing that citizens are more satisfied with federal governments. This design has important merits. One problem is that it cannot adequately control for explanatory factors beyond the four selected (1 through 4).

Powell's study of twenty-eight democracies falls roughly into the most-similar-systems category. He selected "all independent nations of over one million persons that seemed to have both competitive elections and enfranchisement of the majority of citizens for a five-year period before and during the late 1960s."[38] By studying democratic governments with competitive political parties, Powell ran up against another problem of the most-similar design: It allows for no comparison with units left outside the analysis. Because Powell's study did not include countries with weak party systems or with no party systems, it could not disclose the effects of weak parties or no parties on government performance.

We follow the most-different-systems research design, which consists of comparing a large number of very different countries (ideally, every country) with maximally different party systems—competitive and noncompetitive, fragmented and aggregative, volatile and stable—and even countries without political parties. This design focuses on a common set of dependent variables (measures of country governance) and independent variables (measures of party systems) and ignores most of the countless other variables on which the countries differ.[39] Under the logic of this design, if the chosen independent variables have genuine effects on the dependent variables, they should be strong enough to show through the myriad of other differences among the countries—their ethnic and religious differences, their histories, and so on. These differences across many countries would essentially offset one another.

In keeping with this design, we analyze the data on six different indicators of country governance created by scholars at the World Bank for 212 countries in 2007.[40] We determine whether party system traits have any statistically significant effects on country governance across all countries. Although we draw heavily on quantitative data, we present relatively few tables. Instead, we display data graphically in reporting our findings. Moreover, we explain in simple terms alternative methods for scoring data, the meaning of a correlation coefficient, how to interpret a regression equation, and the gist of statistical significance. We think that our presentation is digestible for undergraduate students, even those who have never taken a course in statistics.

We supplement our quantitative analysis by citing where five countries score in the distribution of a summary measure of country governance, from top to bottom:

Iceland: the nation at the top of the 2007 World Bank mean governance scores

United States: a nation scoring high on governance but not at the top (#23)

Korea: a nation scoring near the twenty-fifth percentile, toward the top (#50)

Russia: a nation scoring near the seventy-fifth percentile, toward the bottom (#164)

Somalia: the nation scoring at the bottom of the World Bank scores (#212)

Our book consists of twelve chapters grouped into three parts. Part I, "The Nature of Country Governance," inquires in some detail into the origin and development of the term *governance*, discusses issues in conceptualizing and measuring country governance, and describes the Worldwide Governance Indicators.

Part II, "Environmental Effects on Country Governance," begins by considering whether the quality of country governance is a cause or an effect of environmental conditions. It contends that country governance is clearly affected by country size, which is usually determined long before any particular government is in place. It also argues that country wealth is a cause of country governance, especially in the short term. To assess the relative effects of country size and wealth on country governance, we conduct elementary statistical analysis. To explain the analysis to readers unfamiliar with correlation and regression analysis, we proceed slowly, describing with few formulas (but numerous boxes and graphs) the meanings of essential terms: correlation, statistical significance, regression coefficient, and explained variance. Understanding these terms is essential to understanding the data analysis, which shows strong and consistent effects of country size and wealth on country governance.

Part III, "Party System Effects on Country Governance," addresses the main topic in a series of chapters. This section explains the normative and empirical theory underlying the study. It also describes the data collected to test the theory and various ways to measure party systems. Relying on the statistical knowledge conveyed in Part II, a set of chapters assesses the effects of party systems on country governance, beginning with the twenty-three countries that have no parties. For the other 189 countries, the chapters assess the effects of party system competitiveness, aggregation, and stability. The final chapter reviews the theory and research. It concludes that party systems have significant and mostly consistent effects on improving country governance. The finding should hearten those in international agencies who have spent millions of dollars to strengthen political parties in developing countries on the normative assumption that strong, competitive, stable party systems promote countries' ability to deliver to citizens the benefits of government.

Notes

1. Thomas Carothers, *Confronting the Weakest Link: Aiding Political Parties in New Democracies* (Washington, DC: Carnegie Endowment for International Peace, 2006), 4.

2. Ibid., 13.

3. Ibid., 213.

4. See, for example, Peter Mair, "Comparing Party Systems," in *Comparing Democracies 2: New Challenges in the Study of Elections and Voting*, ed. Lawrence LeDuc, Richard G. Niemi, and Pippa Norris (London: Sage, 2002), 88–107.

5. Democratic Governance Group, *A Handbook on Working with Political Parties* (New York: United Nations Bureau for Development Policy, United Nations Development Programme, 2006), 9. See also Michelle Kuenzi and Gina Lambright, "Party Systems and Democratic Consolidation in Africa's Electoral Regimes," *Party Politics* 11 (July 2005): 423–446.

6. For a comprehensive survey of such aid programs, see Thomas Carothers, *Aiding Democracy Abroad: The Learning Curve* (Washington, DC: Carnegie Endowment for International Peace, 1999).

7. Edward R. McMahon, "Catching the 'Third Wave' of Democratization? Debating Political Party Effectiveness in Africa since 1980," *African and Asian Studies* 3 (2004): 295–320, at 295, 300–303.

8. Allen Hicken, "Stuck in the Mud: Parties and Party Systems in Democratic Southeast Asia," *Taiwan Journal of Democracy* 2 (December 2006): 23–46, at 25.

9. After analyzing trends in survey data in advanced industrial democracies, Russell J. Dalton and Steven Weldon find that "weakening party ties are nearly universal." See Dalton and Weldon, "Is the Party Over? Spreading Antipathy Toward Political Parties," *Public Opinion Pros* (May 2005), www.cses.org/resources/results/POP_May2005.htm.

10. Ingrid van Biezen and Michael Saward, "Democratic Theorists and Party Scholars: Why They Don't Talk to Each Other, and Why They Should," *Perspectives on Politics* 6 (March 2008): 21–35, at 21.

11. Richard Herrera, "The Origins of Opinion of American Party Activists," *Party Politics* 5 (April 1999): 237–252, at 237.

12. S. C. Stokes, "Political Parties and Democracy," *Annual Review of Political Science* 2 (1999): 243–267, at 263.

13. Vicky Randall and Lars Svåsand, "The Contribution of Parties to Democracy and Democratic Consolidation," *Democratization* 9 (2002): 1–10, at 3.

14. E. E. Schattschneider, *Party Government* (New York: Farrar and Rinehart, 1942), 1.

15. Justin Fox, *The Myth of the Rational Market* (New York: HarperCollins, 2009), xii–xiii.

16. According to its own website, *PARADE* magazine appears as a Sunday supplement to 530 U.S. newspapers, reaching over 74 million readers each week. See "A History of *PARADE*," Parade.com, www.parade.com/corporate/parade_history.html.

17. David Wallechinsky, "The World's 10 Worst Dictators," *PARADE*, March 22, 2009, 1. See www.parade.com/articles/editions/2009/edition_03-22-2009/

The-Worlds-10-Worst-Dictators.html. Wallechinsky's 2009 list contained eight of the ten rulers named in 2007, though in somewhat different order. Missing were Islam Karimov (Uzbekistan) and Bashar al-Assad (Syria). They were replaced by Isayas Afewerki (Eritrea) and Gurbanguly Berymuhammedov (Turkmenistan) in 2009. For the 2007 list, see www.parade.com/articles/editions/2007/edition_02-11-2007/Dictators.

18. *PARADE* listed another ten "dishonorable mentions." From eleven to twenty, they were Muammar al-Qaddafi, Libya; Bashar al-Assad, Syria; Teodoro Obiang Nguema, Equatorial Guinea; King Mswati III, Swaziland; Meles Zenawi, Ethiopia; Aleksandr Lukashenka, Belarus; Hosni Mubarak, Egypt; Raúl Castro, Cuba; Choummaly Sayasone, Laos; Idriss Déby, Chad.

19. Jeffrey Gettleman, "The Most Dangerous Place in the World," *Foreign Policy* (March–April 2009): 1.

20. Chad Bray, "Somali Is Charged with Piracy," *Wall Street Journal*, April 22, 2009, A3.

21. Ashraf Ghani and Clare Lockhart, *Fixing Failed States: A Framework for Rebuilding a Fractured World* (New York: Oxford University Press, 2008), 3–4.

22. Jane Perlez, "Taliban Seize Pakistan Area Nearer Capital," *New York Times*, April 23, 2009, 1.

23. Thomas L. Friedman, "(No) Drill, Baby, Drill," *New York Times*, April 12, 2009, WK8.

24. Somini Sengupta, "Line Up and Pick a Dragon: Bhutan Learns to Vote," *New York Times*, April 24, 2007, 1.

25. Peter Wonacott, "Smile Census: Bhutan Counts Its Blessings," *Wall Street Journal*, March 22, 2008, A1.

26. GNH promotes equitable and sustainable socioeconomic development, cultural and spiritual values, the natural environment, and good governance.

27. GNP expresses the value of all goods and services produced annually plus foreign income minus income earned by foreigners in the country.

28. John F. Burns, "At the Polls, Icelanders Punish Conservatives," *New York Times*, April 26, 2009, 8.

29. Charles Forelle, "Turning Page, Iceland Elects New Leaders," *Wall Street Journal*, April 27, 2009, A11.

30. Andrew Batson, "China Turns a Corner as Spending Takes Hold," *Wall Street Journal*, April 11, 2009, 1.

31. "A Breakdown of the Final Bill," *Wall Street Journal*, February 16, 2009, 7A.

32. James T. Areddy and Timothy Aeppel, "China's Stimulus Spurs U.S. Business," *Wall Street Journal*, April 30, 2009, 1.

33. Andrew Batson, "China Rises on Power of Stimulus," *Wall Street Journal*, July 16, 2009, 1.

34. Harry Eckstein, *The Evaluation of Political Performance: Problems and Dimensions* (Beverly Hills, CA: Sage Publications, 1971).

35. G. Bingham Powell Jr., "Party Systems and Political System Performance: Voting Participation, Government Stability and Mass Violence in Contemporary Democracies," *American Political Science Review* 75 (December 1981): 861–879, at 868.

36. Edeltraud Roller, *The Performance of Democracies: Political Institutions and Public Policy* (New York: Oxford University Press, 2005), 3.

37. Adam Przeworski and Henry Teune, *The Logic of Comparative Social Inquiry* (New York: Wiley Interscience, 1970), 32.

38. Powell, "Party Systems and Political System Performance," 861.

39. Ibid., 34–35.

40. See Worldwide Governance Indicators, http://info.worldbank.org/governance/wgi/index.asp.

Part I

The Nature of Country Governance

Chapter 1

Governance:
From Quaint Term to Hot Topic

In the 1950s, the term *governance* was regarded as quaint, and for years afterward it was discarded as obsolete.[1] It was not a topic listed in the seventeen-volume *International Encyclopedia of the Social Sciences* (1968) or even mentioned in its lengthy index.[2] The same was true for the eight-volume *Handbook of Political Science* published in 1975.[3] Governance did not reappear in social science with regularity until the 1980s.[4] By 1988, the term had become enshrined in its own journal, *Governance*.[5] Today, the word "governance" is almost as fashionable as "Google."[6] By 2007, the term even commanded its own encyclopedia: Mark Bevir's *Encyclopedia of Governance* ran more than 1,000 pages with over 550 entries.[7] By 2009, their work on economic governance earned a political scientist and an economist a share in the Nobel Prize for economics.[8]

Still, the concept of governance is problematic.[9] Ask six scholars in different fields what governance means, and you will probably get six different answers. The term has been applied to business firms, labor unions, social clubs, government corporations, and governments at all levels—especially to international organizations.[10] So one might think that all the various uses of governance at least pertain to how well human organizations are run—how well they function. But no, some writers look beyond the process of operating social organizations to their outcomes—what they accomplish. Yet another group dismisses both process and outcomes and defines governance essentially as the institutions that support the authoritative exercise of power. Then there are writers who use governance as a fancy term for government itself.[11]

What then is the correct meaning of governance? No single meaning is right and others wrong. Scholarly terms, such as *governance*, are merely labels applied to concepts, which are nothing more (but nothing less) than "succinct ways of expressing general ideas" about topics under study.[12] Although writers strive to express concepts succinctly (at least most writers do), concepts often reflect complex thought, leading writers to replace concepts with short terms. Terms and concepts themselves are neither right nor wrong. However, both can be more or less useful to thinking and inquiry.

Consider these alternative terms and associated concepts: *largest party*, defined as the political party holding a majority of seats in a parliament or legislature, and *fifth party*, defined as the fifth-place party in number of parliamentary seats. One can imagine how the largest party can affect country politics. One puzzles over what specific effects a fifth party might have. As a concept, fifth party is far less important to political science than largest party.

Just as concepts can be more or less useful in scholarly research, terms that label concepts can be more or less helpful in communication among scholars. Communication may suffer if the same term tags different concepts. Consider the term *gender*. To language teachers, this word has historically pertained to rules governing agreement between nouns, pronouns, and adjectives. To social scientists, it has more recently referred to role differences between men and women. Take a different example: *liberal*. This political term may mean a person who favors political and economic freedom; in contrast, it may describe a person who favors government action to help the poor. The two meanings of "gender" might not confuse writers because they are easily distinguishable in context. That is not so true with the different meanings of "liberal," especially when scholars attempt to communicate with the general public or with scholars outside their narrow field.

The term *governance* raises similar problems.[13] Free to apply labels they like to concepts they use, writers often mean quite different things when they write about governance. Readers concerned with the governance of nations may have to sort through writings on corporate governance that are irrelevant to their interest. Moreover, even readers studying country governance may be interested in quite different aspects of governance. So the issue in answering the question, "What is governance?" is whether its definition advances understanding. In other words, is the concept linked to the term useful to inquiry? If so, how?

This book advances an uncommon definition of governance that focuses on how well country governments function, and it accords with definitions proposed by a few other scholars.[14] The definition is political, in that it refers only to governments—challenging the depolitization characteristic in governance writings.[15] Moreover, it refers to governmental outcomes—not process or institutions—and separates countries that govern well from those that govern poorly. Country governance is defined as the *extent to which a state delivers to its citizens the desired benefits of government at acceptable costs.*[16]

Including the adjective "country" to modify "governance" should help distinguish the concept from its many other formulations.

The definition addresses two issues in assessing the quality of governance. It does not count as benefits of government things that citizens do not want (such as a massive dam or a nuclear power plant) or things that they might want (such as a military for national defense or a cross-national railroad) but only at reasonable costs. In either case, good governance is not at work. This conceptualization of governance, while uncommon, is similar to Marie Besançon's: "Governance is the delivery of political goods—beginning with security—to citizens of nation-states. Good governance results when nation-states provide a high order of certain political goods—when the nation-states perform effectively and well on behalf of their inhabitants."[17] It differs from hers by including the phrase "extent to which," making it a quantitative concept but still a complex one.[18] It is quantitative in that governance in any nation can range from bad to good. It is complex in that the quality of government can be judged according to different views about government benefits. The proposed definition is not necessarily better or even more useful than others in Bevir's *Encyclopedia of Governance*, but it is well suited to our purpose, which is to explain how party systems affect governments' performance. Because we are using country governance as our dependent variable, we need to probe further into its meaning. Researchers need to understand what they are trying to explain.

Issues in Defining Governance

This section reviews five different issues in defining governance: (1) What is the definition's domain of application—that is, to what class of organizations does it refer? (2) To what aspect of organization does it apply: structure, processes, or outcomes? (3) Does it support quantitative measurement? (4) Does it have qualitative dimensions? (5) How does governance relate to democracy?

What Is Governance's Domain of Application?

The word "governance" is not translatable in most foreign languages, which instead use the English.[19] In ordinary English, it has been linked to its root, "govern," meaning to direct and control the actions of people under a sovereign authority.[20] Many writers (mostly political scientists) still conceptualize governance in terms of governmental politics.[21] Let us call this the political application and contrast it with a more recent socioeconomic usage.

In an influential article in the mid-1990s, R. A. W. Rhodes stated, "The term 'governance' is popular but imprecise," having "at least six uses."[22] Rhodes himself favored a definition that extended beyond political sovereignty, saying "governance refers to 'self-organizing, interorganizational networks'" that "complement markets and hierarchies as governing structures for authoritatively allocating resources and exercising control and co-ordination." Later, he reformulated his definition, saying "*governance refers to self-organizing, interorganizational networks* characterized by interdependence, resource exchange, rules of the game and significant autonomy from the state."[23] His definition does not limit governance to interactions between states and citizens. Its domain actually favors nongovernmental applications; hence, we classify it as a socioeconomic usage. In fact, this is how the Nobel Prize Committee used the term in awarding the 2009 prize for work on economic governance.

As is his right, Rhodes (and the Nobel Committee) adopted the term for decision making in all social organizations. Rhodes's intent is clear from the title of his article, "The New Governance: Governing Without Government."[24] To his credit, Rhodes clearly stipulated an alternative concept and applied it to a line of research that generated numerous different but related socioeconomic definitions applying to the domain of all social organization.[25] Our interest in governance is more restricted. Interested in explaining the governance of nation states, we favor a narrower definition targeted to governmental politics, which returns to the term's historical definition. As one scholar put it, "Whilst governance occurs without government, government cannot happen without governance."[26]

Does Governance Refer to Structure, Process, or Outputs/Outcomes?

Scholars often study a given topic in different ways, so even those who apply the concept of governance to the political domain may focus on various aspects of the topic and thus define it differently. Some writers find it useful to view governance in terms of structure; others see it as a process, while still others look at the outputs or outcomes of the process.

Structure. Some definitions of governance focus on institutional structure. That typically occurs in writings that equate governance with government.[27] However, many socioeconomic definitions also focus on governing mechanisms, especially when they are not state institutions.[28] A clear example of a political definition built on a structural conception is reflected in the first sentence of the World Bank's definition: "Governance consists of the traditions and institutions by which authority in a country is exercised."[29] Later we will see that the World Bank expanded its definition, but its structural emphasis is clear.

Process. In contrast, consider definitions of governance that focus on process.[30] The European Union's concept of European governance refers to "the rules, processes and behaviour that affect the way in which powers are exercised at the European level, particularly as regards openness, participation, accountability, effectiveness and coherence."[31] Or consider the definition proposed by the United Nations Economic and Social Commission for Asia and the Pacific (UNESCAP), which said that governance means "the process of decision-making and the process by which decisions are implemented (or not implemented)."[32] Other definitions of government as process abound.[33]

In truth, the World Bank's definition, which focuses on structure, proceeds to include "the process by which governments are selected, monitored and replaced; the capacity of the government to effectively formulate and implement sound policies; and the respect of citizens and the state for the institutions that govern economic and social interactions among them." While it is not always easy to classify definitions of governance as focusing on structure or process, the effort helps uncover differences among the conceptualizations.

Outputs/Outcomes. Definitions of governance that focus on structure or process are quite different from those that focus on outputs or outcomes.[34] These similar terms relate to concepts that are similar themselves. According to a prominent international agency, "Outputs are defined as the goods or services produced by government agencies (e.g., teaching hours delivered, welfare benefits assessed and paid); outcomes are defined as the impacts on social, economic, or other indicators arising from the delivery of outputs (e.g., student learning, social equity)."[35] Both outputs and outcomes refer to the results of processes, but outputs represent more immediate results while outcomes represent longer-range consequences. B. Guy Peters ties the distinction between outputs and outcomes specifically to the measurement of governance:

> We will want to ask the extent to which the processes mentioned previously produced the capacity to govern, or a set of intermediate outputs that could then be related to actual governance. . . .
> [Then] we will want to measure the outcomes of the governance process. What has happened in society because of the interventions of government and the social factors involved with the efforts to govern?[36]

Peters appears to favor measuring governance in terms of outcomes, saying that the basic question for measuring governance "is whether governance has been successful, and indeed, whether governance . . . has actually occurred."[37]

Other writers have also opted to define governance in terms of outcomes. Thomas Remington defines governance "as the provision of public goods and services including secure property rights as well as a minimum of social protection."[38] We find conceptualizing governance in terms of outcomes especially suited to explaining variations in country governance.

Does the Concept of Governance Support Quantitative Measurement?

Scholars commonly write about good governance.[39] A recent book on this topic defines it as expressing "approval not only for a type of government (usually democracy) and its related values (for example respect for human rights) but also for certain kinds of additional components."[40] Presumably, good governance stands opposed to bad governance—while other shades of governance vary from good to bad. Unfortunately, many definitions of governance (especially those that focus on structure and process) do not lend themselves to quantitative measurement—that is, distinguishing less from more. For example, consider Rhodes's definition of governance as comprising "self-organizing, interorganizational networks" that "complement markets and hierarchies as governing structures for authoritatively allocating resources and exercising control and co-ordination." It is hard to conceive of self-organizing networks as ranging from less to more. That does not seem sensible. Or consider the UNESCAP definition of governance as "the process of decision-making and the process by which decisions are implemented (or not implemented)." Can one view process as ranging from less to more? It is not clear what more process might be—or that more process is better than less process.

There is a straightforward way to compare countries on governance, but it would not satisfy many researchers. If we adopt a standard political definition in English dictionaries—directing and controlling the actions of people under a sovereign authority[41]—then governance can be measured by the extent to which citizens are directed and controlled. A totalitarian nation would rate high on governance and an anarchic society low. But few would be satisfied with this view of governance, which might result in scoring the ten so-called worst dictatorships discussed in the introduction as high on governance. It is inadequate to consider simply the amount, or quantity, of governance. For comparative political research, we must consider quantitative variations in different outcomes of governance.

We need a quantitative concept of governance that supports distinguishing bad from good governance outcomes along some implicit measurement scale. One means of providing for measurement in a concept is to incorporate the phrase "extent to which" in its definition. In defining governance as the extent to which certain government outcomes occur, we provide for measuring governance along a scale of bad to good. By requiring that the outcomes be desired by citizens, we call them benefits of government. These considerations underlie our quantitative definition of country governance as the extent to which a state delivers desired benefits of government to citizens at acceptable costs.[42]

Within the United States, many people—even governmental leaders—question the role that government can play in benefiting its citizens. When

President Ronald Reagan delivered his first inaugural address in 1981, the country was experiencing a major economic recession. Reagan acknowledged the problem his new government faced: "These United States are confronted with an economic affliction of great proportions. We suffer from the longest and one of the worst sustained inflations in our national history. It distorts our economic decisions, penalizes thrift, and crushes the struggling young and the fixed-income elderly alike. It threatens to shatter the lives of millions of our people." Then the elected leader of the U.S. government famously proclaimed, "In this present crisis, government is not the solution to our problem; government is the problem." Three decades later, when the nation faced the threat of a financial meltdown in September 2008, a fellow Republican, President George W. Bush, presided over a massive $700 billion government bailout of troubled banks. The bailout did not end the economic decline, but it did avoid the feared meltdown. Bush's resort to government action recalled President Franklin D. Roosevelt's 1933 decision to stop the panicky run on banks by closing them for four days. Putting the banks under government control when they reopened, he effectively ended the bank run.

Despite the positive effects of government action in 1933 and 2008, many Americans doubt government's efficiency and effectiveness. Even after Congress's apparently successful prevention of financial meltdown in September 2008, only 57 percent of Americans polled in December said that they could "trust the United States government to do what is right" versus 43 percent who thought otherwise.[43] Nevertheless, except for anarchists and ardent tea partiers (see Box 1.1), most citizens in the United States and abroad admit that government delivers certain benefits. Sanitation and safe drinking water, roads and bridges, police protection and the administration of justice, public education and financial regulation—these might be on everyone's list of government benefits. People will differ, however, in the value they place on creating parks, providing unemployment compensation, caring for the poor, ensuring health care, and so on. They will differ sharply over whether government should promote religion, allow abortion, censor sexually oriented media, and so on.

Because citizens, especially those in different cultures, value government services very differently, they will not agree on any comprehensive list of government benefits in the form of specific policies or outcomes. Perhaps they can agree on a relatively small set of universal material values, such as providing for sanitation and clean drinking water or delivering adequate electricity twenty-four hours a day, seven days a week. Such benefits, however, may depend more on a country's economic development than on its quality of government. The task is to arrive at some universally prized higher-level values that are normally associated more with the actions of government than economics. These higher-level values, which are necessarily more abstract, we can call metavalues, with "meta" meaning "beyond," "transcending," or

Box 1.1: A Land Without Government

Joel Pett, *Lexington Herald–Leader*, CartoonArts International, *New York Times*, April 19, 2009, WK2. Used with the permission of Joel Pett and the Cartoonist Group. All rights reserved.

"more comprehensive." In principle, we can measure metavalues as having been more or less achieved. By conceiving of government benefits in terms of widely shared metavalues, we can hope to reach more agreement in measuring governance across countries.[44]

Does the Concept of Governance Support Qualitative Dimensions?

Our quantitative conceptualization also recognizes governance's qualitative dimensions. It measures qualities of governance along dimensions of various metavalues deemed to be benefits of government. For example, one universally praised benefit of government (except by anarchists) is the rule of law; another is political stability. Both illustrate distinct qualities of governance. That some countries can slight the rule of law yet enforce political stability indicates that these outcomes are distinct. In principle, one should be able to rate individual countries separately for the extent to which they promote the rule of law and ensure political stability.

One can think of several benefits of government at the level of metavalues that represent qualities of governance. Although the World Bank (as quoted above) formally defined governance in terms of structure and process, it actually created a set of Worldwide Governance Indicators (WGIs) for 212 countries in terms of six specific metavalue outcomes: (1) Government Effectiveness, (2) Rule of Law, (3) Control of Corruption, (4) Regulatory Quality, (5) Political Stability and Absence of Violence, and (6) Voice and Accountability.[45] As the next chapter details, we adopt the six Worldwide Governance Indicators of the qualities of governance to operationalize our concept of governance.[46] Although some researchers have criticized them as biased toward business and not measuring what they claim to measure,[47] these indicators are widely regarded as the best and most comprehensive cross-country data on governance.[48] They will serve as our measures of country governance.

In the language of research (and as Chapter 3 explains), we regard the WGI's six different qualities of governance as dependent variables. That is, we hope to explain variation in countries' scores on the qualities of governance according to variation in their scores on a set of independent variables: country size, wealth, and party system traits. These are independent of the governance scores because they occur prior to them. In contrast, the governance scores are dependent on country size, wealth, and party system traits. By treating governance scores as dependent variables, we depart from much existing empirical research, which usually regards governance scores as independent (causal) variables that explain cross-country variation in international investment, policy reforms, economic growth, and societal development.[49]

How Does Governance Relate to Democracy?

Poets and philosophers may have more interest in the quality of government than its form (see Box 1.2), but others think that the form of government is important too. They may see a similarity between governance (especially as we have defined it) and democracy. If anything, there are even more definitions of democracy than of governance.[50] After reviewing numerous ones, Austin Ranney and Willmoore Kendall noted "general agreement" on the simple proposition "that a democratic government should do what the people want it to do and should not do anything they don't want it to do."[51] Accordingly, one popular understanding holds that democratic government conforms to public opinion. If country governance means "the extent to which a state delivers the desired benefits of government to citizens," is not governance similar to democracy?

We grant that the element of responsiveness to public opinion enters our definition of governance. Most scholars, however, conceive of democracy not in terms of policy outputs or social outcomes but in terms of process—in terms of government procedures rather than substantive results.[52] Some writers seek to combine the element of democratic process with the element of

---

Box 1.2: A Poet and a Philosopher View Government

In his *Essay on Man*, eighteenth-century British poet Alexander Pope wrote,
   For forms of government let fools contest;
   Whate'er is best administer'd is best.
   People who downplay the importance of governmental form often quote these lines.
   In *Leviathan*, seventeenth-century British philosopher Thomas Hobbes described life without government as existence in a "state of nature." Without rules, people would live as predators, stealing and killing for their personal benefit. In his classic phrase, life would be "solitary, poor, nasty, brutish, and short." (Think Somalia.) Hobbes believed that only an all-powerful ruler with unquestioned authority could protect the weak against the strong. He named his all-powerful government "Leviathan," after a biblical sea monster. Those who favor public order, regardless of governmental form, quote Hobbes.

---

beneficial governmental results to form a concept of democratic governance. This is how Scott Mainwaring and Timothy Scully address the issue:

> Democratic governance is conceptually distinct from the quality of democracy and the quality of governance. Democratic governance is mostly a top-down phenomenon that refers to how well democratic government and the state in a democratic regime are functioning. By contrast, the quality of democracy refers to the "democraticness" of the political regime. Most studies of the quality of democracy focus exclusively on democracy's procedural aspects, whereas good democratic governance also involves policy results. It means governing not only democratically, but also effectively. Our focus also differs from analyses of effective governance in general because we specifically analyze democratic governance—that is, good governance under democracy.[53]

Scholars have produced scores of studies on democratic governance. Many do not observe the clear distinction between democracy and governance drawn above by Mainwaring and Scully. Others cloud the distinction by using related terms, such as *responsible governance*,[54] *collaborative governance*,[55] or even *good governance* involving "equality of participation in decision making."[56]

Like Mainwaring and Scully, we explicitly distinguish between governance as outcomes versus democracy as a process involving widespread citizen participation and competition among elites. In fact, some scholars see "tension between governance and democracy" as nonmajoritarian (undemocratic) institutions sometimes produce better governmental outcomes (often economic outcomes) than democratic institutions.[57] Given that this book is about the effects of party systems on country governance and that democracy is explicitly linked to the presences of strong, competitive political parties, we avoid the terminology of democratic governance. Instead, we seek to determine whether party systems contribute to country governance—as proposed in both normative and empirical political theory.

Summary and Conclusion

Above we cited Rhodes's 1996 article on "governing without government. The next year Rhodes published *Understanding Governance,* which expanded on the "new governance." It stressed the rise and influence of policy networks, the increased influence of nonstate actors in making and implementing public policy, and the reduced authority (hollowing out) of the "core executive" in determining public policy.[58] As interpreted by a sympathetic scholar, "The new governance refers to the apparent spread of markets and networks . . . [and] points to the varied ways in which the information authority of markets and networks constitutes, supplements, and supplants the formal authority of governments."[59]

We return to the traditional dictionary definition of governance in terms of sovereign authority of states. For us, that is its domain of application. We judge governance according to its outcomes, not institutional structures or processes. We also view it as a quantitative concept, capable of measurement along an implicit scale of bad to good. Because any government produces many different outcomes, it is also a multidimensional concept. We regard the World Bank's six indicators of the qualities of governance as a suitable operationalization of multiple metalevel qualities of governance. We distinguish between governance as reflecting governmental outcomes and democracy as reflecting governmental processes or procedures. Those are all conceptual aspects of understanding governance. We begin the empirical side of our study by discussing the measurement of country governance.

Notes

1. Andrew Taylor, "Governance," in *Contemporary Political Concepts: A Critical Introduction,* ed. Georgina Blakeley and Valerie Bryson (Sterling, VA: Pluto Press, 2002), 35–53.

2. *International Encyclopedia of the Social Sciences* (New York: Macmillan and The Free Press, 1968).

3. Fred I. Greenstein and Nelson W. Polsby, eds., *Handbook of Political Science* (Reading, MA: Addison-Wesley, 1975).

4. Mark Bevir, *Key Concepts in Governance* (Los Angeles: Sage Publications, 2009), 1–9. See also Cynthia Hewitt de Alcántara, "Uses and Abuses of the Concept of Governance," *International Social Science Journal* 50, no. 155 (1998): 105–113.

5. *Governance: An International Journal of Policy, Administration and Institutions* is now published by Wiley Interscience in association with the International Political Science Association's Research Committee on the Structure and Organization of Government. The first issue in January 1988 described it as "a journal of comparative executive politics" (ii). Its twenty-second volume appeared in January 2009.

6. A Google search for "governance" generates about 50 million hits. Some writers put "governance" in the titles of their works but don't mention it much, if at all, in their texts. See Matthew Shapiro, "A Cross-National Study of Governance and the Sources of Innovation: The Determinants and Effects of International R&D Collaboration" (paper presented at the annual meeting of the Midwest Political Science Association, Chicago, Illinois, April 3–6, 2008).

7. Mark Bevir, *Encyclopedia of Governance*, 2 vols. (London: Sage Reference Publication, 2007). This work contains over "625,000 words written by some 250 international experts" (xxxvi).

8. Political scientist Elinor Ostrom and economist Oliver Williamson won the prize for their studies of rules that govern human interactions. According to the Nobel Committee's statement of October 12, 2009, "Oliver Williamson has formulated a theory of the firm as a conflict resolution mechanism and Elinor Ostrom has subsequently demonstrated how self-governance is possible in common pools."

9. G. G. Candler's own keyword search in the electronic database JSTOR found "little interest in the concept prior to the mid/late 1990s," after which "governance suddenly became important," or "(more likely) the term reflects old wine in new bottles" and renames a phenomenon known as systems theory. See Candler, "Governance, Governança, Gouvernance . . . or Systems Theory?" (paper presented at the annual meeting of the Midwest Political Science Association, Chicago, Illinois, April 22–25, 2010).

10. Hewitt de Alcántara, "Uses and Abuses of the Concept of Governance."

11. Andrew Taylor notes that some writers "further obscure" the meaning of governance by using it as a synonym for government; see his "Governance" at 36–37. Thomas G. Weiss makes the same point in "Governance, Good Governance and Global Governance: Conceptual and Actual Challenges," *Third World Quarterly* 21, no. 5 (2000): 795–814. For examples of such usage, see Matthew Todd Bradley, "'The Other': Precursory African Conceptions of Democracy," *International Studies Review* 7 (September 2005): 407–431; Martin Brusis, "Europeanization, Party Government, or Legacies? Explaining Executive Governance in Bulgaria, the Czech Republic, and Hungary," *Comparative European Politics* 2 (August 2004): 163–184; Anna Grzymala-Busse, "Political Competition and the Politicization of the State in East Central Europe," *Comparative Political Studies* 36 (December 2003): 1123–1147.

12. Georgina Blakeley and Valerie Bryson, eds. *Contemporary Political Concepts: A Critical Introduction* (Sterling, VA: Pluto Press, 2002), 1.

13. For a penetrating analysis of "governance" in the sociology of knowledge, see Claus Offe, "Governance: An 'Empty Signifier'?" *Constellations* 16 (December 2009): 550–562.

14. Marie Besançon, *Good Governance Rankings: The Art of Measurement*, World Peace Foundation Reports 36 (Cambridge, MA: World Peace Foundation, 2003), 1; Jamus Jerome Lim, "Governance Indicators in the Social Sectors" (paper presented at the annual meeting of the Midwest Political Science Association, Chicago, Illinois, April 2–4, 2009); Thomas F. Remington, "Democracy, Governance, and Inequality: Evidence from the Russian Regions" (paper presented at the annual meeting of the Midwest Political Science Association, Chicago, Illinois, April 3–5, 2008).

15. Offe critically reviews the "depolitization of the governance approach" in "Governance: An 'Empty Signifier'?"

16. For a structurally similar definition applied to governance at the microlevel, see Lim, "Governance Indicators in the Social Sectors." He defines microlevel governance as "the extent to which social, political, and institutional structures successfully align the incentives of actors with the overall objectives for which these structures were designed (or evolved) to accomplish" (3). Mark E. Warren says, "The democratic potentials of governance reside in the potentially responsive linkages between what governments do and what citizens receive," in "The Concept of Governance-Driven Democratization" (paper presented at the annual meeting of the Midwest Political Science Association, Chicago, Illinois, April 2–4, 2009).

17. Besançon, *Good Governance Rankings*, 1.

18. Jamus Jerome Lim also uses this phrase in his related definition of microgovernances in "Governance Indicators in the Social Sectors," 3.

19. Offe, "Governance: An 'Empty Signifier'?" 550.

20. This is the first definition listed in the venerable *Oxford University English Dictionary* (Oxford: Oxford University Press, 1937) and the first in the newer *American Heritage Dictionary of the English Language*, 3rd ed. (Boston: Houghton Mifflin, 1992). It is also the historical usage noted by H. K. Colebatch, "Policy Work and the Construction of Governing" (paper presented at the 21st World Congress of the International Political Science Association, Santiago, Chile, July 12–16, 2009).

21. See Taylor, "Governance," 37–40.

22. R. A. W. Rhodes, "The New Governance: Governing Without Government." *Political Studies* 44 (1996): 652–667, at 652. He writes that governance can refer to "the minimal state; corporate governance; the new public management; 'good governance'; socio-cybernetic systems; and self-organizing networks."

23. R. A. W. Rhodes, *Understanding Governance* (Philadelphia: Open University Press, 1997), 15. Emphasis in the original.

24. Ibid.

25. The European Union noted the need "for an all-embracing concept capable of conveying diverse meanings not covered by the traditional term 'government.'" See "What Is Governance?" European Commission, http://ec.europa.eu/governance/governance/index_en.htm. Bevir's *Encyclopedia of Governance* certainly endorses its "all-embracing" interpretation.

26. Taylor, "Governance," 37.

27. Bevir says in *Encyclopedia of Governance*, "Governance can seem to be just a new term for government. However, there are differences between them. Conceptually, governance is less orientated to the state than is government, and it evokes the conduct of governing at least as much as it does the institutions of government" (xxxvii).

28. Gerry Stoker, "Governance As Theory: Five Propositions," *International Social Science Journal* 50, no. 155 (1998): 17–28. See also J. Kooiman and M. Van Vliet, "Governance and Public Management," in *Managing Public Organisations*, ed. K. Eliassen and J. Kooiman, 2nd ed. (London: Sage, 1993).

29. Worldwide Governance Indicators, http://info.worldbank.org/governance/wgi/index.asp. In 1992, however, the World Bank defined governance quite differently, saying, "A general definition of governance is the 'exercise of authority, control, management, power of government.' A more relevant definition for Bank purposes is the management of a country's economic and social resources for development." See World Bank, *Governance and Development* (Washington, DC: World Bank, 1992), 3.

30. B. Guy Peters, "Measurement of Governance," in Blakeley and Bryson, *Contemporary Political Concepts*, 554–558.

31. Ibid.

32. "What Is Good Governance?" United Nations Economic and Social Commission for Asia and the Pacific, www.unescap.org/pdd/prs/ProjectActivities/Ongoing/gg/governance.asp.

33. Other examples of governance defined as process include "systems of rule, as the purposive activities of any collectivity that sustains mechanisms designed to insure its safety, prosperity, coherence, stability, and continuance." See James N. Rosenau, "Change, Complexity and Governance in Globalizing Space," in *Debating Governance: Authority, Steering and Democracy*, ed. J. Pierre (Oxford: Oxford University Press, 2000), 167–200, at 171.

34. Stoker, "Governance As Theory," 17.

35. "Outputs and Outcomes," "Glossary of Statistical Terms," Organization of Economic and Cultural Development, http://stats.oecd.org/glossary/detail.asp?ID=7311.

36. Peters, "Measurement of Governance," 556–557.

37. Ibid.

38. Remington, "Democracy, Governance, and Inequality," 6. See also Joel D. Aberbach and Bert Rockman, "Does Governance Really Matter—and If So, How?" *Governance* 5 (April 1992): 135–152.

39. Weiss, "Governance, Good Governance and Global Governance"; Andrew Taylor, "The Strategic Impact of the Electoral System and the Definition of 'Good' Governance," *British Politics* 2 (April 2007): 20–44; Ruth V. Aguilera and Alvaro Cuervo-Cazurra, "Codes of Good Governance Worldwide: What Is the Trigger?" *Organization Studies* 25, no. 3 (2004): 417–446.

40. B. C. Smith, *Good Governance and Development* (New York: Palgrave, 2007), 4.

41. *Oxford University English Dictionary* and *American Heritage Dictionary of the English Language*, 3rd ed.

42. After formulating our definition, we encountered a similar definition in Besançon, *Good Governance Rankings*, 1. She says, "Governance is the delivery of political goods—beginning with security—to citizens of nation-states. Good governance results when nation-states provide a high order of certain political goods—when the nation-states perform effectively and well on behalf of their inhabitants."

43. A December 17–21, 2008, poll of 1,000 registered voters asked, "How much do you trust the United States government to do what is right—a great deal, some,

not very much, or not at all?" In percentages, the responses were 11 "a great deal," 46 "some," 36 "not very much," and 7 "not at all." See Andy Barr, "Poll Finds Low Trust in Feds," *Politico*, January 14, 2009, www.politico.com/news/stories/0109/17424.html.

44. Neil Walker and Gráinne de Búrca, "Reconceiving Law and New Governance" (EUI Working Paper, Law 2007/10, European University Institute, San Domenico de Fiesole, Italy, 2007).

45. World Bank, *A Decade of Measuring the Quality of Governance* (Washington, DC: World Bank, 2006). See Worldwide Governance Indicators, http://info.worldbank.org/governance/wgi/index.asp.

46. To "operationalize" a concept is to identify specific empirical indicators used to measure it in research.

47. Marcus J. Kurtz and Andrew Schrank, "Growth and Governance: Models, Measures, and Mechanisms," *The Journal of Politics* 69, no. 2 (May 2007): 538–554; Sandra Botero and Katherine Schlosse, "What We Talk About When We Talk About Governance: Measurement and Conceptual Issues in the World Governance Indicators" (paper presented at the annual meeting of the Midwest Political Science Association, Chicago, Illinois, April 22–25, 2010).

48. Steven Radelet said they are "the best set of governance indicators currently available" in *Challenging Foreign Aid: A Policymaker's Guide to the Millennium Challenge Account* (Washington, DC: Center for Global Development, 2003), 34.

49. Christiane Arndt and Charles Oman, *Uses and Abuses of Governance Indicators* (Paris: Development Centre of the Organisation for Economic Co-Operation and Development, 2006), chap. 1, "Why All the Interest in Governance," 15–19.

50. David Collier and Steven Levitsky, "Research Note: Democracy with Adjectives: Conceptual Innovation in Comparative Research," *World Politics* 49 (April 1997): 430–451; Tatu Vanhanen, *Democratization: A Comparative Analysis of 170 Countries* (London: Routledge, 2002), 48–49.

51. Austin Ranney and Willmoore Kendall, *Democracy and the American Party System* (New York: Harcourt Brace and Company, 1956), 28.

52. Kenneth Janda, Jeffrey Berry, and Jerry Goldman, *The Challenge of Democracy* (Boston: Wadsworth, 2009), 32–37.

53. Scott Mainwaring and Timothy R. Scully, "Latin America: Eight Lessons for Governance," *Journal of Democracy* 19 (July 2008): 113–127, at 113–114.

54. Steven G. Kovan, *Responsible Governance: A Case Study Approach* (Armonk, NY: M. E. Sharpe, 2008).

55. Arwin van Buuren and Jurian Edelenbos, "Collaborative Governance," in Bevir, *Encyclopedia of Governance*, 104–106.

56. Michael D. Mehta, "Good Governance," in Bevir, *Encyclopedia of Governance*, 359–362, at 359.

57. Mark Bevir, "Governance," in Bevir, *Encyclopedia of Governance*, 379.

58. Rhodes, *Understanding Governance*. Recently, Rhodes published "Understanding Governance: Ten Years On," *Organization Studies* 28 (2007): 1243–1264.

59. Bevir, "Governance," 368.

Chapter 2

Science and Art in Measuring Country Governance

"If you cannot measure it, you cannot improve it." So supposedly said Lord Kelvin, the nineteenth-century British physicist who devised a scale to measure absolute temperature. On the Kelvin scale, $0°$ represents the complete absence of heat, when all molecular action theoretically ceases. (That point corresponds to $-459.67°$ Fahrenheit and $-273.15°$ Celsius.) Today, the Kelvin scale is accepted internationally and used widely in scientific research. Granting that measuring country governance is a difficult task, we doubt that it is more challenging in the twenty-first century than measuring thermodynamic temperature was in the nineteenth century. If people want to improve country governance, they must first measure it. Like creative artists, they must be imaginative in choosing aspects of governance to measure.[1] As social scientists, they must be skilled in employing research methods to pin numbers on the chosen phenomena. In the measurement process, scholars will improve our understanding of governance—even if their efforts are imperfect.

Attempts to measure narrow aspects of governmental performance in the United States have a long history in the field of public administration, but such efforts were rarely, if ever, described as measuring state governance.[2] As interest in the concept of governance grew in the late 1980s, scholars and practitioners became involved in its measurement across countries. One of the earliest and most sustained efforts was begun in 1991 by scholars at the World Bank.[3] In 1996, its researchers began to collect cross-national data more systematically and to generate indicators of governance.[4] Other organizations soon started collecting cross-national data for similar purposes.

By 2003, interest had spread, leading Harvard's John F. Kennedy School of Government to sponsor "The Conference on Measuring Governance." A report on the conference listed forty-seven data sets pertaining to different ways of measuring governance across countries.[5]

Even those who agree with our definition of governance (the extent to which a state delivers to citizens the desired benefits of government at acceptable costs) may disagree over which benefits of government are desirable. Some people desire government that produces an equitable distribution of wealth, while others favor government that encourages economic inequality in order to promote economic growth. Some people desire government that encourages literacy among all citizens, while others see little benefit in educating women. A major challenge for measuring government across countries throughout the world is to develop measures that also travel across cultures (e.g., socialist versus capitalist, Christian versus Islamic).

As mentioned in Chapter 1, citizens in different cultures often disagree on any comprehensive list of government benefits in the form of specific policies or outcomes. Chapter 1 also argues that we can meet this measurement challenge by identifying some comprehensive, universally accepted values called metavalues that relate to specific qualities of governance—for example, ensuring citizen safety, responding to public opinion, and eliminating public corruption. There is no finite list of key values or functions of government, and different scholars may come up with different lists.[6] Fortunately, scholars at the World Bank, who created what are widely recognized as the best measures of country governance, artfully focused on metavalues that travel well across cultures. The measures of government used in this book rely solely on the results of their monumental, multiyear effort, "A Decade of Measuring the Quality of Governance."[7]

An Overview of the Worldwide Governance Indicators Project

The Worldwide Governance Indicators (WGI) project originated in the Research Department of the World Bank in the late 1990s.[8] Daniel Kaufmann and Aart Kraay launched the effort, assisted initially by Pablo Zoido-Lobatón and later by Massimo Mastruzzi.[9] Accordingly, the measures are sometimes called the KK, KKZ, or KKM indicators, and we will refer to the most recent authors as KKM. The project started with about 150 countries but had expanded to 212 by 2006. These 212 countries (or polities) include not only all 192 nations in the United Nations but 20 nonmember nations (such as Taiwan) and some entities (such as Guam and Hong Kong) not normally regarded as independent nations.

KKM wrote frequently and at length about their project's methodology in documents freely available via the Internet.[10] They detailed their sources of information, discussed issues of data quality control, and published estimates of error rates for individual indicators. While these details are important, they lie beyond the scope of this chapter, which seeks only to describe the methodology adequately for readers to understand how KKM measured governance. Readers who wish to learn more should consult the WGI Internet site, especially KKM's responses to their critics.[11]

Country governance is inherently a complex concept with countless aspects. Selecting some to study demands artistic insight and imagination as much as scientific knowledge. KKM chose just six metaqualities of country governance to measure in the Worldwide Governance Indicators:

Rule of Law (RL): measuring perceptions of the extent to which agents have confidence in and abide by the rules of society, particularly the quality of contract enforcement, property rights, the police, and the courts, as well as the likelihood of crime and violence

Government Effectiveness (GE): measuring perceptions of the quality of public services, of the civil service and the degree of its independence from political pressures, and of policy formulation and implementation, as well as the credibility of the government's commitment to such policies

Control of Corruption (CC): measuring perceptions of the extent to which public power is exercised for private gain, including both petty and grand forms of corruption, as well as "capture" of the state by elites and private interests

Regulatory Quality (RQ): measuring perceptions of the ability of the government to formulate and implement sound policies and regulations that permit and promote private-sector development

Voice and Accountability (VA): measuring perceptions of the extent to which a country's citizens are able to participate in selecting their government, as well as freedom of expression, freedom of association, and a free media

Political Stability and Absence of Violence (PS): measuring perceptions of the likelihood that the government will be destabilized or overthrown by unconstitutional or violent means, including politically motivated violence and terrorism[12]

The perceptions underlying the six Worldwide Governance Indicators came from individuals or firms with firsthand knowledge of the country, from experts in international agencies, and from global networks of correspondents. Each indicator was constructed from multiple measures. KKM write, "For the 2007 round of the WGI, we rely on a total of 340 individual variables measuring different dimensions of governance. These are taken from 35 different sources, produced by 32 different organizations."[13] Appendix A provides the list of sources and the information used in scoring each indicator. Data were difficult to acquire for certain countries, especially small and lesser-known ones. In 2007, the median number of sources per country ranged from eight to thirteen, depending on the indicator. While most indicators were based on multiple sources, indicators for a few countries were based on only one.[14] A total of 205 countries were scored on all six indicators. The fewest countries (207) were scored for Regulatory Quality, but all 212 countries were scored for Governmental Effectiveness. Although these six qualities do not exhaust the concept of governance, we accept them as central to it and will use them as our indicators, as other scholars have done.[15]

Not all scholars are convinced that the KKM indicators satisfactorily measure different dimensions of country governance. Marcus Kurtz and Andrew Schrank have accused them of bias toward commercial and risk-assessment sources, resulting in "good governance" being linked to "limited government."[16] Conducting an ingenious analysis of the KKM data sources, Sandra Botero and Katherine Schlosse did not find clear support for systematic business bias, but nor did they find support that each set of indicators was "actually measuring [its] respective underlying concept."[17] In later chapters we discuss some limitations of the KKM measures. For now, we accept them as useful and meaningful dependent variables.

From Raw Scores to Z-Scores

Using multiple sources to create composite scores for all countries on the six indicators, KKM were left with six different distributions of raw scores—each with different means (i.e., averages) and different standard deviations (i.e., measures of dispersion; see Box 2.1).[18] To help compare country scores on one indicator with those on another, KKM standardized them by subtracting the mean from each score and then dividing by the standard deviation of the distribution. This process transformed the original noncomparable raw values into easily compared values called z-scores, which have a mean of 0 and a standard deviation of 1.[19]

Why trouble to transform data from raw scores to z-scores? Because it facilitates analysis (see Box 2.2). Think of the difference in using the Fahrenheit and Celsius scales to measure temperature. On the Fahrenheit scale, water freezes at the odd value of 32°; on the Celsius scale, water freezes at 0°. The Celsius scale, with its more useful reference point, facilitates laboratory research. (Many scientists even prefer to use the Kelvin scale, which fixes 0° even more understandably as the absence of heat.)

Creating z-scores helps comparisons across unlike scales by fixing a common 0 point at the mean for every data distribution. In measuring countries on any trait, all countries become scored on a common metric—in relationship to one another—regardless of the trait being measured.[20] Let us transfer

Box 2.1: Measuring Dispersion: The Standard Deviation

Distributions of data typically show dispersion around an average value, the mean. Some cases deviate above the mean and some below. The standard deviation expresses the average deviation from the mean in terms of squared differences—not simple differences. Here is its formula:

$$\text{Standard deviation} = std.dev. = \sqrt{\frac{\sum(X_i - \overline{X})^2}{N}}$$

Read it as follows: (1) compute the mean value, $\overline{X}$, of all the values; (2) subtract the mean, $\overline{X}$, from every value, X_i, in the distribution; (3) square each observed difference (which eliminates any negative signs); (4) sum all the squared differences; (5) divide by the total number of values, N; (6) compute the square root of the result. The result is the standard deviation, the most common measure of how much a group of observations deviates around their mean value.

The table below applies the formula to the number of parliamentary parties seated in five countries. The mean number of parties is 5.6, and the standard deviation is 4.8.

	Number of Parties X_i	(2) $X_i - \overline{X}$	(3) $(X_i - \overline{X})^2$
Iceland	5	5 – 5.6 = –0.6	0.36
United States	2	2 – 5.6 = –3.6	12.96
South Korea	7	7 – 5.6 = +1.4	1.96
Russia	14	14 – 5.6 = +8.4	70.56
Somalia	0	0 – 5.6 = –5.6	31.36

$$\sum_i^N X_i = 28$$

(4)
$$\sum(X_i - \overline{X})^2 = 117.2$$

(1)
$$\frac{\sum_i^N X_i}{N} = 5.6 = \overline{X}$$

(5)
$$\frac{\sum(X_i - \overline{X})^2}{N} = 23.44$$

(6)
$$\sqrt{\frac{\sum(X_i - \overline{X})^2}{N}} = 4.8$$

this measurement logic to governance scores. A country that scores 0 on an indicator (say, Rule of Law) stands exactly at the mean of the distribution of all countries: It is average. By extension, a positive z-score on Rule of Law shows that the country stands above the mean score, while a negative z-score tells that it stands below the mean. The larger the magnitude of the

Box 2.2: Transforming Data into Z-Scores

Assume that you had the following data on the percentage of literacy among adult males for the first ten countries in an alphabetical list of all countries. Over all ten countries, the mean percent literate is 88.6 and the standard deviation is 16.06. If the countries' male literacy rates were plotted on a graph, they would distribute as follows:

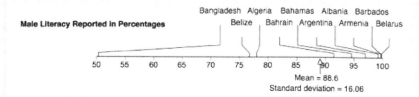

Let us transform these countries' raw literacy percentages into z-scores. Subtract the mean (88.6) from each country's percentage (X_i) and divide the difference by the standard deviation (16.06). Performing this calculation for all ten scores produces a mean of 0 and a standard deviation of 1. The graph below plots the literacy rates after transformation into z-scores.

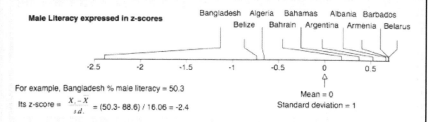

For example, Bangladesh % male literacy = 50.3

Its z-score = $\frac{X_i - \bar{X}}{s.d.}$ = (50.3 - 88.6) / 16.06 = -2.4

Note that there is absolutely no change in the relative positions of any nation as a result of the transformation. The values were simply rescaled. The mean for male literacy in z-scores becomes 0 (instead of 88.6), and the standard deviation becomes 1 (instead of 16.06).

z-score (in either direction), the further the country is from the average for Rule of Law. In practice, nearly all z-scores range between −3.00 and +3.00, providing convenient and interpretable boundaries for measurement. In the case of the 2007 Worldwide Governance Indicators, all but one fell between those boundaries.

Are the Measures Reliable?

In measurement theory, alternative indicators of any proposed concept should demonstrate both reliability and validity. Reliability means that the alternative (but imperfect) measures should produce similar scores for the object being measured. In practice, this means that they should intercorrelate highly. Validity means that they are measuring what they intend to measure. In practice, this means that the indicators should (1) appear on the surface to make sense (called face validity) and (2) correlate as theorized with other phenomena (called criterion validity). This section assesses measurement reliability. We will take up validity later.

Although KKM scored the countries separately on six conceptually distinct qualities of governance, all indicator scores were significantly intercorrelated, as displayed in Figure 2.1.[21]

Figure 2.1 Intercorrelations among all six Worldwide Governance Indicators

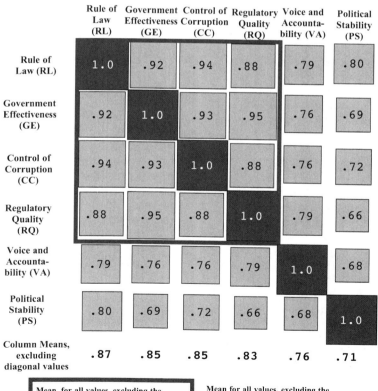

	Rule of Law (RL)	Government Effectiveness (GE)	Control of Corruption (CC)	Regulatory Quality (RQ)	Voice and Accountability (VA)	Political Stability (PS)
Rule of Law (RL)	1.0	.92	.94	.88	.79	.80
Government Effectiveness (GE)	.92	1.0	.93	.95	.76	.69
Control of Corruption (CC)	.94	.93	1.0	.88	.76	.72
Regulatory Quality (RQ)	.88	.95	.88	1.0	.79	.66
Voice and Accountability (VA)	.79	.76	.76	.79	1.0	.68
Political Stability (PS)	.80	.69	.72	.66	.68	1.0
Column Means, excluding diagonal values	.87	.85	.85	.83	.76	.71

Mean, for all values, excluding the diagonal, within the shaded square	.92	Mean for all values, excluding the diagonal, outside the shaded square	.74

The diagonal values of 1.0 in Figure 2.1 express the perfect correlation of each variable with itself. The sizes of the squares off the diagonal correspond to the magnitude of the correlation coefficients compared with a perfect correlation coefficient of 1.0 (see Box 2.3).

Let us compare the highest correlation coefficient of 0.95 (between Regulatory Quality and Control of Corruption) and the lowest of 0.66 (between Regulatory Quality and Political Stability) by plotting the relationships between the two pairs of variables. The coefficient states that the relationship between RQ and CC is stronger than that between RQ and PS. Figures 2.2a and 2.2b illustrate how much stronger. The tiny circles represent each of the two hundred plus countries jointly scored on each pair of variables. The magnitude of the correlations expresses how closely the circles fit the line that provides the "best fit" to the swarm. In statistics, this line of best fit is termed the *regression line* (see Box 2.4). The fit is much closer between Regulatory Quality and Government Effectiveness than between Regulatory

---

Box 2.3: Interpreting a Correlation Coefficient

The mathematical symbol for a correlation coefficient is r. Correlation coefficients measure the direction and extent of relationships between pairs of variables. The coefficient's sign (+ or –) tells whether the variables are positively or negatively related. The coefficient's value (magnitude) indicates how strongly they are related. Whether a correlation coefficient is statistically significant depends on the number of cases (sample size). Given about two hundred cases (approximately the number of countries), a correlation as large as $r = 0.12$ could occur by chance as often as five times in one hundred. Fewer than five times in one hundred (typically expressed as the 0.05 level of significance) is a standard yardstick for significance in social research. Correlations larger than $r = 0.12$ between any pair of variables suggest that the observed correlation reflects a non-chance relationship between them. All the correlation coefficients in Figure 2.1 are highly significant—meaning that they are likely to occur far less than five times in one hundred.

The value of a correlation coefficient is a guide to the strength of the relationship between the variables, but the coefficient's value only has direct interpretations at its extremes: at 0 (no relationship) and at 1 (perfect relationship). Between these extremes, larger coefficients indicate stronger relationships than smaller coefficients. Fortunately, one can precisely determine the strength of the relationship between two variables by squaring the correlation coefficient, but to understand this procedure, one must first learn the function of the regression line, which is introduced below and discussed more in Chapter 3. See Box 4.2 for calculating the precise strength of relationship between two variables.

Figure 2.2a Scatter plot of 0.95 correlation [see Figure 2.2b]

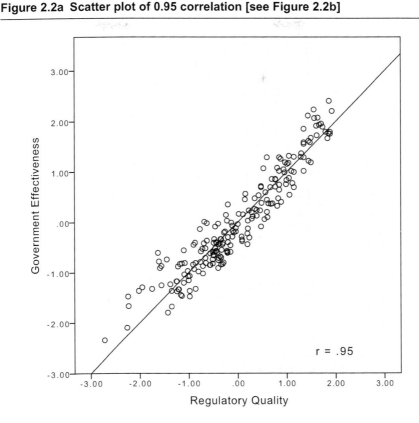

Quality and Political Stability. As the correlation drops from 0.95 to 0.66, some countries deviate substantially from the regression line.

All the correlations in Figure 2.1 are statistically significant far beyond the customary 0.05 level of significance (i.e., they would be due to chance fewer than five times in one hundred; see Box 2.3). This implies that they are fairly reliable (i.e., they are measuring a common property). However, they are not equally reliable, which suggests that some may be measuring different things.

Compare the high correlations inside the shaded area of Figure 2.1 with the low correlations outside of it. Note that the lowest correlation within the shaded square exceeds the highest correlation outside it. This pattern indicates that the first four indicators (RL, GE, CC, and RQ) are all measuring common properties of governance. With an average intercorrelation of 0.92, they are highly reliable indicators; one is about as good as another. RL, GE, CC, and RQ, however, have somewhat less in common with VA and PS.

Figure 2.2b Scatter plot of 0.66 correlation [see Figure 2.2a]

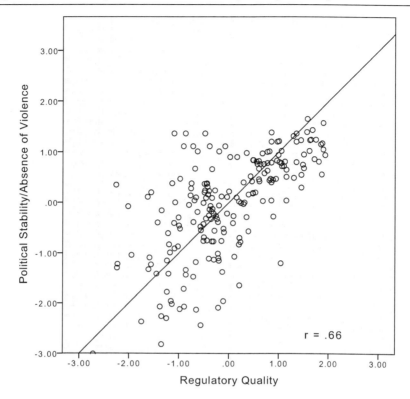

Moreover, VA is only correlated 0.68 with PS. Perhaps VA and PS, respectively, are measuring qualities of governance that are quite different from those measured by the other indicators.[22] Henceforth, we refer to the first four as the administrative variables, in contrast to the two political variables, VA and PS. Most recent research has treated only the administrative measures of governance, while using VA separately as a measure of democracy and ignoring PS completely.[23]

Despite the lower correlations of Voice and Accountability and Political Stability with the other four WGI measures of governance, we note that all six measures are strongly intercorrelated, indicating that they are all fairly reliable measures of the same property. We choose to view that property as governance. We examine the validity of our choice next.

Box 2.4: Meaning of the Regression Line

The line of regression, also known as the least-squares line, represents the best-fitting line that can be drawn through the points that minimizes the sum of the squared deviations calculated from each point to the line. The term *regression* comes from Sir Francis Galton, a pioneer in statistical analysis, who studied physical traits (such as height) that children inherited from parents. Correlating the heights of parents and children, he noted that tall parents tended not to produce even taller children, just as short parents tended not to produce even shorter children. (If they did, then our population would split, over time, into very tall and very short people!) Instead, children of tall and short people both tended to regress toward average heights. Thus, the line that fit the correlations was called the line of regression. For more information, see Daniel J. Denis, "The Origins of Correlation and Regression: Francis Galton or Auguste Bravais and the Error Theorists?" York University, June 29, 2000, www.york.ac.uk/depts/maths/histstat/bravais.htm.

Testing Measurement Validity

As a first test of measurement validity, we can recall our discussion in the introduction of *PARADE*'s list of the world's ten worst dictators. The question here is, Are the WGI measures really measuring governance? If they are, and if we assume that the worst dictatorships produce bad governance, we should expect their countries to rank low on the WGI indicators. Which indicators should we use to test this relationship? For the purpose of this illustration, let us accept the substantial intercorrelations among the six indicators and build an average governance score by computing the mean of all six z-scores. Later in this chapter, we unpack the measures and treat each one separately as the WGI authors intended, but we think that combining them is useful for this illustration.[24]

First, imagine a country that practiced "average" governance. It would likely have z-scores at or near 0 for all six governance indicators. After averaging, its mean z-score would also be at or near 0. Next, imagine governance in the ten worst dictatorships. You would expect them to practice bad governance and to have negative z-scores on all or most of the six indicators, yielding mean z-scores with large negative values.

As Figure 2.3 shows, all ten of *PARADE*'s world's worst dictatorships (countries in boldface) rank below the mean z-score calculated over all six governance indicators. For comparison, the five countries we are tracking are in italics, while three others are in normal type. In the language of research, the boldfaced countries offer evidence of criterion validity because the WGI

Figure 2.3 Average governance scores, top ten dictatorships and selected countries

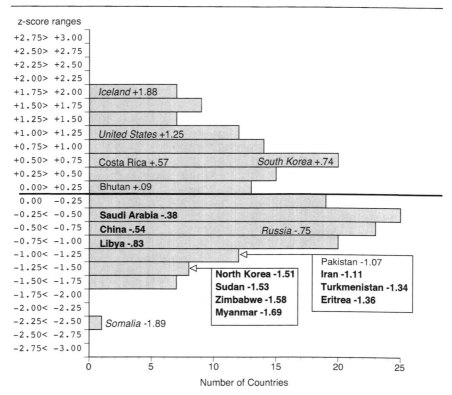

z-score ranges

Boldface marks *PARADE's* ten worst dictatorships. Italics marks the five countries we are tracking.

measure corresponds to an external standard or criterion—*PARADE*'s list of the world's ten worst dictators. Among the ten worst, moreover, there is some understandable variation. Saudi Arabia and China, both of which are powerful states, do not rate as low on governance as the other dictatorships, supporting the validity of the measurement. Furthermore, Somalia, mentioned in the introduction as a failed state without a government, rates by a good margin at the absolute bottom on governance of all 212 countries. In addition, Pakistan, mentioned in the introduction for failing to maintain control over its Swat Valley and ceding authority there to the Taliban, also has a low governance score.

In contrast, note the positive governance score for the Latin American country, Costa Rica, mentioned for its environmental record. Also, note that tiny Bhutan, an absolute monarchy in 2007, nevertheless rated about average in governance, while similarly small but staunchly democratic Iceland stood at the top of the scale in 2007.[25] Solidly on the positive side of the scale is the United States, but it stands only twenty-third in the ranking. This indicates that governance in the United States was not rated as highly as governance in some other countries.

Do the governance measures discriminate among countries thought to vary in the quality of governance? They pass this crude test of criterion validity very well. In order to proceed to more demanding validity tests, we need to study their construction in more detail, beginning with the issue of measurement error.

Dealing with Measurement Error

Attempts to measure any concept carry some degree of measurement error, even in the natural sciences. In the social sciences, measurement error is often more substantial, and error certainly exists in measuring governance. KKM acknowledge that their measures "provide a noisy or imperfect signal of the true, but unobserved, level of governance in a country."[26] Moreover, they compute and report estimates of the "standard error" for all the measures (which differs somewhat from the definition of standard error in statistics[27]). For KKM, the standard error of a given indicator reflects variation in observed values for governance based on different sources.[28] Their reported standard errors depend on two factors: "cross-country differences in the number of sources in which a country appears, and differences in the precision of the sources in which each country appears."[29] As the WGI project progressed over time, more and better sources were added, enabling KKM to say, "In 2007 the standard error ranges from 0.18 to 0.23 for five of our six indicators, while for Political Stability it is slightly higher at 0.26"[30] (see the discussion in Box 2.5).

Because we averaged all six governance indicators together in creating Figure 2.3, we cannot use the separate KKM error estimates to calculate margins of error. Nevertheless, we must allow for measurement error in evaluating the scores of −1.69, −1.58, −1.53, and −1.51, respectively, for Myanmar, Zimbabwe, Sudan, and North Korea. Allowing for error, all these scores are much the same, meaning that these observed differences do not matter much. Moreover, the scores of −1.36 and −1.34 for Eritrea and Turkmenistan are probably not significantly different from the score of −1.51 for North Korea. The point: One should recognize that measurement error exists in the WGI data and not make much of small differences between country scores. Due to margin of error, Costa Rica's score of +0.57 is not significantly different from South Korea's score of +0.75; nor is China's score of −0.54 that different from Russia's −0.74. However, the differences between the scores for the dictatorships on the one hand and for Bhutan, Costa Rica, and the United States on the other hand reflect differences in governance scores not due to measurement error.

Box 2.5: Margins of Error in Governance Scores

These WGI standard errors can be converted into something like the margins of error reported for large national sample surveys. Typically, a national poll of 1,500 respondents has a margin of error of ±3 percentage points at the 0.05 level of significance. *Example:* If a poll showed that 35 percent of the respondents were satisfied with their economic condition, the true percentage (allowing for sampling error) could be between 32 and 38—with a 95 percent chance of being correct.

Roughly speaking, this notion of converting margin of error into WGI scores can be translated as follows: (1) Double the standard error to yield a margin of error, and (2) add and subtract the result from the observed governance score to yield a likely range of values at the 95 percent level of confidence. *Example:* A WGI standard error of 0.18 should be doubled to 0.36, yielding a margin of error of ±0.36. Thus, an observed governance score of 1.36 could be expected to range between 1.00 and 1.72 with a 95 percent probability. As KKM note, "Small differences in estimates of governance across countries [as observed among some of the dictatorships in Figure 2.3] are not likely to be statistically significant."[1]

Note

1. Daniel Kaufmann, Aart Kraay, and Massimo Mastruzzi, "Governance Matters VII: Aggregate and Individual Governance Indicators, 1996–2007" (Working Paper 4564, World Bank, Washington, DC, June 2008), 18.

Recognition of WGI measurement error guides our choice of five countries to follow in subsequent chapters in terms of the effects of size, wealth, and party systems on country governance. We excluded the dictatorships because most of them have governance scores that do not differ significantly from one another. Instead, we chose countries that differ both significantly and widely. Two of our choices—Iceland and Somalia—stand poles apart at the top and bottom of the average governance scores as countries #1 and #212. There is nothing special about the ranking of our third choice, the United States (#23 puts it in about the tenth percentile of all nations). We selected it because most readers of the book are likely to be U.S. citizens, as is the primary author.

The fourth country chosen is the Republic of Korea, whose name we shorten to South Korea to distinguish it from the Democratic People's Republic of Korea (designated as North Korea in Figure 2.3). We selected South Korea because Jin-Young Kwak, my colleague in this research, is its citizen, and many additional readers are likely to be citizens of South Korea. Moreover, South Korea (#50 in the average scoring) conveniently stands in about the twenty-fifth percentile of all 212 nations.

The final country is Russia (#164 in the average ranking), which stands in about the seventy-fifth percentile, nicely counterbalancing South Korea in the twenty-fifth percentile. Moreover, Russia is a powerful country whose governance since the collapse of communism in the early 1990s has been called into question. Choosing Russia invites us to consider the issue of measuring governance over the years from 1996 to 2007 for which the WGI data are available.

Measuring Governance over Time

Are the Worldwide Governance Indicators sensitive enough to measure change in governance for a single nation over time? KKM contend that they are, saying, "In assessing trends over time, we find that 31 percent of countries experience significant changes over the decade 1998–2007 in at least one of the six indicators (roughly evenly divided between significant improvements and deteriorations). This highlights the fact that governance can and does change even over relatively short periods such as a decade."[31] Starting with 1996, the WGI project has published comparable data for all six of its governance indicators. At first, data were collected and published in two-year intervals, but the scores were published annually beginning with 2002. For 1996, the indicators were only available for 150 countries, growing to 212 by 2006. Over time, the number of data sources—and thus the reliability of the scoring—also increased. We can obtain more insight into the WGI data by plotting over time the governance scores for our five selected countries, all of which were included in the scoring beginning with 1996. Figure 2.4a–f displays the plots for 1996 through 2008.

Recall that countries are measured for governance in relationship to one another and not according to some fixed standard. Because the mean governance score in any year is 0, all the countries cannot shift over time toward "better" governance scores. Their mean score will always be 0. But compared with governance in all other countries, certain countries can move up or down from year to year.

The first thing to notice in Figure 2.4a–f is that governance plots are relatively constant over time for each country over each indicator. If one believes that most country governments do remain fairly stable from year to year, that pattern is reassuring. The WGI scores do not jump about wildly from year to year. Most of the observed variation may be due more to measurement error than to substantive differences in governance.

**Figure 2.4a Governance scores for our five selected countries:
Rule of Law**

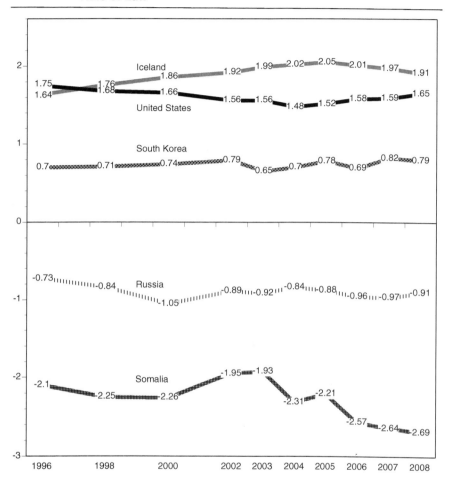

The second thing to notice is that abrupt changes sometimes do occur between years. For example, see the spikes for Somalia in 2002 for Government Effectiveness (Figure 2.4b) and Control of Corruption (Figure 2.4c). Perhaps this reflects cautious optimism following the creation of a Transnational National Government in late 2000 to forge a permanent national Somali government.[32] An even more dramatic (and telling) example occurred in the sharp drop in the score for Political Stability and Absence of Violence for the United States between 2000 and 2002. Recall that this indicator measures perceptions of the likelihood that the government will be destabilized

Figure 2.4b Governance scores for our five selected countries: Government Effectiveness

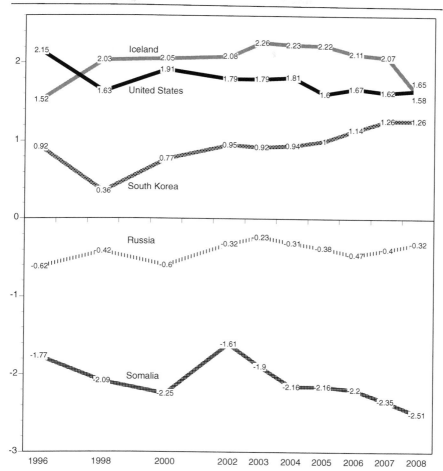

or overthrown by unconstitutional or violent means, including politically motivated violence and terrorism. Accordingly, the drop clearly reflects the terrorist attack of September 11, 2001, the creation of the Department of Homeland Security, and the continuing threat of terrorist attacks.

The third thing to notice is the presence of upward and downward trends in some indicators for some countries. For example, Iceland rated at or below the United States on every indicator in 1996, but by 2007 Iceland had significantly higher scores than the United States on every indicator except Regulatory Quality, for which the two countries were essentially tied. Over ten

Figure 2.4c Governance scores for our five selected countries: Control of Corruption

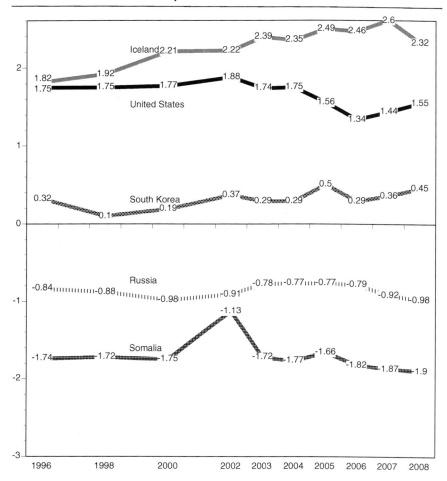

years, Iceland mostly moved ahead in governance scores, while the United States stayed in place or declined. But in 2008 Iceland experienced sharp drops in its Regulatory Quality (Figure 2.4d) and Political Stability (Figure 2.4f). Although all nations suffered from the 2008 worldwide financial melt-down, Iceland, which had extended itself in global lending, became virtually bankrupt. It suffered a fall not only in its Regulatory Quality score but also in Political Stability, as its long-governing free market party was swept from office, replaced by a leftist coalition.

South Korea and Russia offer other examples. South Korea rose steadily in Governmental Effectiveness from 1998 to 2007. Russia, in contrast,

Figure 2.4d Governance scores for our five selected countries: Regulatory Quality

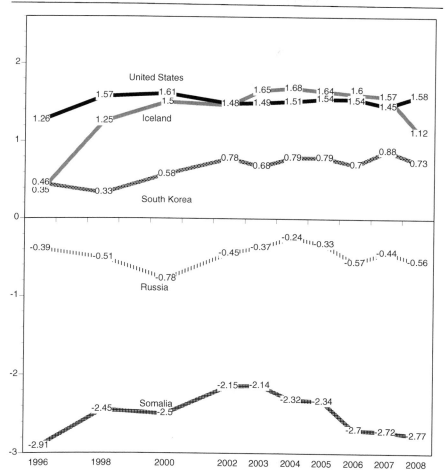

dropped almost as steadily in Voice and Accountability from 2002 to 2007. South Korea's rise corresponds with the nation's first peaceful transfer of power following the 1997 elections and the 2002 election of the progressive president Roh Moo-hyun.[33] Russia's drop fits with Vladimir Putin's efforts to stifle dissent. One observer wrote that Putin's government "had taken over national television, emasculated the power of the country's governors, converted parliament into a rubber stamp, jailed the main financier of the political opposition and intimidated the most potent would-be challengers" from running against him for reelection.[34]

**Figure 2.4e Governance scores for our five selected countries:
Voice and Accountability**

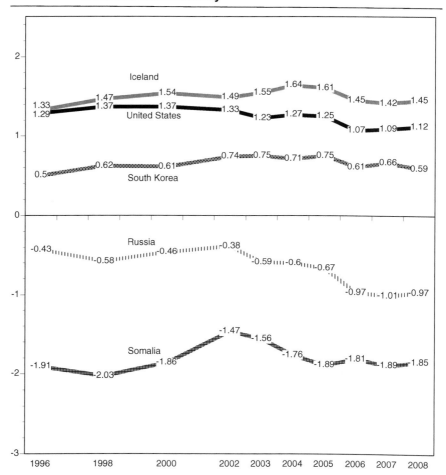

Unpacking the Average Governance Measure

Earlier, to simplify discussion of measuring governance, we combined all six WGI variables to create an average measure of government used in Figure 2.3. We promised to unpack this average measure to show how all countries distributed on each of the six governance indicators in 2007. Although expressing country scores as z-scores automatically rescales the data to produce a mean of 0 for each indicator, rescaling does not affect the way the scores are distributed around the mean, which conveys important information:

**Figure 2.4f Governance scores for our five selected countries:
Political Stability**

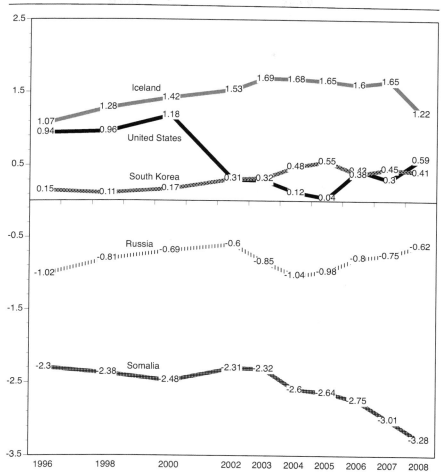

Do the countries cluster around a single most frequent value? Is that value (called the mode) centered on the mean? Are the countries symmetrically distributed around the mean, or are they skewed toward low or high governance scores? Studying the distributions of each variable as displayed in Figure 2.5a–f reveals something about country governance worldwide.

In Figure 2.3, the 212 countries were distributed fairly symmetrically in bell-shaped (unimodal) form around the mean of 0 for the average measure combining all six indicators. The world's countries are not distributed in symmetrical bell-shaped forms in Figure 2.5a–f. The pattern for Regulatory Quality (Figure 2.5d) most closely resembles the symmetrical distribution

Figure 2.5a Variable distributions: Rule of Law

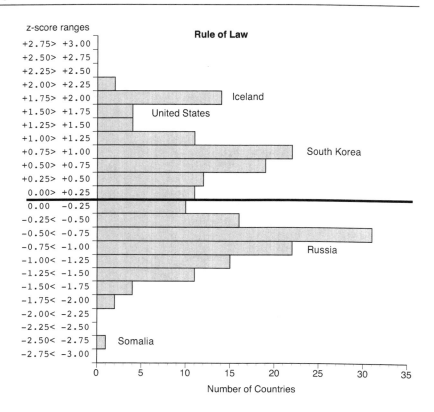

in the earlier figures, but many countries score fairly high on Regulatory Quality, while a few are skewed far below.

The graphs for the other governance indicators depart substantially from the unimodal, symmetrical pattern. For example, the one for Rule of Law (Figure 2.5a) shows countries bunching into separate groups above and below the mean (represented by the horizontal line), approximating a bimodal distribution. This suggests that countries cluster around two poles: those that tend to practice the Rule of Law and those that do not. This pattern suggests a fundamental division among countries concerning the Rule of Law.

Although the measures for Rule of Law and Governmental Effectiveness correlated at 0.92 in Figure 2.1, the distributions of nations on the two variables are quite different. In contrast to the graph for the Rule of Law, the two graphs for Government Effectiveness (Figure 2.5b) and Control of Corruption (Figure 2.5c) show most nations clustering around low governance scores. They suggest that most countries in 2007 were rated as having ineffective government and a substantial degree of corruption.

Figure 2.5b **Variable distributions: Government Effectiveness**

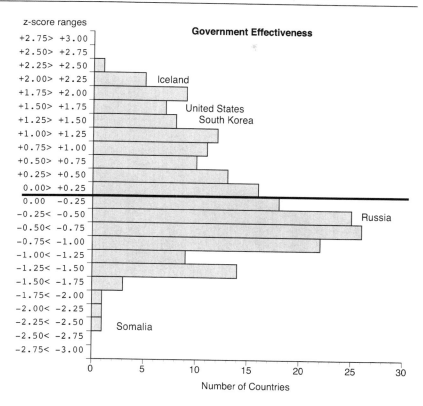

The graph for Voice and Accountability (Figure 2.5e) is more promising from the standpoint of good governance. Many countries bunch around high governance scores for Voice and Accountability, counterbalanced by a smaller number of countries far below. This pattern is accentuated in the distribution of Political Stability and Absence of Violence (Figure 2.5f). Most countries rate high on this indicator of governance, but some have dismal ratings.

Studying All 212 Countries

Although the Worldwide Governance Indicators project covers 212 countries, one might ask why bother to include all 212 in this study? Many of the countries are tiny. Niue (pronounced new-way), an island in the South Pacific Ocean encompassing 260 square kilometers, is only 1.5 times the area of Washington, DC, and is inhabited by fewer than 2,000 people. While Niue

Figure 2.5c Variable distributions: Control of Corruption

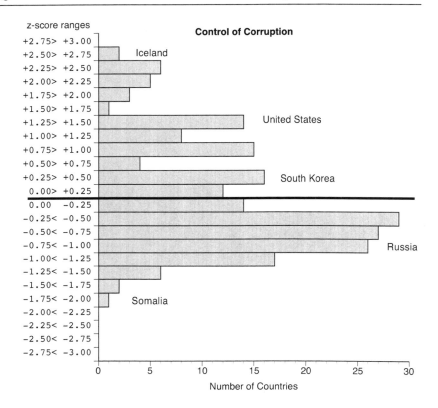

is self-governing, it is associated with New Zealand, which is responsible for its defense and external affairs. Niue is just the smallest of eleven countries with fewer than 50,000 people. Another eight have up to 100,000 people, and twenty-six only have between 100,000 and 500,000. In contrast, 79 of the 212 countries have more than 10 million people. What sense is there in comparing, say, Niue and China for quality of governance?

In fact, some distinguished political scientists have argued against large-N comparisons involving all members of the United Nations.[35] One objection is that many of these units "do not possess the requisite capacity for autonomous political action."[36] Then there is Galton's problem: Countries, particularly those close to one another, often share features by cultural diffusion, so the cases are not statistically independent.[37] Also, something seems wrong with treating Niue and China as equal cases in statistical analysis. Finally, there is the considerable practical problem that one cannot obtain adequate data for so many countries to test the theory at hand.

Figure 2.5d Variable distributions: Regulatory Quality

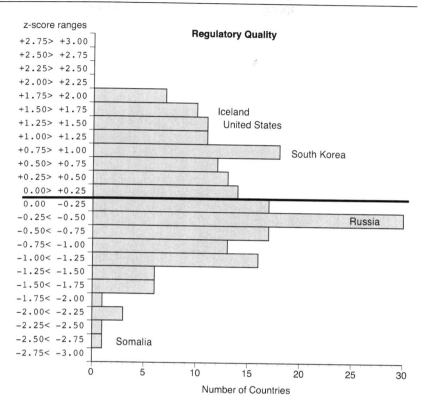

Notwithstanding these objections, four important considerations argue for including all two hundred plus countries in this study. First, the most-different-systems design for comparative politics ideally includes all countries to insure maximum differences among the countries. Second, the z-score calculations of the Worldwide Governance Indicators are based on all the available data on each indicator, which varied from 205 to 212 countries. Because every country is scored in relationship to every other country, using all the countries preserves the integrity of the scoring. Third, one lessens the risk of selection bias in comparative research by studying the whole population of cases, which means all the countries studied.[38] Fourth, one of the theoretically important variables, country size, can only be studied by including small countries—precisely the cases targeted for exclusion.

For example, one study found, contrary to its hypothesis, that population size and geographical area "had no effect on governmental performance" in a study of 110 countries. However, the 110 countries were larger ones

Figure 2.5e Variable distributions: Voice and Accountability

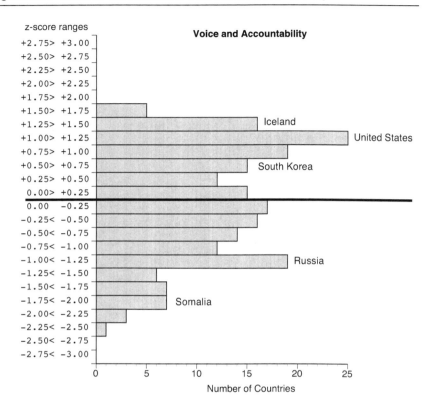

and did not include very small countries.[39] As Chapter 4 shows, small size does have a significant effect on governance when the analysis includes all countries—large, medium, and small.

Summary and Conclusion

Measuring country governance is not an easy task, but scholars at the World Bank have shown that it can be done with reasonable results. They created a set of six broad indicators of country governance that appear to travel well across cultures. Their indicators demonstrate criterion validity, in the sense that the "top ten" dictatorships for 2009 rate quite low on our average measure of governance for 2007. Moreover, their indicators admit the presence of measurement error, which warns users that countries with close governance scores do not differ significantly from one another. Acting on this warning, we selected five countries—Iceland, the United States, South Korea, Russia,

Figure 2.5f Variable distributions: Political Stability

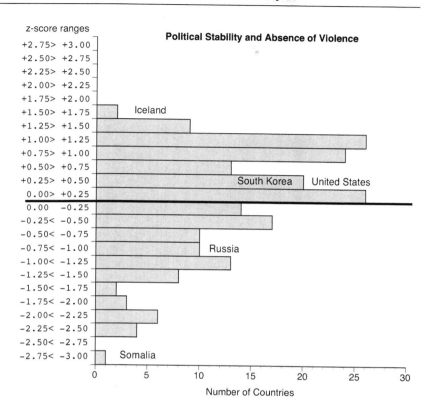

and Somalia—that differed widely in governance scores to track in subsequent chapters explaining the effects of size, wealth, and party systems on country governance. When plotted for these five countries from 1996 to 2008, the WGI scores reveal a reassuring stability over time while occasionally displaying interpretable deviations from stability. These theoretically expected patterns lend support to the general validity of the WGI measures.[40]

Finally, we saw that countries across the world generated different distributions for each of the six WGI measures of governance, which argues for analyzing each indicator separately in subsequent chapters rather than limiting analysis to the average measure. In general, countries clustered toward the top of the ratings for Voice and Accountability and Political Stability, while they clustered toward the bottom of the rating concerning Rule of Law, Government Effectiveness, Control of Corruption, and Regulatory Quality. These observations support our belief in the overall utility of the WGI measures of country governance, despite the understanding that they are not perfect.

Notes

1. The artistic metaphor in measuring governance is also used by Marie Besançon, *Good Governance Rankings: The Art of Measurement,* World Peace Foundation Reports 36 (Cambridge, MA: World Peace Foundation, 2003).

2. Partia de Lancer Julnes and Marc Holzer, eds., *Performance Measurement: Building Theory, Improving Practice* (Armonk, NY: M. E. Sharpe, 2008), especially chap. 1, "Making the Case for Performance Measurement," 3–20. The index to the entire book contains no entry for "governance."

3. World Bank, *Governance: The World Bank's Experience* (Washington, DC: World Bank, 1994), xv.

4. Daniel Kaufmann, Aart Kraay, and Pablo Zoido-Lobatón launched the first major cross-national set of indicators in what became the Worldwide Governance Indicators.

5. Besançon, *Good Governance Rankings,* 9.

6. For example, Ashraf Ghani and Clare Lockhart offer their own list of "ten functions of the state" in *Fixing Failed States: A Framework for Rebuilding a Fractured World* (New York: Oxford University Press, 2008), chap. 7, "The Ten Functions of the State," 124–126. Their first function is "rule of law," a Worldwide Governance Indicators measure that also serves as the feature indicator for our analysis.

7. The booklet "A Decade of Measuring the Quality of Governance" is available at Worldwide Governance Indicators, http://info.worldbank.org/governance/wgi/resources.htm.

8. See "A Decade of Measuring the Quality of Governance: Governance Matters 2006" (Washington, DC: World Bank, 2006), 1. Documents pertaining to the Worldwide Governance Indicators are available at http://info.worldbank.org/governance/wgi/resources.htm.

9. Daniel Kaufmann, Aart Kraay, and Pablo Zoido-Lobatón wrote the first major report, "Governance Matters" (Policy Research Working Paper 2196, World Bank, Washington, DC, 1999) and subsequent reports to 2002. The 2003 through 2008 editions of "Governance Matters" were authored by Daniel Kaufmann, Aart Kraay, and Massimo Mastruzzi.

10. See Worldwide Governance Indicators, http://info.worldbank.org/governance/wgi/resources.htm.

11. See Daniel Kaufmann, Aart Kraay, and Massimo Mastruzzi, "Worldwide Governance Indicators Project: Answering the Critics" (Policy Research Working Paper 4149, World Bank, Washington, DC, 2007), available from the Social Science Research Network at http://papers.ssrn.com/sol3/papers.cfm?abstract_id=965077.

12. From Daniel Kaufmann, Aart Kraay, and Massimo Mastruzzi, "Governance Matters VII: Aggregate and Individual Governance Indicators, 1996–2007" (Policy Research Working Paper 4564, World Bank, Washington, DC, June 2008), 7–8. The order of the indicators was changed from the original.

13. Ibid., 8.

14. An average of 7 percent of the countries had scores from only one source. Ibid., 17.

15. See, for example, Marko Grdesic and Viktor Koska, "Governance in the Weak State–Weak Society Settings of Eastern Europe" (paper presented at the 21st World Congress of the International Political Science Association, Santiago, Chile, July 12–16, 2009).

16. Marcus J. Kurtz and Andrew Schrank, "Growth and Governance: Models, Measures, and Mechanisms," *The Journal of Politics* 69, no. 2 (May 2007): 538–554.

17. Sandra Botero and Katherine Schlosse, "What We Talk About When We Talk About Governance: Measurement and Conceptual Issues in the World Governance Indicators" (paper presented at the annual meeting of the Midwest Political Science Association, Chicago, Illinois, April 22–25, 2010), 34.

18. Standard deviation measures the variation of scores for a single variable (X) around its mean 0 according to this formula: s.d. $= \sqrt{\frac{\sum(X_i - \bar{X})^2}{N}}$.

19. Standard scores with means of 0 and standard deviations of 1 are commonly called z-scores. They are calculated by this formula $z_i = \frac{X_i - \bar{X}}{s.d.}$.

20. Suppose we measured the same ten countries in Box 2.2 for literacy among adult females. Their mean literacy rate for women is 84.2, somewhat lower than that for men, and the standard deviation is much higher at 22.7. Suppose you were told that 59.6 percent of the women in Algeria were literate, compared with 78 percent of the men. To judge whether those scores were "high" or "low" compared with other countries, you would need four pieces of information: the means for both distributions and the amount of variation in both distributions. But knowing that the z-score for Algerian men was –0.66 and that for Algerian women was –1.08, you would know immediately that the Algerian literacy rate was below the mean for the ten other countries (the sign is negative) and that, relatively speaking, the literacy rate for Algerian women ranked even lower than the rate for Algerian men. (Because the women's z-score of –1.08 has a greater magnitude than the men's z-score of –0.66, the women's score stands further from its mean.)

21. Correlations in Figure 2.1 were computed using pairwise case deletion. The numbers of cases underlying each correlation vary between 205 and 211.

22. Factor analysis shows a single factor explaining 85 percent of the variance among all six indicators. The mean correlations reported in Figure 2.1 correspond according to their loadings on the principal component.

23. Irina Denisova et al., "Who Wants to Revise Privatization? The Complementarity of Market Skills and Institutions," *American Political Science Review* 103 (May 2009): 284–304. See also Kurtz and Schrank, "Growth and Governance," who hold that VA and PS "are not conterminous with governance" (543).

24. In fact, the authors of the Worldwide Governance Indicators have gone to great lengths to measure different qualities of governance and warn against undoing their efforts by combining all six indicators into an overall measure of governance. We understand their point from the standpoint of serious research, but we think that the combination is useful here as a learning heuristic. For more on this issue, see Christiane Arndt and Charles Oman, *Uses and Abuses of Governance Indicators* (Paris: Development Centre of the Organisation for Economic Co-Operation and Development, 2006), 44–45.

25. In 2006, Iceland was 0.01 behind Finland in overall governance score. In 2008, Iceland still had strong governance scores but dropped to thirteenth place. In 2007, however, Iceland had the highest aggregate governance score.

26. Kaufmann, Kraay, and Mastruzzi, "Governance Matters VII," 97.

27. In statistics, standard error refers to the standard deviation of the sampling distribution of an infinitely large sample of the particular statistic (e.g., the mean) under consideration.

28. The authors write, "The output of our aggregation procedure is a distribution of possible values of governance for a country, conditional on the observed data for that country. The mean of this conditional distribution is our estimate of governance, and we refer to the standard deviation of this conditional distribution as the 'standard error' of the governance estimate." See Kaufmann, Kraay, and Mastruzzi, "Governance Matters VII," 17n12. At that point, the authors cite an earlier paper for more information about computing the standard errors. See Daniel Kaufmann, Aart Kraay, and Massimo Mastruzzi, "Governance Matters III: Governance Indicators for 1996, 1998, 2000, and 2002," *World Bank Economic Review* 18 (2004): 253–287.

29. Kaufmann, Kraay, and Mastruzzi, "Governance Matters III," 264.

30. Ibid., 17.

31. Kaufmann, Kraay, and Mastruzzi, "Governance Matters VII," 2.

32. See the introduction to Somalia in the 2002 CIA *World Factbook*, at www.umsl.edu/services/govdocs/wofact2002/index.html.

33. Sook-Jong Lee, "The Transformation of South Korean Politics: Implications for U.S.–Korea Relations" (Washington, DC: The Brookings Institution, September 2004).

34. Peter Baker and Susan B. Glasser, "The Rollback of Democracy in Vladimir Putin's Russia," *Washington Post*, June 7, 2005, A01.

35. Philippe C. Schmitter, "Watch Out! The Units You Are Comparing May Not Be What They Used to Be," in *The Future of Political Science: 100 Perspectives*, ed. Gary King, Kay Lehman Schlozman, and Norman H. Nie (New York: Routledge, 2009), 176–179.

36. Ibid.

37. Raoul Naroll, "Galton's Problem: The Logic of Cross-Cultural Research," *Social Research* 32 (1965): 428–451.

38. Simon Hug, "Selection Bias in Comparative Research: The Case of Incomplete Data Sets," *Political Analysis* 11 (2003): 255–274.

39. Alicia Adsera, "Are You Being Served? Political Accountability and Quality of Government," *Journal of Law Economics & Organization* 19 (October 2003): 445–490.

40. More demanding tests of construct validity are described in Kurtz and Schrank, "Growth and Governance."

Part II

Environmental Effects on Country Governance

Chapter 3

Country Governance:
Chicken or Egg?

Should governance be viewed as the chicken or the egg? Is the quality of governance primarily a cause of environmental conditions (the chicken) or a consequence (the egg)? In the language of research, should governance be treated as an independent variable (an explanatory factor) or a dependent variable (the thing to be explained)?

Most studies that employ the Worldwide Governance Indicators (WGI) have used them as independent variables, or explanatory factors, to predict to one or more dependent variables, which are usually economic in nature. In their one-hundred-plus-page report for the Organization for Economic Development, Christiane Arndt and Charles Oman found that international investors use governance indicators to identify potential investment locations; aid donors use them to determine where to provide aid; and analysts and academics use them to study the effects of governance infrastructure on foreign direct-investment inflows and outflows.[1] Consider also these three studies in 2009: One used all six WGI indicators in predicting to economic development in 129 countries.[2] Another used all the indicators except Political Stability to predict public opinion about support for privatization of state enterprises in twenty-eight postcommunist countries.[3] In contrast, another selected Political Stability as an independent variable to explain foreign trade as a manifestation of globalization.[4] Yet another incorporated Voice and Accountability, Political Stability, and Rule of Law in a model to predict rates of economic growth for 125 countries.[5]

Some theorists instead argue forcefully that the qualities of governance are more often a result, rather than a cause, of economic conditions.[6] In this vein, a few scholars have treated governance not as an independent but as a dependent variable—something to be explained. Those who used the WGI scores for this purpose tended to focus on selected indicators, such as the Rule of Law[7] and Government Effectiveness.[8] They also studied subsets of countries. No previous research has attempted to explain, in general, how social conditions worldwide affect multiple qualities of governance—using all six WGI measures and all 212 countries scored on those measures.

Sorting Out Causality

Especially in the social sciences, events and behavior flow from no single cause but from multiple causes. Because so many social, economic, psychological, and political variables affect social behavior at any given time, one can argue that causal explanation in social science is more complex than in physical science. Moreover, the effects of relevant variables are more likely to change over time in the social sciences. (Think of the shifting roles of newspapers, television, and the Internet in politics over only the last two decades.) Finally, explaining social behavior often raises the question of the causal arrow, with which we began. Is governance more often a cause or effect of social conditions?

Even in the physical sciences, establishing causation is a complicated task. Just consider the debate over the cause of global warming and the problem of determining the causes of cancer. In the social sciences, it is difficult to pin down the cause of any type of event or behavior. Most likely, governance and social conditions are subject to reciprocal causation, meaning that they influence each other simultaneously or are too close in time to sort out cause and effect.

Philosophers of science hold that we never actually prove that one event causes another—which is why science can never prove the truth of empirical theories. We can only demonstrate that one event necessarily precedes another in an understandable connection.[9] Therefore, establishing the time sequence of events is crucial for claiming causality. Controlling events through experimental design is the standard scientific method for investigating causality. While experimentation is not possible when analyzing real countries, researchers sometimes mimic experimental conditions by studying social phenomena over time. Such research designs are often called time-series or time-panel analyses. In contrast, a cross-sectional design is, in effect, a snapshot of phenomena occurring at or near the same time in different countries. Researchers who rely on a cross-sectional design typically rely on theory to impute causality to the variables in their causal models. That is what we do here.

We argue that features of a country's party system and two other factors—country size and country wealth—help explain variations in the qualities of country governance. In the language of research, the governance qualities that we seek to explain are called endogenous variables. The explanatory factors are called exogenous variables (the terms mean "inside" and "outside," respectively).[10] Figure 3.1 depicts in its simplest form the causal model that guides our study.

Strictly speaking, there should be no reciprocal causation between exogenous and endogenous variables in a causal model. In our model, that is certainly true for country size. Size is a true exogenous variable unaffected by any of the endogenous governance indicators. For virtually all countries, their size (whether measured by population or area) was settled by history before their contemporary governments came into being. Excluding the rare cases of territorial changes due to strife, governance can have no effect on country size, but country size can theoretically affect governance.

Treating country wealth as exogenous is more problematic because of suspected reciprocal causation. Above we cite studies that use governance scores to predict to economic development, typically measured by country wealth. That would make governance a cause of wealth, contrary to the model in Figure 3.1. While some theorists think as we do—that wealth is more likely a cause than an effect of governance—some might think that treating country

Figure 3.1 A basic model for explaining country governance

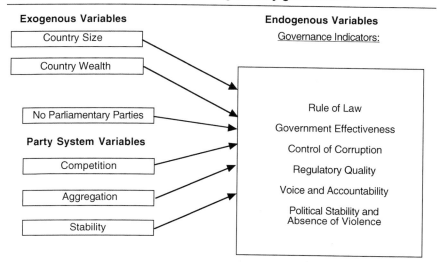

wealth as an exogenous variable presents a serious problem with our model. We argue otherwise. Although governments have more control over country wealth than they have over country size, country wealth is largely a function of geology, geography, and history. Countries tend to be poor, rich, or in between—and they remain relatively fixed in place over generations or even centuries. Nevertheless, countries can substantially rise or decline in wealth over a decade or two (think of China and Russia) due to government actions. Unlike country size, therefore, country wealth is not a pure exogenous variable. When measured at any particular time, however, wealth is sufficiently independent of governance to be regarded as an exogenous causal factor.

Whether the political party system variables—competition, stability, and aggregation—are causes or consequences of country governance is a more complex question explored in Chapter 6. For now, we contend that they function more as causes, which permits us to treat them as independent variables predicting to country governance.

Exogenous Variables: Country Size and Wealth

Our theory asserts that the traits of a country's political party system affect the quality of its governance. The theory does not hold that party system traits are the only, or even the main, cause of country governance. Indeed, two other country factors—size and wealth—are presumed to affect its governance independently of its party system. Our theory only holds that party system traits have significant effects on country governance after controlling for the prior effects of country size and wealth. Chapters 4 and 5, respectively, examine the separate effects of country size and wealth. We can encapsulate the reasoning behind their effects in a few sentences.

Country Size

Country size can be expressed in terms of area or population. Countries large in area also tend to be large in population. The correlation between country area and population is strong but not perfect. Governments in countries with vast areas find it difficult to extend their control over the entire nation. Governments in countries with huge populations find it difficult to tend to conflicting needs of their people. At least in the short run, country governments have no control over their countries' area or population.

The effects of country size on governance depend on whether we measure size as area or population. As we will show, country area is more important for most qualities of governance, but population has the greater effect on some qualities. These effects of country size are not large, but they are significant.

Country Wealth

A country's total wealth can be expressed in terms of its annual gross domestic product (GDP), which is the total value of all goods and services produced in the country in a given year.[11] To adjust for country population, a country's wealth is commonly measured by dividing its GDP by its population, yielding GDP per capita. Henceforth in this book, country wealth should be understood as GDP per capita.

Clearly, country wealth affects a government's ability to deliver to its citizens such material benefits as clean water and electricity. It also affects a government's ability to deliver metavalues not specifically tied to material goods. Government faces fewer administrative problems in a wealthy country than in a poor one. Wealth brings better schools, which graduate better-educated officials, who are better paid and therefore less susceptible to bribes. Although recent scholarship shows that some sources of country wealth—oil, for example—create governmental and social problems, we will consider only the effects of GDP per capita, regardless of the source of the country's wealth. We will demonstrate that wealth effects are quite substantial in explaining variations in country governance.

Exogenous Variables: Country Politics

Both country size and country wealth fix parameters for country governance. A scholar writing about the world's poorest countries says, "Good governance and policy help a country to realize its opportunities, but they cannot generate opportunities where none exist, and they cannot defy gravity."[12] Within the parameters of country size and wealth, we expect that country politics exert separate effects. Politics, however, plays only a partial role in explaining country governance. Unlike size and wealth—both of which are readily translated into quantitative concepts—country politics is a vague umbrella term that encompasses a wide range of political structures, processes, and outcomes. Under the umbrella, for example, lie these political factors: presidential versus parliamentary government, proportional versus majority electoral system, unitary versus federal structure, voting requirements, voter turnout, government spending as percentage of GDP, spending for military and police, democratic nature of the government, and operation of the party system. We discuss only two here.

Democracy and Governance

Readers might presume that democratic governments will score higher on governance qualities than nondemocratic governments. Some scholars do link satisfaction with governance to the presence of democracy.[13] Many, however, question whether democracy improves governance,[14] and some writers argue that democracy actually weakens governance.[15] They contend that democracy generates conflicting demands, leading to incoherent policies that frustrate governance. Or they hold that governance today inevitably relies on nongovernmental institutions that are by design—and properly so—outside of popular control.[16] We are interested in governmental institutions that are, in principle, susceptible to some degree of shaping. We are further interested in major dimensions of their party systems, which are often regarded as indicators of democracy. As in the case of democracy and governance, scholars disagree about whether political parties help or hinder governance.[17]

Party Systems and Governance

As scholars who specialize in the comparative analysis of political parties and party systems, we study here the effects of political party systems on country governance. A party system can be defined as the set of one or more political parties seeking to place their avowed representatives into government positions.[18] Party systems can be classified in different ways and measured for different attributes. The most popular classifications of party systems are based on the number of parties that afford realistic opportunity for access to office.[19] Jan-Erik Lane and Svante Ersson list fifteen other bases of classification and methods of measurement.[20] For our analysis, we choose only three of the most commonly used measures: competition among the parties in the system, the stability of parliamentary party representation, and the party system's aggregation of socioeconomic interests. These concepts and how they are measured are explained in Part III.

Even after controlling for country size and wealth, we find that party system competition has small but significant effects on most qualities of governance, that party system stability has similar effects within electoral democracies, and that party system aggregation has different and contradictory effects on individual qualities of governance.

Summary and Conclusion

Do social and political conditions affect country governance, or does governance affect social and political conditions? In both the social and physical sciences, establishing cause-and-effect relationships is problematic. The problem of reciprocal causation—variables influencing one another more or less simultaneously—is especially troublesome in the social sciences. No doubt, country governance is reciprocally related to social and political conditions, but causal priorities can be argued in some cases. For example, country size certainly affects country governance rather than vice versa. Country wealth plausibly precedes country governance too. As for party systems, their complex connections to country governance need more discussion, which we will undertake in Part III.

Notes

1. Christiane Arndt and Charles Oman, *Uses and Abuses of Governance Indicators* (Paris: Development Centre of the Organisation for Economic Co-Operation and Development, 2006), chap. 3, "Uses of Governance Indicators," 35–48.

2. André Faria and Paolo Mauro, "Institutions and the External Capital Structure of Countries," *Journal of International Money and Finance* 28 (April 2009): 367–391.

3. Irina Denisova et al., "Who Wants to Revise Privatization? The Complementarity of Market Skills and Institutions," *American Political Science Review* 103 (May 2009): 284–304.

4. Luisita Cordero and Richard N. Rosencrance, "The 'Acceptance' of Globalization," in *No More States? Globalization, National Self-Determinism, and Terrorism*, ed. Richard N. Rosencrance and Arthur A. Stein (Lanham, MD: Rowman & Littlefield, 2006), 23–34.

5. Michael Alexeev, Kim P. Huynh, and David T. Jacho-Chávez, "Nonmonotonic Growth and Governance Relationships: Robust Nonparametric Inference" (paper presented at the annual meeting of the Midwest Political Science Association, Chicago, Illinois, April 2–4, 2009).

6. Arthur A. Goldsmith, "Is Governance Reform a Catalyst for Development?" *Governance: An International Journal of Policy, Administration, and Institutions* 20 (April 2007): 165–186; Marcus J. Kurtz and Andrew Schrank, "Growth and Governance: Models, Measures, and Mechanisms," *The Journal of Politics* 69, no. 2 (May 2007): 538–554.

7. Svend-Erik Skaaning, Niels Bossen, and Jeppe Kehlet Sørensen, "What Explains Respect for the Rule of Law? Evidence from a Cross-National Analysis of Structural Conditions" (paper presented at the annual meeting of the Midwest Political Science Association, Chicago, Illinois, April 3–6, 2008).

8. Marko Grdesic and Viktor Koska, "Governance in the Weak State–Weak Society Settings of Eastern Europe" (paper presented at the 21st World Congress of the International Political Science Association, Santiago, Chile, July 12–16, 2009). Some scholars also use governance measures from non–World Bank sources, such as the International Country Risk Guide. See Deborah A. Bräutigam and Stephen Knack, "Foreign Aid, Institutions, and Governance in Sub-Saharan Africa," *Economic Development and Cultural Change* 52, no. 2 (2004): 255–285.

9. The eighteenth-century philosopher David Hume famously expounded this concept in *A Treatise of Human Nature*.

10. The terms *exogenous* and *endogenous* are used in different ways. For a nontechnical discussion of their application in comparative politics, see Jan-Erik Lane and Svante Ersson, *Democracy: A Comparative Approach* (London: Routledge, 2003), 82–85.

11. See "G," "Glossary," Energy Information Administration, www.eia.doe.gov/glossary/glossary_g.htm, for the difference between GDP and gross national product, or GNP, which essentially includes net foreign investment. For both figures for the United States see Econ Stats, www.econstats.com/gdp/gdp__q10.htm.

12. Paul Collier, *The Bottom Billion: Why the Poorest Countries Are Failing and What Can Be Done About It* (Oxford: Oxford University Press, 2007), 64.

13. Christopher J. Anderson, "Parties, Party Systems, and Satisfaction with Democratic Performance in the New Europe," *Political Studies* 46 (1998): 572–588; Carlos Santiso, "Governance Conditionality and the Reform of Multilateral Development Finance: The Role of the Group of Eight," G8 Governance 7, G8 Information Centre, 2002, www.g8.utoronto.ca/governance/santiso2002-gov7.pdf.

14. S. C. Stokes, "Political Parties and Democracy," *Annual Review of Political Science* 2 (1999): 243–267; Mark Bevir, "Governance," in *Encyclopedia of Governance*, ed. Mark Bevir (London: Sage Reference Publication, 2007), 1:379; Robert B. Albritton and Thawilwadee Bureekul, "Are Democracy and 'Good Governance' Always Compatible? Competing Values in the Thai Political Arena" (paper presented at the 21st World Congress of the International Political Science Association, Santiago, Chile, July 12–16, 2009).

15. Timothy J. Colton and Stephen Holmes, eds., *The State After Communism: Governance in the New Russia* (Lanham, MD: Rowman & Littlefield, 2006); Thomas F. Remington, "Democracy, Governance, and Inequality: Evidence from the Russian Regions" (paper presented at the annual meeting of the Midwest Political Science Association, Chicago, Illinois, April 3–5, 2008). Philip Keefer finds that young democracies in particular tend to underperform in governance; see his "Clientilism, Credibility, and the Policy Choices of Young Democracies," *American Journal of Political Science* 51, no. 4 (October 2007): 804–821.

16. Bevir, "Governance," 378–379.

17. Sylvain Brouard cites "two essentially divergent views on the relationship between political parties and governance" in "Political Party," in *Encyclopedia of Governance*, ed. Mark Bevir (London: Sage Reference Publication, 2007), 2:720.

18. Kenneth Janda, *Political Parties: A Cross-National Survey* (New York: The Free Press, 1980), 5.

19. Alan Siaroff, "A Typology of Contemporary Party Systems" (paper presented at the 20th World Congress of the International Political Science Association, Fukuoka, Japan, July 9–13, 2006).

20. Jan-Erik Lane and Svante Ersson, *Politics and Society in Western Europe*, 3rd ed. (London: Sage Publications, 1994), 180.

Chapter 4

The Effects of Country Size

Is there a relationship between the size of a country and the quality of its government? For centuries, political philosophers (e.g., early Greeks, Montesquieu, Rousseau) thought there was. In their pioneering book *Size and Democracy*, Robert Dahl and Edward Tufte write, "Until quite recently—around the end of the eighteenth century—there was little dissent among political philosophers from the view that a democracy or a republic had to be small: a democracy had to be a city-state, by modern standards quite tiny."[1] They continue, "Smallness, it was thought, enhanced the opportunities for participation in and control of the government in many ways."[2] More poetically, the ancient Chinese philosopher Laozi wrote of bigness, "Governing a large country is like frying a small fish. You spoil it with too much poking."[3]

Later theorists have thought otherwise. The development of elected representative assemblies made democracy possible in large nation-states. Indeed, James Madison in *Federalist* 10 argues that "the greater [the] number of citizens and extent of territory," the easier for the majority to counter the pernicious effects of minority factions. Dahl and Tufte counter that the more citizens there are in the political system, the harder it is for them to communicate their preferences to, and to control, decision makers. Other theorists have thought the same.[4]

Dana Ott's comprehensive study of 222 polities published in 2000 found that small states "were significantly more likely than large states to be democratic, particularly when small states are defined as those countries having . . . 1.5 million population or less."[5] Although country size has long been argued to have effects on democratic government, democracy and governance are essentially different concepts. Of the six WGIs, only Voice and Accountability has any logical connection to democracy.[6] Even authoritarian states can theoretically pursue the Rule of Law, Government Effectiveness, Control of Corruption, Regulatory Quality, and Political Stability. Putting the question differently, is there any relationship between the size of a country and the quality of its governance?

Several scholars have hypothesized that the larger the country, the lower the quality of governance. Marcus Kurtz and Andrew Schrank supply the reasoning: "Larger societies are more complex and in principle more difficult to administer."[7] Although their own research predicting to Government Effectiveness produced only weak support for the hypothesis, research by others using Control of Corruption provided stronger support.[8] Before the recent interest in the concept of governance, a much earlier study of political system performance (quite similar to governance) tested for country size but found no significant effects.[9] Still others seeking to explain the Rule of Law found mixed results concerning country size.[10]

One limitation of previous research is that it treated country size as a control variable among other variables and not as a prime causal factor. However, the case is very strong for treating size as an early, independent cause of the quality of governance. Cause must precede effect, and country size is certainly fixed long before contemporary governments take power. It is also fixed before virtually any other likely causes of governance (e.g., wealth or politics). In statistical terms, country size is a classic example of an exogenous variable—one whose value is independent of the other values in the explanatory model. It stands outside the system of variables that it affects. This argues for assessing the direct effects of country size alone on governance.

Measuring Country Size

Previous research on country size did not devote much attention to measurement options. Of the four studies cited above that considered the effects of country size on governance, three measured size according to population; only one measured it according to territory.[11] Dahl and Tufte's book does suggest measurement alternatives: "A territorial entity has several dimensions of size: population, area, density, and others."[12] Although they do not explore the effects of these options, they offer that "most discussions of the relation between size and democracy refer explicitly or implicitly to *absolute size*: the number of people, the number of square miles, the percentage of the population in cities of more than 20,000 people, and the like."[13] They also note that absolute size is sometimes less significant than relative size, particularly in international relations.

We need to look more closely at the relationship between the two major options—number of people versus area in square miles or kilometers—for measuring country size. As Figure 4.1(a, b) shows, the distribution of the

Figure 4.1 Distribution of 212 countries by (a) population and (b) area

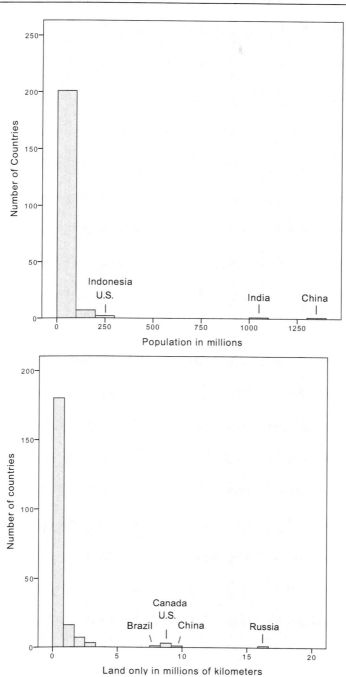

world's countries by size is highly skewed—whether measured by population or by land area.[14] Ranked by population, China and India, with over 1 billion inhabitants, are so large that they prevent most other countries from getting any space on the scale. Judged by land area, however, Russia rates as the world's biggest country. China is next biggest, followed closely by Canada, the United States, and Brazil. India is not among the largest countries in area, and only China and the United States register among the biggest countries for both population and area. Clearly, country size differs depending on how one measures it.

Figure 4.2 plots all 212 countries by both population and area. This plot suggests that only a modest correlation exists between the alternative measures of country size. (See Box 2.3 for how to interpret a correlation coefficient.) Some countries, like Canada and Australia, occupy large amounts of territory but are sparsely settled. India, on the other hand, is large but very densely populated. In fact, the correlation between country population and country area is only 0.47, but the high degree of positive skew for both variables affects that correlation—a few countries have very high values for both population and land area. The top eight big countries according to one or the other of the two measures are identified by name.

Figure 4.2 Plot of population and area for 212 countries

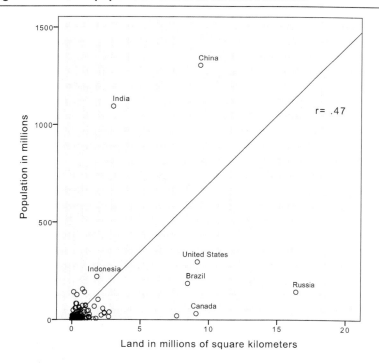

Figure 4.2 portrays a common problem in political research. Many important variables—for example, personal wealth, GDP, and deaths in wars—are dramatically skewed toward high values. Consider the personal wealth of Bill Gates, whose fortune is tracked daily on a critic's Web site.[15] In July 2010, the site estimated Gates to be worth over $63 billion. Gates is a distant outlier toward the positive side of any distribution of personal wealth in the United States. He and other very rich people have so much money that perhaps we should not measure personal wealth in terms of raw dollars but on a different scale, one that devaluates money as income increases. In fact, that is what economists do. They argue that the marginal utility (the relative worth) of $10,000 is far less for a wealthy person like Bill Gates than it is for someone making $40,000 a year. A $10,000 increase in salary is a 25 percent raise for a person with an income of $40,000, and a 20 percent raise for someone making $50,000, but less than a 0.00001 percent increase for Bill Gates. Perhaps personal income should be measured in a way that squeezes together values at the high end of the scale while not altering values much at the lower end.

A standard method for deflating extreme values in highly skewed distributions is to replace the raw values with their common logarithms. The common logarithm of a number, X, is the exponent to which the base number of 10 must be raised to produce X. Thus, the common logarithm of 10,000 is 4. That is, 10 to the power of 4 is 10,000. Here are the corresponding logarithms (rounded to the first decimal) for the above examples of personal income:

4.6 is the log of 40,000.
4.7 is the log of 50,000.
10.8 is the log of 63,000,000,000.

As this example illustrates, transforming raw data for personal wealth or income into logarithms keeps an income of $50,000 barely ahead of an income of $40,000, and $63 billion in wealth becomes less than three times $50,000 in income—not 1 million times. Whereas the z-score discussed in Chapter 2 is a linear transformation that does not change the relative position of any value on the scale, a logarithm is a nonlinear transformation performed with the purpose of changing the relative positions of the values.

A rationale similar to the marginal worth of money justifies a nonlinear transformation of the skewed values for country size measured by population and area. An additional 10 million people has less effect on a country with a billion inhabitants than on one with fewer than 10 million. Another 10,000 square kilometers means less for a country with 15 million square kilometers than for one with fewer than 1,000. Figure 4.3(a, b) displays the distributions of the raw data for country population and country area after they have been transformed into logarithms. Note that India, China, and Russia no longer stand as distant outliers, although they still top the distributions for population and area. Note also that both logarithmic distributions tend to

Figure 4.3a Distribution of 212 countries by population logarithm[a]

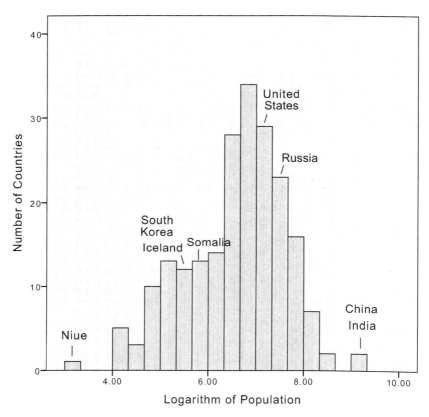

[a] Estimates of population for 2006 came from various sources, usually the CIA *World Factbook.* Computing logarithms compresses small differences in raw data estimates.

Country	Population	Logarithm	
Niue	1,800	3.26	Fewest people
Iceland	296,750	5.47	
Somalia	8,227,826	6.92	
South Korea	48,294,143	7.68	
Russia	143,113,650	8.16	
United States	296,410,404	8.47	
India	1,094,583,000	9.04	
China	1,304,500,000	9.12	Most people

Figure 4.3b Distribution of 212 countries by land-area logarithm[a]

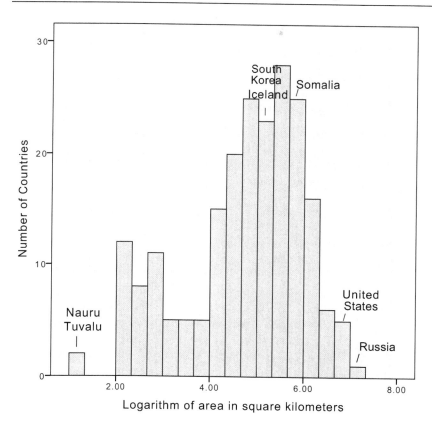

[a] Estimates of land area came from various sources, usually the CIA *World Factbook*. Computing logarithms compresses small differences in raw data estimates.

Country	Sq. kilometers	Logarithm	
Nauru	21	4.32	Smallest country
Tuvalu	26	1.415	
South Korea	98,700	4.99	
Iceland	100,300	5.00	
Somalia	627,300	5.80	
United States	9,161,900	6.96	
Russia	16,381,000	7.21	Largest country

be more unimodal and symmetrical than their corresponding raw distributions in Figure 4.1.

Some readers may think that transforming data into logarithms is unacceptable data manipulation rather than justifiable data rescaling. In fact, research has demonstrated that logarithms appropriately capture important human experiences. According to one university laboratory,

> Logarithmic scales allow one to examine values that span many orders of magnitude without losing information on the smaller scales. . . . Many aspects of nature are logarithmic. The human eye responds to changes in light intensity on a logarithmic scale. Since the difference in light intensity between sunlit areas and shade is so great, if your eyes did not work on a logarithmic scale, you would never be able to discern details in the shade! The intensity of the light from stars is often described using the magnitude scale, which is a logarithmic scale relating large changes in light intensity to the response of the human eye.[16]

Even people familiar with the Richter scale for measuring earthquakes may not realize that it too is based on logarithms. Each one-point increase on the Richter scale really measures ten times the quake's magnitude. For example, a "moderate" quake of 5.0 is ten times greater than a "light" quake of 4.0, a "strong" quake of 6.0 is ten times greater than a moderate quake, and a "major" quake of 7.0 is ten times greater than a strong quake.[17]

For our purposes, the question becomes, Does transforming country population and land area into logarithms help us in measuring country size? Recall that country population and area correlated only 0.47 when expressed as raw values in Figure 4.2. As displayed in Figure 4.4, the correlation between the logarithms for country population and country size becomes a robust 0.87, and the plot of the cases is fairly even around the regression line.

Both the high correlation in Figure 4.4 and the tighter clustering of cases suggests that country population and area have much in common. The seven big countries that were widely scattered in Figure 4.2 are more neatly grouped toward the top on both population and area. When alternative indicators of a single property (here, country size) are so highly correlated, researchers often combine them into a single measure, assuming that the combination measures the property more reliably than the individual indicators. We tried that approach, adding country population to country area and creating one measure of country size.[18] We show, however, that doing so is not entirely satisfactory, for country population and country area have somewhat different effects on each of the six governance indicators.

Analyzing Effects of Country Size

Earlier in this chapter, we proposed that smaller countries are easier to govern than larger countries because (in the words of Kurtz and Schrank) "larger

Figure 4.4 Plot of population (log) and area (log) for 212 countries

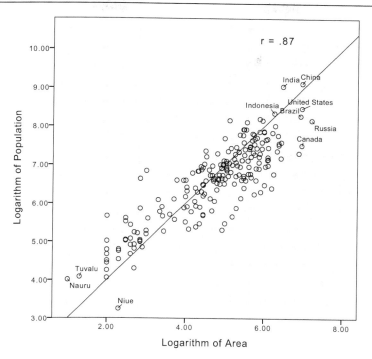

societies are more complex and in principle more difficult to administer."
What makes this so? Are larger countries complex because they have more
people? Or are they complex because their people are spread over more
territory? Having two independent measures of country population and land
area, we can determine whether one has more effect on governance than the
other. (See Box 4.1 for issues in comparing countries by area and population.)

In this and the next chapter, we rely on one indicator, Rule of Law (RL), to
illustrate our statistical analysis of variable effects on the governance indicators. According to Table A.1 in Appendix A, Daniel Kaufmann, Aart Kraay,
and Massimo Mastruzzi scored countries on Rule of Law using such items of
information as losses and costs associated with crime, fairness of the judicial
process, presence of an independent judiciary, quality of police, security of
contracts, and so on. Rule of Law showed the highest average intercorrelation
(0.87) with the other five indicators (see Figure 2.1), and it was scored on
211 of the 212 countries (Niue being the exception). We should distinguish
between Rule of Law (capitalized) as a WGI measure of country governance
and rule of law (lowercase) as a concept central to many notions of country
governance. Ashraf Ghani and Clare Lockhart refer to rule of law as the
"glue" that "binds all aspects of the state, the economy, and society,"[19] and
the U.S. Agency for International Development calls rule of law its "strategic
focus" because it fosters order and security, legitimacy, checks and balances,

---

Box 4.1: Country Area and Population: Measurement Issues

Both total land area and total population are crude measures of country size in themselves. Both measures only allow rough comparisons among all countries while ignoring huge differences among specific countries.

Take the case of land area in Greenland. Greenland covers over 2 million square kilometers and is among the largest countries of the world. However, its fewer than 60,000 people are concentrated among coastal towns, mainly in the southwest. Because nearly all its interior is uninhabited, Greenland has the lowest population density of any country in the world. Should uninhabited areas be included in measuring country size?

Contrast Greenland with Indonesia, the fourth most populous nation in the world. Its nearly 240,000,000 inhabitants are spread over almost 2 million square kilometers—an area almost as big as Greenland. However, Indonesia is an archipelago spread over 17,500 islands, with more than 6,000 inhabited. Should lack of contiguity in land area be considered when measuring country size?

Measurement issues also arise concerning country population. Consider China and India, the two most populous countries in the world. Each country has more than 1 billion citizens, but China's population is more homogeneous. More than 90 percent are ethnic Han, nearly everyone is literate in the written Chinese language, about two-thirds speak the Mandarin dialect, and there are no major religious schisms. In contrast, only about 70 percent of Indians are ethnic Indo-Aryan, only about 40 percent speak the main language (Hindi), and India has major religious divisions. Should issues of population heterogeneity be considered in population size as an indicator of complexity?

Although we acknowledge these issues in measuring country size, we do not consider them in our elementary statistical analyses. They remain to be treated in more sophisticated research.

---

fairness, and effective enforcement.[20] As Thomas Carothers notes, however, aid practitioners are uncertain of the meaning of the phrase "rule of law," which is a topic "of great conceptual and practical complexity."[21] Rachel Kleinfeld identifies different meanings and ways of defining it.[22]

Note that rule of law differs from democracy. Writing about the decision at the Fifteenth Congress of the Chinese Communist Party in 1997 "to give priority to the rule of law rather than democracy," Yingyi Qian and Jinglian Wu observe, "The rule of law is not the same as democracy. For example, the two most free market economies, Hong Kong and Singapore, observe the rule of law but are not democracies by Western standards."[23] Rule of law, they say, is necessary for a modern market economy but does not "directly and immediately threaten the governing power of the Party." After illustrating the analysis for Rule of Law, we summarize the results for all six indicators. The causal effects are quite similar for most indicators but not for all six. We will theorize about why the relationships differ.

At this point, we engage in elementary statistical analysis. Readers who know some statistics may be impatient with the slow pace of the presentation, whereas those unfamiliar with statistics may find the pace too fast and the discussion quite challenging. For them, reading will take some time and considerable thought. After chewing on and eventually digesting this chapter, however, they should be able to read and understand the remaining chapters comfortably. So, for the statistically knowledgeable, we ask your tolerance; for those learning new analytical skills, we request your attention over the next few pages. We think you will find what you learn rewarding.

The Rule of Law and the other governance indicators are the dependent variables in our analysis. The extent to which all countries vary above and below the mean on these indicators is called the total variation, measured by computing the sum of the squared distances of every country's value on an indicator from the indicator's mean value over all countries (see Box 4.2). Because our indicators are measured using z-scores, the total variation for each indicator equals the number of countries (ranging from 205 to 212) on which it was scored.[24]

Ideally, researchers hope to account for the total variation around each governance indicator with one or more independent variables. We hope to explain much of the variation in governance scores using country size, wealth, and party system traits as independent variables. To simplify the analysis, we will score the independent variables such that an increase in each factor produces an increase in governance. Accordingly, we rescore our three measures of country size by multiplying the associated logarithm by -1 as follows:

SmallArea $= -1 \times$ log of the land area in square kilometers, converted to z-scores (see Box 2.2)

SmallPop $= -1 \times$ log of the population, converted to z-scores

Henceforth, we refer to the rescored country size variables by these names: SmallArea and SmallPop. Furthermore, we convert both small size variables to z-scores to correspond to the governance indicators, also measured in z-scores. This helps in interpreting the data analysis below.

Although researchers hope to account for most of the total variation in their dependent variables of interest, in practice, they often fall far short of their desires. Let us see how much of the total variation in Rule of Law the single variable SmallArea can explain through correlation and regression analysis. Figure 4.5 reports the results for all 211 countries, clearly identifying the specific predictions for our five tracking countries.

Box 4.2: The Concept of Total Variation

This graph illustrates the concept of total variation. It plots 211 country scores for Rule of Law against an uncorrelated variable assigned by chance to each country. The correlation between Rule of Law and the random variable is 0.00, signifying the complete absence of any relationship.

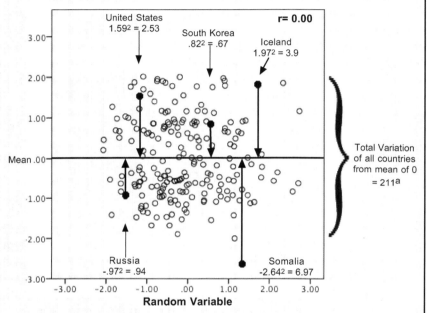

Variation computed for five countries = 15.01

[a] Total variation in z-scores = Number of countries (see note 24)
Variation for five countries = Sum of squared deviations from 0 = 2.53 + 0.67 + 3.90 + 0.94 + 6.97 = 15.01

Black dots mark the countries we are tracking. Their positions on the horizontal *x* axis are randomly assigned. They rate relatively high or low on governance, measured here by Rule of Law on the vertical *y* axis.

The squared deviations from the mean for these five countries are quite large. For example, the United States scored 1.59 on Rule of Law. The mean for all countries is 0, so the U.S. deviation from the mean is 1.59. Squaring 1.59 yields a squared deviation of 2.53. The sum of all deviations from the mean is the total variation. Because most countries are much closer than the United States to the mean of 0, they contribute much less to the total variation. We seek to explain this variation—why countries vary about the mean.

The line drawn here at the mean of 0 is the best-fitting regression line. When two variables are uncorrelated, as in this figure, the best-fitting line is simply a flat line drawn through the mean of the *y* variable, Rule of Law. A flat line drawn through the mean of the *y* variable has no predictive value in terms of variation in the *x* variable. In this example of no correlation, knowing a country's score on the random variable on the *x* axis does not help in predicting its score for Rule of Law on the *y* axis.

Note that the regression line in Figure 4.5 is no longer flat. The upward slope indicates that the smaller the country in area, the higher its predicted score on Rule of Law. Drawn according to a mathematical formula better left to statistics texts, the regression line provides the best fit to all 211 RL scores. It is the best fit in the sense that it minimizes the deviations to the line for all country scores. For statistical reasons, however, the deviations are not simple differences but squared differences. The general formula for a regression line (using these variables) is as follows:

$$\text{Predicted country RL value} = \beta \times \text{observed value for country size} \qquad (4.1)$$

A computer performed the regression analysis using a statistical program, which read the data for all countries—their RL scores and their population or land area—and then calculated the line that best fit the swarm of data points. The best-fit line minimizes the sum of the squared deviations between the countries' observed RL scores and their scores predicted by the regression line. The line's slope is expressed by a numerical value called a regression coefficient that states the expected increase in Rule of Law (the vertical y axis) for each one-unit increase in country size (the horizontal x axis).

Figure 4.5 Rule of Law related to SmallArea for 211 countries

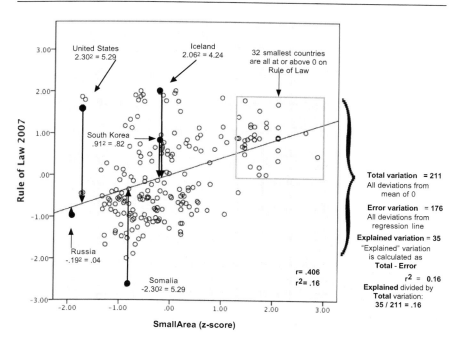

In Equation 4.1, β (called beta) is the regression coefficient by which the observed value of the independent variable (SmallArea) is multiplied (×) to yield the best overall prediction of the dependent variable (Rule of Law).[25] The best prediction also means the highest correlation between the variables. Given the data on Rule of Law and SmallArea for 211 countries, the statistical program computed a value of 0.41 for β to produce this regression equation:

$$\text{Rule of Law} = 0.41 \times \text{SmallArea}_{z\text{-score}} = .41\text{SmallArea} \qquad (4.2)$$

The mathematical formula that computes β is discussed in statistics texts and need not concern us here. Take it on faith that Equation 4.2 constitutes the best fit of a straight line to the swarm of country observations on both Rule of Law and SmallArea.

It will help to see how the regression formula is applied to the data on country size and Rule of Law. Chapter 2 states that the mean value for data scaled into z-scores is 0. Given that both Rule of Law and SmallArea are expressed in z-scores, both means equal 0. An "average" country has a Small-Area z-score of 0. When the score of 0 for an average country is multiplied by 0.41 in Equation 4.2, the predicted value for Rule of Law is still 0. In other words, an average-size country displays an average score on Rule of Law. Countries' Rule of Law scores will increase or decrease depending on the value of their SmallArea z-scores—whether they are positive (indicating smallness) or negative (indicating bigness).

The β coefficient of 0.41 can be interpreted as the effect of SmallArea. Each 1.0 (one unit) increase in the SmallArea z-score increases the predicted value for Rule of Law by 0.41. As theorized, therefore, as countries get smaller, Rule of Law improves. In general, the larger the β coefficient for the independent variable, the greater its effect on the dependent variable—in this instance, the greater the effect of SmallArea on Rule of Law. In general, you can judge the effects of independent variables by looking at the size of their β coefficients.

Although the regression formula produces a precise line, the country scores do not fit very closely to it. Table 4.1 reports the observed Rule of Law scores, the scores predicted by small country area, the differences between observations and predictions, and the squared deviations (differences) from the line. These deviations represent errors in prediction. For example, Russia (the largest country) deviates only –0.19 from its predicted position on the regression line. Russia's squared deviation (–0.19 × –0.19) is only 0.04—not much error. In contrast, the predicted position of the United States (nearly as large as Russia) deviates 2.3 from the regression line, for a squared deviation of 5.3—a great deal of error. (Note that by squaring, larger deviations count more toward error than smaller deviations.) Of the three other countries,

Table 4.1 **Five Tracking Countries: Rule of Law, Actual and Predicted Scores**

Country	Land Area (1,000 km²)	SmallArea Z-Score	Rule of Law Actual Score	Rule of Law Predicted Score	Deviations (Actual-Predicted)	Squared Deviations from Predicted
Iceland	100.3	−0.22	1.97	−0.09	2.06	4.244
United States	9,161.9	−1.74	1.59	−0.71	2.30	5.290
South Korea	98.7	−0.22	0.82	−0.09	0.91	0.828
Russia	16,381.0	−1.93	−0.97	−0.78	−0.19	0.036
Somalia	627.3	−0.84	−2.64	−0.34	−2.30	5.290

South Korea's RL score is not far away from that predicted, but Iceland's and Somalia's positions are also badly predicted by country size.

However, many countries do cluster closer to the regression line. Consider the box at the upper right of Figure 4.5. It contains thirty-two countries—15 percent of the total.[26] All thirty-two countries are smaller than 1,000 square kilometers, and all score at or above the mean on RL. Most are tiny island polities, such as Palau, a group of islands southeast of the Philippines inhabited by 20,000 people on only 460 square kilometers of land.[27] (In 2009, Palau offered to accept some of the Chinese Muslim detainees held by the United States at Guantánamo Bay.[28]) Perhaps the centuries-old philosophy that democracy is only possible in tiny countries has relevance here. As Philip Keefer observes, "The demand for roads or the costs of providing education or ensuring the rule of law are different in large, thinly populated countries than in small, densely populated countries."[29] At least, countries that are very small in area seem better able to extend the Rule of Law across their limited domains.

The correlation coefficient ($r = 0.41$) in Figure 4.5 shows that there is some relationship between the variables.[30] The relationship is statistically significant—meaning that it is unlikely to have occurred by chance. However, it is not especially strong—referring to its explanatory power. (See Box 4.3 for more discussion of significance and strength in a correlation.) By squaring the correlation coefficient, r, we create a more informative statistic, r^2. It tells how much of the total variation in the dependent variable—the one to be explained—stems from variation in the independent (explanatory) variable. Given that $r^2 = 0.16$, we can say that 16 percent of the variation in Rule of Law scores is associated with variation in SmallArea scores.[31] Clearly, factors other than country area explain why the United States has a high RL score while Russia rates very low on Rule of Law. More generally, country area is not closely linked to RL scores except for very small polities.[32] As we add other variables to the analysis, we increase the value of r^2 and thus the explained variation in Rule of Law.

Box 4.3: Significance Versus Strength of a Correlation

A correlation coefficient computed between two random variables will be close to 0. Chance factors usually prevent it from being exactly 0. The more cases that are observed, the smaller the role of chance and the more the expected coefficient tends toward 0. A formula (based largely on the number of cases) computes the likelihood of observing the value of a correlation between two variables if chance is the only factor. The likelihood is expressed in probabilities (e.g., 1 time in 100, 1 time in 1,000). By convention, a correlation is said to be statistically significant (not likely by chance) if it is likely to occur fewer than five times in one hundred, according to chance factors. This is called the 0.05 level of significance. The correlation (0.41) in Figure 4.5 is called significant because it would occur fewer than five times in one hundred if SmallPop and GDP per capita were related only by chance.

Researchers compute levels of significance to guard against claiming a relationship when none probably exists. Once significance is established, attention turns toward the correlation's strength, measured by r^2, which expresses the percentage of variation in one variable explained by the other. The correlation of 0.41 in Figure 4.5 accounts for only 16 percent of the variance in Rule of Law explained by SmallArea (allowing for rounding). The relationship is not especially strong, although it is significant. Unless otherwise noted, all correlations reported in this book are significant at least at the 0.05 level.

Nevertheless, country size seems to exert a partial explanation for variation in Rule of Law over all 211 countries. The r^2 value of 0.16 in Figure 4.6 indicates that the logarithm of country area in square kilometers explains 16 percent of the total variation in Rule of Law.[33] This 16 percent reduction in variation allows us to state, through regression analysis, that country area "explains" 16 percent of Rule of Law.

We used correlation and regression analysis to determine what effects different measures of country size have on all six WGI governance indicators. Figure 4.6 summarizes the results. The β values in horizontal bars show the different effects of country size on each indicator. The r^2 values in pie charts depict the proportion of variation explained by the country size. Land area as a measure of country size had the highest correlation with five of the six governance indicators.[34] In theory, the smaller the territory over which governments must extend these capabilities, the better governance they get. For example, Singapore's small size as a city-state has made it easier to police and combat corruption.[35]

However, Figure 4.6 reveals that SmallPop works better than SmallArea in explaining Political Stability and Absence of Violence. This finding may

Figure 4.6 Effects of country size on all six governance indicators and percentage of explained variance

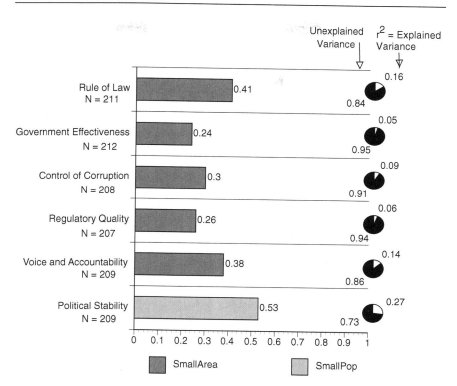

reflect political dynamics. Threats of revolution and terrorism issue from people who oppose governments. A major source of political hostility lies in volatile ethnic divisions, which may occur less often in smaller populations.[36] Because land without people cannot oppose governments, measuring country size in terms of people rather than land may serve better in explaining Political Stability and the Absence of Violence. On the other hand, measuring country size by population may better predict to Political Stability simply because (as reported in Appendix A, Table A.6) the indicator counts instances of violent demonstrations and political killings without compensating for country population.

Summary and Conclusion

For centuries, political philosophers contended that democracy could only be practiced in small countries. More recently, political scientists have inquired into the relationship between country size and the quality of governance without giving much consideration to whether country size should be measured by number of inhabitants or by land area. In fact, the absolute values of country population and country area in square kilometers correlate at only 0.47. Because the raw values of both variables are highly skewed toward large populations and large land areas, they should be transformed into logarithms. After logarithmic transformation, country population and country area correlate at 0.87, which suggests that both are alternative, but not equivalent, measures of country size and that both should be studied for their effects on country governance.

To facilitate statistical analysis, we converted our measures of country size to country "smallness." In that way, all the factors that we use to predict to governance will have positive effects, making it easier to add them together. Accordingly, we scored countries as being small in land area and being small in population. We also converted our country smallness scores to z-scores to match the measurement of the governance indicators.

Logically, cause must precede effect. Because country size, however measured, is fixed long before country governance and rarely changes,[37] the case is strong for treating country size alone as a causal factor of country governance. We illustrated our statistical analysis of the effect of country size on governance using the WGI measure Rule of Law. Elementary correlation analysis showed that SmallArea related more highly to Rule of Law than SmallPop. Simple regression analysis showed, as expected, a significant negative relationship between Rule of Law and SmallArea, which explained 16 percent of the variation in that indicator of governance.

Similar analyses showed that country smallness alone explained from 6 to 28 percent of the variation in all six WGI governance measures. For five measures of government capabilities, SmallArea was a better predictor than SmallPop, while population size better predicted to Political Stability and the Absence of Violence. As Chapter 2 shows, those four indicators of government capabilities tend to intercorrelate at much higher levels than the other two indicators. SmallArea also predicted to Voice and Accountability better. For these five indicators, the larger the territory governed, the poorer the governance.

For Political Stability and Absence of Violence, SmallPop was a better predictor. That indicator refers to what governments can prevent from happening—revolution and terrorism. Threats of revolution and terrorism issue from people who oppose governments, not from land area. Therefore, people become more important than land in measuring country size for Political Stability. The smaller the population, the greater the political stability.

Our ultimate objective is to determine the effects of political party systems on country governance—realizing that other factors may promote or retard country governance. In this chapter, we learned that country size, measured in understandably different ways, explains from 5 to 27 percent of the variation in the six WGI indicators of governance. Country size, however measured, does nothing to explain the relatively high scores achieved on all the governance indicators by Iceland, the United States, and South Korea. Perhaps their relatively high wealth facilitates governance in these countries. We pursue this line of investigation in Chapter 5.

Notes

1. Robert A. Dahl and Edward R. Tufte, *Size and Democracy* (Stanford, CA: Stanford University Press, 1973), 4.

2. Ibid., 5.

3. "Tao De jing," Verse 60. Whether Laozi actually said the second line is questionable. See "Talk:Laozi," Wikiquote, en.wikiquote.org/wiki/Talk:Laozi.

4. See the summary in Dana Ott, *Small Is Democratic: An Examination of State Size and Democratic Development* (New York: Garland, 2000), chap. 2, "Small Is Beautiful: Theories of Small State Behavior," 24–59.

5. Ott, *Small Is Democratic*, 197.

6. From Chapter 2, Voice and Accountability measures "perceptions of the extent to which a country's citizens are able to participate in selecting their government, as well as freedom of expression, freedom of association, and a free media." In fact, Voice and Accountability was used as a measure of democracy in Irina Denisova et al., "Who Wants to Revise Privatization? The Complementarity of Market Skills and Institutions," *American Political Science Review* 103 (May 2009): 284–304.

7. Marcus J. Kurtz and Andrew Schrank, "Growth and Governance: Models, Measures, and Mechanisms," *The Journal of Politics* 69, no. 2 (May 2007): 545. Kurtz and Schrank rephrased a claim by Xiaohui Xin and Thomas K. Rudel, "The Context for Political Corruption: A Cross-National Analysis," *Social Science Quarterly* 85 (June 2004): 294–309.

8. Xin and Rudel, "The Context for Political Corruption."

9. Powell, G. Bingham Jr., "Party Systems and Political System Performance: Voting Participation, Government Stability and Mass Violence in Contemporary Democracies," *American Political Science Review* 75 (December 1981): 861–879.

10. Svend-Erik Skaaning, Niels Bossen, and Jeppe Kehlet Sørensen, "What Explains Respect for the Rule of Law? Evidence from a Cross-National Analysis of Structural Conditions" (paper presented at the annual meeting of the Midwest Political Science Association, Chicago, Illinois, April 3–6, 2008).

11. Skaaning, Bossen, and Sørensen used territory.

12. Dahl and Tufte, *Size and Democracy*, 17.

13. Ibid., 18. Emphasis in original.

14. Data on land area is available from multiple sources. The United Nations GEO-3 Data Compendium gives land area in square kilometers for 2003 for 190 nations. An Excel file is available from the authors on request. A more comprehensive list of 233 nations is available at "List of Countries and Outlying Territories by Total Area," Wikipedia, http://en.wikipedia.org/wiki/List_of_countries_and_outlying_territories_by_total_area. The CIA's *World Factbook* site at https://www.cia.gov/library/publications/the-world-factbook/index.html reports country size by square kilometers for individual countries.

15. See "Bill Gates Personal Wealth Clock," Philip Greenspun, http://philip.greenspun.com/WealthClock.

16. See "A Refresher on Logs," Astronomy at WKU, astro.wku.edu/labs/m100/logs.html.

17. See "Richter Scale," *Encyclopedia Britannica*, www.britannica.com/EBchecked/topic/502877/Richter-scale.

18. When combining two variables in an additive scale, it is important to weight each variable equally. We do this by converting the logarithms of population and area into z-scores, insuring that each variable has a mean of 0 and a standard deviation of 1. We then add together the z-scores and divide by 2 to create a single measure of country size.

19. Ashraf Ghani and Clare Lockhart, *Fixing Failed States: A Framework for Rebuilding a Fractured World* (New York: Oxford University Press, 2008), 125.

20. USAID devotes a Web page to its focus on the rule of law at "Democracy & Governance," USAID, www.usaid.gov/our_work/democracy_and_governance/technical_areas/rule_of_law.

21. Thomas Carothers, ed., *Promoting the Rule of Law Abroad: In Search of Knowledge* (Washington, DC: Carnegie Endowment for International Peace, 2006), 19, 26.

22. Rachel Kleinfeld, "Competing Definitions of the Rule of Law," in *Promoting the Rule of Law Abroad: In Search of Knowledge*, ed. Thomas Carothers (Washington, DC: Carnegie Endowment for International Peace, 2006), 31–73.

23. Yingyi Qian and Jinglian Wu, "China's Transition to a Market Economy: How Far Across the River?" (paper presented at the Conference on Policy Reform in China at the Center for Research on Economic Development and Policy Reform [CEDPR], Stanford University, November 18–20, 1999 [revised May 2000]), 11.

24. Technically, for sample data, the total variation is divided by the number of degrees of freedom, which is $N - 1$, not N. A related term, *total variance*, divides the total variation by the number of countries, yielding the average sum of squared deviations. By means of the z-score transformation discussed above, the total variance conveniently equals 1 for each indicator.

25. Here, all formulas are expressed using standardized β (beta) coefficients instead of unstandardized b coefficients because the data are standardized scores. When a regression equation is expressed using β coefficients, the convention is to drop the constant term or intercept (a), for the regression line passes through the means of both variables, which are 0.

26. The thirty-two countries in increasing order of size are Nauru, Tuvalu, Anguilla, Aruba, Bermuda, Cayman Islands, Cook Islands, Macao, Monaco, San Marino,

American Samoa, Liechtenstein, Marshall Islands, Grenada, Maldives, Malta, Virgin Islands, Antigua and Barbuda, Barbados, Saint Kitts and Nevis, Saint Vincent and Grenadine, Andorra, Guam, Palau, Seychelles, Saint Lucia, Bahrain, Kiribati, Micronesia, Singapore, Tonga, and Dominica.

27. Carsten Anckar found that "islandness" among small states (and Christian religion) helped explain democratic government (not governance). See his "Size, Islandness, and Democracy: A Global Comparison," *International Political Science Review* 29 (September 2008): 433–459. For a related analysis, see Dag Anckar, "Dominating Smallness: Big Parties in Lilliput Systems," *Party Politics* 3 (April 1997): 243–263.

28. Mark Landler, "U.S. Hopes to Send Chinese Guantánamo Detainees to Palau, Officials Say," *New York Times,* June 10, 2009, A6.

29. Philip Keefer, "Clientilism, Credibility, and the Policy Choices of Young Democracies," *American Journal of Political Science* 51, no. 4 (October 2007): 804–821, at 814.

30. When there is only one independent variable in regression analysis, the value of β, the regression coefficient, equals the value of r, the correlation coefficient. That is not true for multiple regression, which has two or more variables, used in Chapter 5.

31. Squaring a correlation of 0.41 yields 0.17, not 0.16, but the slight difference is due to rounding.

32. The plot in Figure 4.5 exhibits the statistical condition of heteroscedasticity: unequal variance in the dependent variable over the range of values in the independent variable. The contrasting condition of homoscedasticity exists when data points are arrayed fairly evenly above and below the regression line along the full range of the independent variable.

33. Put another way, the total sum of squares for RL is 211 when calculated from the mean of 0, but only 175.4 when calculated from the regression line in Figure 4.5. This difference of 34.6 amounts to 16 percent of the total variation of 211.

34. Others have used the logarithm of land area as a measure of country size. See Luisita Cordero and Richard N. Rosencrance, "The 'Acceptance' of Globalization," in *No More States? Globalization, National Self-Determinism, and Terrorism*, ed. Richard N. Rosencrance and Arthur A. Stein (Lanham, MD: Rowman & Littlefield, 2006), 23–34.

35. Jon S. T. Quah, "Singapore's Experience in Curbing Corruption," in *Political Corruption: A Handbook*, ed. Arnold Heidenheimer, Michael Johnson, and Victor Levine (New Brunswick, NJ: Transaction Books, 1989), 846.

36. However, the correlation for 183 countries between the log of population size in 2002 and Alberto Alesina's measure of ethnic fractionalization is not significant, according to cross-national data posted by Pippa Norris at "Pippa Norris Data," John F. Kennedy School of Government, Harvard University, March 1, 2009, www.hks.harvard.edu/fs/pnorris/Data/Data.htm.

37. Special cases arise when new countries emerge from former countries and thus change dramatically in size. In 1990, for example, the Federal Republic of Germany essentially became a new country when the former West and East Germanies were united. In 1991, the former Soviet Union was dissolved and replaced by the Commonwealth of Independent States, consisting of twelve former Soviet republics, of which Russia was the largest and acted independently. However, both events created new countries for this analysis instead of dramatically changing the size of existing countries.

Chapter 5

The Effects of Country Wealth

When they deliver benefits to citizens, governments spend money. Governments' capacity to spend is linked with country wealth. Wealthy countries, therefore, have more governing capacity than poor countries and should rate higher in all six measures of governance.[1] In cross-national studies, total country wealth is typically measured by estimates of gross domestic product (GDP), the total value of the goods and services produced in a country in a given year. Because countries with large populations generate more GDP than smaller countries, GDP is typically divided by population, yielding GDP per capita, a measure of country wealth standardized by population.

Virtually all researchers find strong positive relationships between country wealth (using GDP per capita) and country governance (regardless of the measures used).[2] Scholars differ over how to interpret that relationship. Many studies, perhaps most, theorize that governance produces wealth through economic growth. One of the founders of the Worldwide Governance Indicators project said, "The evidence points to the causality being in the direction of better governance leading to higher economic growth."[3] In direct contrast, other scholars have argued that "good governance is in all likelihood a consequence, rather than a cause, of economic growth."[4]

Regardless of which statement is closer to the truth,[5] neither applies to the analysis at hand, which considers the level of country wealth, not its rate of growth. The amount of wealth at a given time (the level) is quite different from the change in that amount over two points in time. Statistics on annual growth in GDP per capita—the change from one year to the next—are quite volatile. Country statistics on the level of wealth in a given year, however, vary relatively little from year to year. As mentioned in Chapter 3, country wealth is largely a function of geology, geography, and history. Nevertheless, some scholars argue vigorously that "the great differences in the wealth of nations are mainly due to differences in the quality of their institutions and economic policies."[6] Despite this argument, countries tend to be poor, rich, or in between, and they remain relatively fixed in place over generations.

Measuring Country Wealth

Like measures of country size, wealth is heavily skewed, with a few very rich countries and many poor ones. Accordingly, researchers typically adjust for the skewed distribution by taking the logarithm of the distribution of GDP per capita in dollars, as we did with measures of country size in population and area. Figure 5.1 (a, b) presents the distributions of wealth for raw data in U.S. dollars and for the logarithm of the raw data. The richest country in 2006 was Luxembourg, which boasted a GDP per capita of over $60,000, benefiting from its location in Europe and its booming financial sector. Next was Norway, with a GDP per capita of over $40,000 from rich natural resources, including oil. Once again, taking the log of U.S. dollars per capita pulls in these very wealthy countries while stretching out the wealth differences at the lower end of the scale.

We use 2006 data on GDP per capita, but earlier or later years would have served about as well. As stated above, countries do not change much in their levels of wealth. This stability is portrayed in Figure 5.2, which plots, for 104 countries, GDP per capita in 1960 versus 2006—forty-six years later![7] The correlation between the measures separated by almost fifty years is $r = 0.84$. Some countries, however, did shift in status dramatically over this period. Three—Botswana, Oman, and South Korea—substantially improved their relative positions in wealth during the interval. Botswana, one of the few economic success stories in Africa, transformed itself from one of the poorest countries in the world to a middle-income country, thanks largely to diamond mining but also to fiscal management. Oman benefited from modernization under a new sultan, who came to power in 1970 and expanded Oman's oil and gas production. South Korea exemplifies one of Asia's several success stories, as it moved from below-average to above-average wealth levels through government programs integrating it into the high-tech world economy.

In contrast to these economic achievers since 1960, several countries— Zimbabwe, Liberia, Congo-Brazzaville, and Burundi (all in Africa)—lost ground relative to others in the world. Once-promising Zimbabwe, weakened by involvement in the Congolese war, embarked on a disastrous land reform program under President Robert Mugabe that damaged its commercial sector and led to astronomical inflation. Liberia suffered fourteen years of civil war until 2003, which (along with government mismanagement) destroyed much of its productive economy. The former French Congo-Brazzaville—once

Figure 5.1a Distribution of GDP/CAP in 2006 in raw dollars[a]

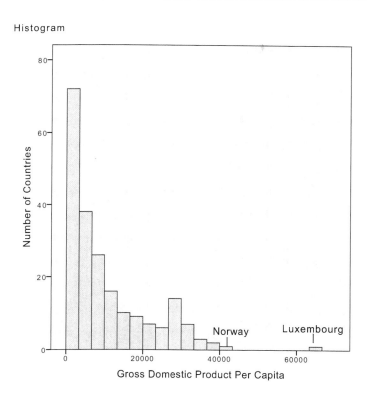

Histogram

Gross Domestic Product Per Capita

[a] Estimates of GDP per capita for 2006 came from various sources, usually the CIA *World Factbook.* Computing logarithms compresses small differences in raw data estimates. The countries are plotted by their logarithms in Figure 5.1b.

Country	GDP per capita	Logarithm	
Malawi	569	2.76	Poorest country
Somalia	600	2.78	
Russia	10,179	4.01	
South Korea	21,419	4.33	
Iceland	33,269	4.52	
United States	39,496	4.59	
Norway	40,005	4.60	
Luxembourg	63,609	4.80	Richest country

Figure 5.1b Distribution of GDP/CAP in 2006 in logarithm of raw dollars

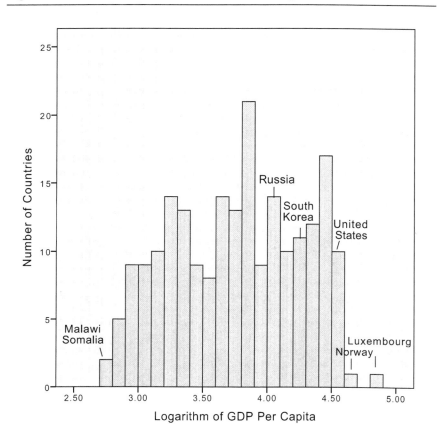

one of Africa's largest oil producers—abandoned its Marxist experiment in 1990 and later endured ethnic and political unrest while its oil production declined. Burundi suffered a dozen years of ethnic strife between the governing Tutsi minority and the majority Hutu rebels, resulting in over 200,000 deaths and hundreds of thousands of refugees and displaced persons.

These seven illustrations of countries' economic progress and decline from 1960 to 2006 demonstrate that country wealth is not rigidly static. Over a long period, intelligent government—or lack of it—can have profound implications for a country's economy. In the short run, however, the relative levels of country wealth do not change much. So, we theorize that, in any given year, country governance depends on the level of wealth, interpreted as a measure of governing capacity.

Critics, however, say that GDP per capita is a poor measure of a country's wealth.[8] For one thing, it does not reflect how equally wealth is distributed

Figure 5.2 Stability in GDP per capita for 104 countries, 1960–2006

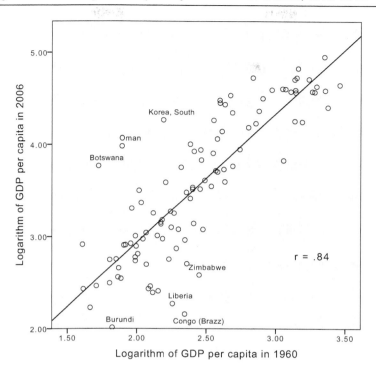

among the population. Vast income from oil production in Africa's Equatorial Guinea, divided by its population of 500,000, calculated in 2006 to a per capita income of about $34,000—almost as much as that for the United States. However, only about half the African country's population has access to safe water. (More generally, income from oil is suspect when it constitutes the main source of country wealth.[9]) Nevertheless, GDP per capita is the standard measure, and we use it in our analyses, while admitting problems in acquiring comparable data for all 212 countries.[10]

Assessing Effects of Country Wealth, Given Country Size

Before assessing the joint effects of country size and country wealth on governance, we must examine the relationship between the independent variables, size and wealth. If the size of a country strongly affects its wealth, then these variables are not independent of each other and cannot serve as separate causes of governance. In fact, as Table 5.1 shows, a statistically significant, but weak, relationship exists between both measures of country smallness and

Table 5.1 Measures of Smallness Correlated with Wealth for 212 Countries

	SmallArea (Log)	SmallPop (Log)
GDP/CAP (log)	$r = 0.24$	$r = 0.19$
GDP/CAP (log)	$r^2 = 0.06$	$r^2 = 0.04$

Note: Both correlation coefficients are significant at the 0.01 level for 212 cases (countries).

the log of GDP per capita. Smaller countries tend to be wealthier than larger countries. Nevertheless, the correlations are weak enough to treat both size and wealth as separate causes of governance. Figure 5.3 depicts the weakness of the correlation between SmallArea and GDP per capita ($r = 0.24$). The r^2 value of 0.06 means that SmallArea explains only 6 percent of the variation in GDP per capita. Countries vary widely on wealth regardless of size.

We are now positioned to assess the joint effects of country wealth and country size on governance. We do so using a technique called multiple regression analysis, which is very similar to the analysis in the previous chapter.

Figure 5.3 Plot of GDP per capita (log) against SmallArea (log)

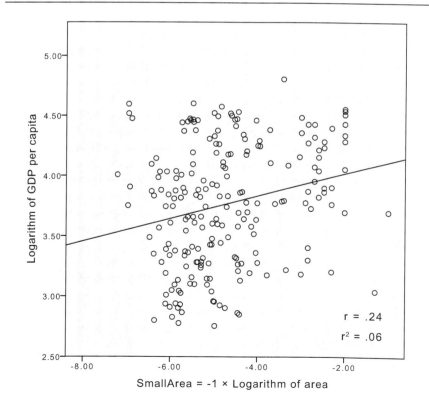

There, regression analysis computed a line of best fit for points plotted on the joint distribution of a dependent and an independent variable. Here, multiple regression allows prediction to a dependent variable from more than one independent variable. Through mathematical formulae better left to statistics tests, multiple regression determines the best combination of two, three, or more variables in predicting to a dependent variable. Moreover, the β_k coefficients express the effect of each independent variable on the dependent variable while controlling for the effects of other independent variables in the equation. A multiple regression equation has this form:

$$\text{Dependent} = \beta_1 \times \text{variable}_1 + \beta_2 \times \text{variable}_2 + \beta_3 \times \text{variable}_3 \ldots \tag{5.1}$$

For the present analysis involving two variables, the general formula is

$$\text{Rule of Law} = \beta_1 \times \text{SmallArea}_{z\text{-score}} + \beta_2 \times \text{Wealth}_{z\text{-score}} \tag{5.2}$$

The specific formula computed by the regression analysis is

$$\text{Rule of Law} = .23\text{SmallArea} + .73\text{Wealth} \qquad R2 = 0.66 \;(5.3)$$

The predicted Rule of Law score increases 0.23 for each 1.0 (one unit) rise in the z-score for SmallArea, plus it increases 0.73 for each 1.0 rise in the z-score for Wealth. Because the effects of both independent variables are additive, the combined effects of both variables predict a 0.96 increase in Rule of Law for each 1.0 rise in both SmallArea and Wealth.[11] Again, comparing the β coefficients reveals the relative effects of the variables. Wealth has more than three times SmallArea's effect on Rule of Law.

The symbol R instead of r differentiates the correlation coefficient associated with multiple regression from that for simple regression. R represents the correlation between the dependent variable and a computed predicted variable weighted by the β coefficients. For Equation 5.3, the multiple correlation is $R = 0.84$. Like r, R can be squared to express the percentage of variance in the dependent explained by the weighted combination of independent variables. For $R = 0.84$, $R^2 = 0.66$. Therefore, using two variables instead of just one increases the explanation of Rule of Law from 16 to 66 percent! Figure 5.4(a, b) compares the plot of countries' Rule of Law scores against countries' predicted score using Equation 4.2 in Chapter 4 and Equation 5.3 in this chapter.

Note the extraordinary differences in accuracy of prediction between the two graphs in Figure 5.4. The first, which predicts to Rule of Law using only SmallArea, is adapted from Figure 4.5 in the previous chapter. The second adds Wealth to the explanatory equation. The percentage of explained variation rises fifty points with the second variable, and the five countries

Figure 5.4 Two models predicting Rule of Law for 211 countries: (a) by SmallArea only and (b) by SmallArea and GDP per capita

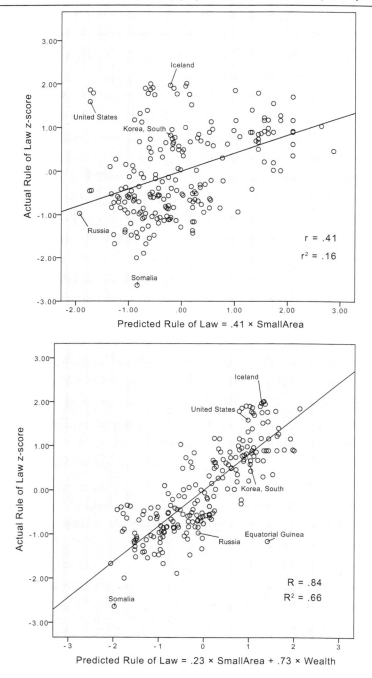

being tracked lie much closer to the regression line. South Korea's Rule of Law score is now almost perfectly predicted by its size and wealth. The high Rule of Law scores for both the United States and Iceland move closer to predictions, benefiting from both countries' high wealth. Russia's position, in contrast, falls further off the predicted line. Despite Russia's great size, its moderate wealth suggests that it should rate higher in Rule of Law than it does. Somalia's position at the bottom remains essentially unchanged. Of some interest is the isolated position of Equatorial Guinea, mentioned earlier as high in GDP per capita but also high in income inequality. Its unique position as a very small nation showered with great wealth from oil sets it apart from the others—far below its predicted position on Rule of Law based on great wealth and small size.

As in Chapter 4, we conducted regression analyses for all of the six governance indicators. Figure 5.5 summarizes the results. As shown by the β coefficients, country wealth had a greater effect than country size on every indicator. Although country size effects were reduced in each case after adding wealth into the equation, size continued to be significant for all governance indicators. The R^2 values show the proportion of variation explained by both small country size and high country wealth. The two

Figure 5.5 Effects of country size and wealth on all six governance indicators and percentage of explained variance

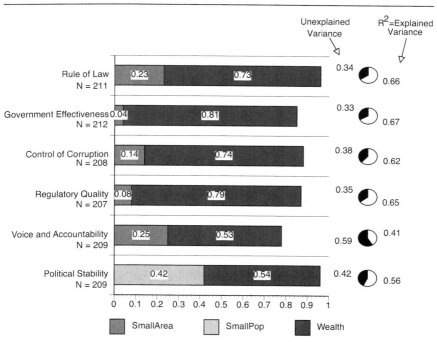

variables together substantially increased the percentage of explained variance in country governance.

Compared with the first four variables, the explanatory story in Figure 5.5 differed somewhat for Voice and Accountability and Political Stability. First, the effect of country wealth, while strong, was much weaker for these two indicators. Second, the joint effects of country size and wealth explained far less of the variation—only 56 percent for Political Stability and merely 41 percent for Voice and Accountability. Other variables not in our model presumably account for the unexplained variation.

Summary and Conclusion

Does wealth affect governance, or does governance affect wealth? Given that GDP per capita in 1960 correlates at 0.84 with GDP per capita in 2006, relative country wealth appears more a function of geology, geography, and history than of government. Wealth, in turn, provides the resources needed for governments to provide benefits to citizens, and it is a major factor in explaining country governance. In conjunction with country smallness, wealth explains from 41 to 67 percent of the variation in all six governance indicators for 212 countries. For each indicator, moreover, wealth has more effect on governance than country size. In light of these findings, poor countries certainly face strong odds against rating high in quality of governance. They may simply lack the resources to deliver sufficient benefits to citizens.

So far, we have found that almost one-half to two-thirds of the variation in all six Worldwide Governance Indicators in 2007 can be explained by two factors: country size, which essentially has not changed over time, and country wealth, which has changed relatively little over almost half a century since 1960. Because the substantial variations in Rule of Law across the world in 2007 systematically co-vary with variations in two variables that are themselves stable over time, our analysis suggests that variations in Rule of Law (and in the other five governance indicators) are largely, but not entirely, deterministic.

If country size and relative wealth are fixed in time, they will determine relative country governance for 2008, 2009, and so on into the foreseeable future. What can a country do (besides getting smaller or wealthier) to improve future World Bank governance scores? The United States and the United Nations, as well as other international agencies, link quality of governance to quality of political party system, described as the weakest link in popular control of government.[12] Specifically, a UN publication ties democratic governance to the development of "robust, transparent, internally democratic and accountable political parties," saying, "Political parties represent a keystone of democratic governance."[13] Would governance improve if countries had a more competitive and stable political party system? We examine the theory concerning party system effects on governance in Chapter 6.

Notes

1. In the language of research, wealth becomes a proxy variable for state capacity. See Joseph Wright, "Do Authoritarian Institutions Constrain? How Legislatures Affect Economic Growth and Investment," *American Journal of Political Science* 52, no. 2 (April 2008): 322–343.

2. See Marcus J. Kurtz and Andrew Schrank, "Growth and Governance: Models, Measures, and Mechanisms," *The Journal of Politics* 69, no. 2 (May 2007): 538–554; Jerome F. Venteicher, "Huntington's Third Wave—Cresting, Crashing, or Chimerical? A Comparison of International and Domestic Factors on Democratic Transitions" (paper presented at the annual meeting of the Midwest Political Science Association, Chicago, Illinois, April 5, 2008); Xiaohui Xin and Thomas K. Rudel, "The Context for Political Corruption: A Cross-National Analysis," *Social Science Quarterly* 85 (June 2004): 294–309.

3. Daniel Kaufmann, "10 Myths About Governance and Corruption," *Finance & Development* 42 (September 2005): 41–43.

4. Kurtz and Schrank, "Growth and Governance," 540.

5. In some ways, this controversy is similar to that over democracy and economic growth. Recent research holds that there is no relationship between the two. See Hristos Doucouliagos and Mehmet Ali Ulubasoglu, "Democracy and Economic Growth: A Meta-Analysis," *American Journal of Political Science* 52, no. 1 (January 2008): 61–83.

6. Mancur Olson, "Big Bills Lefts on the Sidewalk: Why Some Nations Are Rich, and Others Poor," in *Democracy, Governance, and Growth*, ed. Stephen Knack (Ann Arbor: University of Michigan Press, 2003), 29–55, at 47.

7. This correlation was calculated from data for 1960 and 2006 provided at "Economy Statistics > GDP (Per Capita) (1960) by Country," NationMaster, www.nationmaster.com/red/graph/eco_gdp_percap-economy-gdp-per-capita&date=1960. Data for other periods came from "Sort the Nations of the World," MrDowling.com, www.mrdowling.com/800gdppercapita.html.

8. One critic points out that GDP measures economic activity, not economic benefits. See Eric Zencey, "G.D.P. R.I.P.," *New York Times*, August 10, 2009, A15. Also see Joseph E. Stiglitz, "GDP Fetishism," in *The Economists' Voice* 6, no. 8 (September 2009), www.bepress.com/ev.

9. See Moisés Naím, "The Devil's Excrement: Can Oil-Rich Countries Avoid the Resource Curse?" *Foreign Policy*, September–October 2009, www.foreignpolicy.com/articles/2009/08/17/the_devil_s_excrement?page=0,1.

10. Sources sometimes disagree on both a nation's GDP and its population, providing two sources of discrepancy when calculating GDP per capita. There are also different methods for measuring GDP per capita. One major method is based on purchasing power parity (PPP), which adjusts for currency exchange rates. Another utilizes nominal GDP, which "does not reflect differences in the cost of living in

different countries." See the discussion of the two at www.en.wikipedia.org/wiki/List_of_countries_by_GDP_%28PPP%29_per_capita. We use GDP per capita in PPP.

11. Note that effect of 0.23 for SmallArea entering GDP per capita into the analysis is much smaller than the 0.41 effect reported in Chapter 4 (equation 4.2) for Small-Area alone. Because SmallArea and GDP per capita are correlated at 0.24, some of the effect of SmallArea (when used alone) is picked up by the correlated variable, GDP per capita. If SmallArea and GDP per capita were completely independent ($r = 0$), then the effects of each variable computed separately would be identical to their effects when both variables were entered in a multiple regression equation.

12. Thomas Carothers, *Confronting the Weakest Link: Aiding Political Parties in New Democracies* (Washington, DC: Carnegie Endowment for International Peace, 2006).

13. Democratic Governance Group, *A Handbook on Working with Political Parties* (New York: United Nations Bureau for Development Policy, United Nations Development Programme, 2006), v.

Part III

*Party System Effects on
Country Governance*

Chapter 6

Party Systems Effects: The Theory

With Jin-Young Kwak

The chapters in Part III analyze the effects of political party systems, not individual parties, on country governance. Newcomers to political science may be surprised to learn that party systems and political parties are distinct units of analysis.[1] Maurice Duverger formalized the distinction in his pioneering 1951 study *Les Partis Politiques*, which was divided into Book I, "Party Structure," and Book II, "Party Systems."[2] Many texts since have followed that format.[3] Often, however, scholars write entire books about political parties[4] or party systems[5] with little cross-reference between the two.

Before studying the effects of party systems, let us consider how different properties of individual parties can affect country governance. A political party can be defined as an organization that seeks to place its avowed representatives in government positions (e.g., in the national legislature or parliament).[6] Typically, party members gain parliamentary office through elections (usually free, sometimes not), but occasionally they fill the legislature without elections—as we will see. Very little research on political parties per se has sought to explain governance in terms of metavalues (e.g., Rule of Law, Control of Corruption) as we do here, but much research has tried to explain governmental outputs, outcomes, or policies according to differences in party traits or properties.

Theories of Political Party Effects

Most policy research concerning political parties has asked whether public policies differ under governments controlled by different types of parties—especially parties with different ideologies.[7] An early, seminal study in the late 1970s (when communism was still a force in the world) found that macroeconomic policies concerning inflation and unemployment in capitalist countries varied according to whether leftist or rightist parties controlled government. In general, leftist government pursued policies that lowered unemployment, while rightist government favored combating inflation, a policy theoretically incompatible with lowering unemployment.[8] A 1982 book, *The Impact of Parties*, largely supported these findings and also looked at government policies concerning the distribution of wealth.[9] A review of this research, titled "Partisan Theory After Fifteen Years," concluded, "Parties behave to a significant degree 'ideologically,' meaning that they promote policies broadly consistent with the objective interests and revealed preferences of their core constituencies."[10] Although interest in studying the governmental consequences of party ideology faded with the collapse of European communism and the rise of globalization, similar research continued afterward.[11]

For a hundred or so of the most established nations, scholars can readily determine which major parties are leftist, centrist, or rightist. For the next hundred nations, placing parties on an ideological continuum becomes very difficult. Moreover, ideology is only one property on which political parties vary. They differ in when and how they were formed, as well as in their electoral and legislative strength, degree of organization, centralization of power, social composition, legislative cohesion, factionalism, autonomy from other organizations, and so on.[12] Such data are difficult to gather across many nations, some of which have multiple parties. Often parties are ephemeral, appearing and disappearing over short periods. Sometimes they split into different parties or merge with others. Parties' more interesting aspects are usually not published in public records but must be inferred from close observation and creative research. In short, it is not easy to collect comparative data on political parties across nations. This vastly limits studying the effects of party properties—other than ideology—on governance.

Still, some researchers have done so. Philip Keefer, for example, considers the age of the main governmental party, whether it or the largest opposition party is programmatic. He finds that older parties are more programmatic and that programmatic political parties are related to lower corruption and higher bureaucratic quality but have no effect on the rule of law.[13] Ruben Enikolopov and Ekaterina Zhuravskaya also find positive effects on governance for countries with older main parties.[14] Cross-national research that measures the properties of individual parties, such as their programmatic orientation or even their age, makes heavy demands on availability of data and consequently is limited in scope. The cited studies involve only about one hundred countries and favor developed over developing democracies.[15]

Perhaps the properties of a nation's parties can help to explain its governance, but we do not address that question in this study. Instead, we concentrate our data collection and explanation on the effects of party systems, which conforms to a programmatic shift in democracy assistance. Whereas most Western aid programs for democracy assistance have sought to strengthen individual political parties in developing countries, Thomas Carothers sees that as a problem and proposes an "alternative way to view (and try to assist) party development."[16] He suggests focusing not on improving the organizational capacity of individual parties but "on the shape and function of the party system as a whole." That raises our question, Do different properties of party systems have different effects on country governance?

A Theory of Party System Effects

Scholars encounter difficulty in defining a party system. Most contend that a party "system" requires more than one party. Giovanni Sartori provides a typical definition: A party system is "the system of interactions resulting from inter-party competition."[17] Earlier and later writers agree that a party system requires competition between at least two parties.[18] However, the same writers often talk blithely about one-party systems.[19] For example, an eminent scholar once wrote in the concluding essay to his edited book on comparative political parties, "Only the co-existence of at least one other competitive group makes a political party real."[20] Nevertheless, his book included a chapter titled "Communist Party of the Soviet Union." Especially during the Soviet era, Western scholars argued at length that one-party states did not really have a one-party system.[21]

Today, a Google search for "China" and "one-party system" returns half a million hits. Because comparative party scholars also talk about one-party systems, a realistic definition of party system should be independent of the number of parties. Accordingly, we define a party system as the pattern of interactions of one or more political parties with government, citizens, and other parties. In short, we broaden the concept of a party system to include the government and the public as relevant political actors—not just other parties.[22] That allows us to speak of one-party systems because even a single party (as in China) must interact with the government and the public. In short, a one-party system is a political system that involves only one political party. In this study, however, we also narrow the concept's application to parties represented in parliaments or legislatures, excluding their interactions in elections. (We favor using the word "parliament" instead of the equivalent "legislature.")

As discussed in the introduction, our theory of party system effects on country governance originates in a normative theory: It is good to have political parties competing to control government in open elections. Underlying that normative theory is an empirical assumption: Countries with competitive party systems perform better than those without competitive party systems. We unpack that assumption in a testable, empirical theory explaining why and how competitive party systems perform better, resulting in better country governance, defined in Chapter 1 as the extent to which a state delivers to its citizens the desired benefits of government at acceptable costs.

Assumptions

Like all empirical theories with testable propositions, our theory of party system effects on country governance rests on a number of assumptions. In the logic of inquiry, assumptions are untested empirical assertions. They are untested primarily because they are too general or too vague to test—as, for instance, is the assumption in economics that actors behave rationally. We make similar assertions about political parties, formalized as follows:

A1. *A popularly elected government is more responsive to public opinion than one not popularly elected.* Popularly elected means chosen by citizens in free elections. Candidates for office may or may not be members of political parties. In a few countries, elections to the legislature or parliament are nonpartisan (e.g., in Micronesia).

A2. *A party government is more responsive to public opinion than a nonparty government.* A nonparty government is headed and staffed by kings, generals, oligarchs, revolutionaries, and so on. A party government is headed and staffed by party members, most of whom are outside government. Rank-and-file party members offer more contact with ordinary citizens than members of the royal family, the military, the oligarchy, revolutionary groups, and so on.[23] Single-party regimes exhibit some constraints even on authoritarian rule.[24]

A3. *Governing parties seek to retain control of government.* Governing parties do not pass all their desired laws and then withdraw from politics.

A4. *To the extent that elections decide control of parliament, governing parties respond to public opinion.* The threat of losing office induces governments to be responsive to the electorate. According to Adam Przeworski, Susan C. Stokes, and Bernard Manin, "Elections serve to hold governments responsible for the results of their past actions. Because they anticipate the judgment of voters, governments are induced to choose policies that in their judgment will be positively evaluated by citizens at the time of the next election."[25]

A5. *Public opinion favors government policies that serve general interests more than those serving special interests.* Although political parties articulate special interests in election campaigns, parties that control parliament must aggregate interests in the process of governing, which also increases their chances of reelection.

A6. *General interests are served when governments deliver benefits that serve shared metavalues.* As described in Chapter 1, metavalues are widely shared abstract values that transcend differences dividing the electorate.

A7. *The likelihood that governing parties will retain control of parliament depends on various factors:*

A7.1. *The competitiveness of the party system:* Some governing parties face little or no threat of electoral defeat by rival parties. Opposition parties may be outlawed, they may be restricted in various ways, their votes may not be counted fairly in elections, or they may be too weak to pose a credible threat. Genuine threat comes only from rival parties strong enough to succeed in challenging the governing parties.

A7.2. *The aggregation of the party system:* Party system aggregation and its converse, fragmentation, refer to the variety and strength of political parties at any point in time. A highly aggregative system has few parties that appeal to broad segments of society. A highly fragmented system implies numerous, sharp divisions in political interests, which make it difficult to please the broad electorate.

A7.3. *The stability of the party system:* Predictability in electoral behavior over time is the hallmark of a stable party system. Parties can calculate the electoral effects of their actions only in a stable party system. If the electorate is capricious, swinging wildly between elections in support of different political parties that may pop up or pop out, parties cannot reliably anticipate voting behavior, and governing parties cannot expect electoral rewards for good performance.

Propositions

In contrast to assumptions, which are simply accepted as given, a theory's propositions are empirical assertions intended, at least in principle, to be tested against data. We derive four propositions from the above assumptions:

P1. *Countries with popularly elected **nonpartisan** parliaments score higher on governance than those with unelected **nonparty** parliaments, which score lower on governance than those with parties in parliament.* (Derived from A1 and A2.)

P2. *The more **competitive** the party system, the better the country governance.* (Derived from A3, A4, A5, A6, and A7.1.)

P3. *The more **aggregative** the party system, the better the country governance.* (Derived from A3, A4, A5, A6, and A7.2.)

P4. *The more **stable** the party system, the better the country governance.* (Derived from A3, A4, A5, A6, and A7.3.)

These propositions employ abstract concepts—nonpartisan, nonparty, competitive, aggregative, and stable—that must be specified before they can be tested in practice. In the language of research, concepts must be made operational; researchers must state the operations used to measure the concept. For example, we operationalize country governance using the six Worldwide Governance Indicators:

> Rule of Law
> Government Effectiveness
> Control of Corruption
> Regulatory Quality
> Voice and Accountability
> Political Stability and Absence of Violence

Chapter 7 describes the data that we collect to operationalize the abstract concepts on party systems. Chapters 8 to 10 explain how we use those data to operationalize the concepts, and we match the concepts in the four propositions with empirical measures or indicators to form parallel hypotheses for testing with data about party systems and country governance. If the empirical evidence supports the hypotheses that flow from the propositions, the evidence implies support for the propositions. If the evidence does not support the hypotheses, the propositions may still be true. The hypotheses may have failed because of poor indicators used to measure the concepts. The attempt to validate a theory is inevitably an interactive process involving formulating the theory, operationalizing its concepts, and testing its hypotheses.

Party System Properties: Cause or Effect?

To this point, our theory has assumed that party system properties affect country governance—and not that country governance affects party system properties. Is the reverse possible instead? As in the question raised in Chapter 3, is the party system the chicken or the egg?

Consider the governance indicator Rule of Law and the party system properties competitiveness and stability. Does a more competitive and stable party system contribute to a high score on Rule of Law, or does a competitive and stable party system merely reflect the extent to which countries enforce the rule of law? It is easy to argue that party system competitiveness and stability are simply the effects of rule of law. When countries observe the rule of law, opposition parties are freer to compete with governmental parties for political power in multiple elections. According to this argument, positive properties of the party system are the effect, not the cause, of the Rule of Law indicator.

Staying with P2 and P4, it is hard to argue the contrary case: that party system competitiveness and stability cause countries to promote the rule of law. Indeed, Carothers's *Promoting the Rule of Law Abroad* reveals that even rule-of-law practitioners do not know what factors advance their objective. Primarily lawyers, they focus on revising specific laws or entire legal codes, training judges and paying better salaries, improving court records, reforming police and prosecutors, broadening access to courts, and so on. Carothers says, "Even when aid programs are able to facilitate fairly specific changes in relevant institutions, it is rarely clear what the longer-term effects of those changes are on the overall development of the rule of law in the country in question."[26] Reviewing ten analyses in his book, he finds, "Many of the chapter authors also urge aid organizations to be more political in their approach to promoting the rule of law. These authors' broad command 'to take politics more fully into account' has many variations."[27] Authors of some chapters in Carothers's volume contend that the authoritarian nature of regimes (e.g., in the Arab world) blocks progress in implementing the rule of law, while coalitions built across parties (e.g., in Africa) sometimes support reforms. Similarly, democratic winds of change in Latin America helped the criminal justice reform movement, while at least a period of political change temporarily advanced legal reforms in Russia.

Not all political parties see value in promoting the rule of law. Parties in uncompetitive systems manipulate the law to perpetuate their power.[28] In contrast, promoting the rule of law serves the purposes of leading parties in a competitive and stable system. Because voters prefer government by rule of law in contrast to government by rulers, the rule of law meshes with parties' strategic goals: to win votes and seats.[29] Although we have couched our argument for treating party system as the cause and governance as the effect in terms of the specific variable Rule of Law, it can be made more general: A competitive party system tends to promote country governance, of which Rule of Law is just one indicator. Recall our earlier definition of governance as the extent to which a state delivers to its citizens the desired benefits of government at acceptable costs. Competitive political parties propose government benefits in order to win votes and seats. Hence, they promote Rule of Law, as well as the other Worldwide Governance Indicators: Government Effectiveness, Control of Corruption, Regulatory Quality, Voice and Accountability, and Political Stability.

The test of our argument that party systems are primarily causes and not effects of country governance rests with the findings reported in later chapters. Let us grant that one can reasonably argue that Rule of Law causes party system competitiveness. A similar argument cannot easily be made for the other indicators. Take Government Effectiveness. Why should Government Effectiveness produce more competitive parties? What argument could one

102 ☀ *Chapter 6*

construct that would favor that reasoning? Nor is it easy to argue that party competitiveness is a reasonable consequence of Control of Corruption or Regulatory Quality. If we find that a competitive party system is significantly related to all or most indicators of country governance, the findings will suggest that the nature of the party system is causal, not consequential.

Summary and Conclusions

More research has studied the effects of individual political parties on government policies than the effects of party systems on government performance. Most scholars have defined a party system as requiring at least two political parties, ruling out the possibility of a one-party "system." Nevertheless, ordinary people and scholars alike still refer to one-party systems. Reflecting ordinary and scholarly language, we define a party system as the pattern of interactions of one or more political parties with government, citizens, and other parties. In short, we broaden the concept of a party system to include the government and the public as relevant political actors—not just other parties—which allows us to speak of one-party systems. We regard a one-party system as a political system that involves only one political party.

Party theory has a normative basis: It is good to have political parties competing to control government in open elections. Underlying that normative theory is an empirical assumption: Countries with competitive party systems perform better than those without competitive party systems. That assumption is in turn based on a series of other assumptions that we set forth. From these assumptions we derive four propositions that together contend that country governance is a positive function of party systems, especially competitive, aggregative, and stable party systems. Using the Worldwide Governance Indicators to operationalize country governance and our own data on party systems in 212 countries, we will generate and test a series of hypotheses derived from the four assumptions.

Notes

1. Alan Ware, *Political Parties and Party Systems* (Oxford: Oxford University Press, 1996), 6.
2. This was published in English in 1954 as *Political Parties* and is available now in many reprintings.
3. Ware's, *Political Parties and Party Systems* adopts a similar format. See also Giovanni Sartori, *Parties and Party Systems: A Framework for Analysis* (London: Cambridge University Press, 1976).

4. Robert Harmel and Kenneth Janda, *Parties and Their Environments: Limits to Reform?* (New York: Longman, 1982); Richard S. Katz and Peter Mair, eds., *Party Organizations: A Data Handbook* (London: Sage Publications, 1992).

5. Peter Mair, *Party System Change: Approaches and Interpretations* (Oxford: Clarendon Press, 1997); Arend Lijphart, *Electoral Systems and Party Systems: A Study of Twenty-Seven Democracies, 1945–1990* (Oxford: Oxford University Press, 1994).

6. "Avowed representatives" means that candidates must compete under the party's name or publicly identify with the party when in office. See Kenneth Janda, *Political Parties: A Cross-National Survey* (New York: The Free Press, 1980), 5.

7. Hans Keman, "Parties and Government: Features of Governing in Representative Democracies," in *Handbook of Party Politics*, ed. Richard S. Katz and William Crotty (London: Sage Publications, 2006), 160–174, at 161.

8. Douglas A. Hibbs Jr., "Political Parties and Macroeconomic Policy," *The American Political Science Review* 71 (December 1977): 1467–1487.

9. Francis G. Castles, ed., *The Impact of Parties: Politics and Policies in Democratic and Capitalist States* (London: Sage Publications, 1982). However, in the case of income redistribution, the relationship of leftist political parties to the labor unions was also important.

10. Douglas A. Hibbs Jr., "Partisan Theory After Fifteen Years," *European Journal of Political Economy* 8 (1992): 361–373, at 363.

11. See Carles Boix, "Political Parties and the Supply Side of the Economy: The Provision of Physical and Human Capital in Advanced Economies, 1960–90," *American Journal of Political Science* 41 (July 1997): 814–845.

12. See Janda, *Political Parties*, for a list of more than one hundred variables pertaining to political parties. The relevant portion of the book is available at International Comparative Political Parties Project, see http://janda.org/ICPP/index.htm.

13. Philip Keefer, "Programmatic Parties: Where Do They Come From and Do They Matter?" (WPS4185 Post-Conflict Transitions Working Paper 1, World Bank, Washington, DC, August 2007).

14. Ruben Enikolopov and Ekaterina Zhuravskaya, "Decentralization and Political Institutions," *Journal of Public Economics* 91, no. 11–12 (December 2007): 2261–2290.

15. This shortcoming has been noted by Joseph W. Robbins, "Party System Institutionalization and Government Spending" (paper presented at the annual meeting of the Midwest Political Science Association, Chicago, Illinois, April 3–5, 2008).

16. Thomas Carothers, *Confronting the Weakest Link: Aiding Political Parties in New Democracies* (Washington, DC: Carnegie Endowment for International Peace, 2006), 68–69.

17. Sartori, *Parties and Party Systems*, 44. Emphasis removed.

18. Ware, *Political Parties and Party Systems*, 7; Steven B. Wolinetz, "Party Systems and Party System Types," in *Handbook of Party Politics*, ed. Richard S. Katz and William Crotty (London: Sage Publications, 2006), 51–62, at 52.

19. Sartori, however, never speaks of a one-party system, which he refers to instead as a "party-state system" (*Parties and Party Systems*, 45).

20. Sigmund Neumann, ed., *Modern Political Parties: Approaches to Comparative Politics* (Chicago: University of Chicago Press, 1965), 395.

21. This point is made by Luciano Bardi and Peter Mair, "The Parameters of Party Systems," *Party Politics* 14 (March 2008): 147–166, at 150.

22. Like Myron Weiner and Joseph LaPalombara, we "treat parties, whether in totalitarian or democratic systems, as a generic phenomenon," recognizing "the need for linking the individual to the state," which is typically done by political parties. See Weiner and LaPalombara, eds., *Political Parties and Political Development* (Princeton, NJ: Princeton University Press, 1966), 433–434.

23. See the argument in Rudolf Wildenmann, "The Problematic of Party Government," in *Visions and Realities of Party Government*, ed. Francis G. Castles and Rudolf Wildenmann (New York: Walter de Gruyter, 1986), 1–30, especially at 8.

24. Joseph Wright, "Do Authoritarian Institutions Constrain? How Legislatures Affect Economic Growth and Investment," *American Journal of Political Science* 52, no. 2 (April 2008): 322–343. A more pointed argument occurs in Mary Gallagher and Jonathan K. Hanson, "Coalitions, Carrots, and Sticks: Economic Inequality and Authoritarian States," *PS: Political Science & Politics* 42 (October 2009): 667–672, at 668.

25. Adam Przeworski, Susan C. Stokes, and Bernard Manin, eds., *Democracy, Accountability and Representation* (New York: Cambridge University Press, 1999), 29.

26. Thomas Carothers, ed., *Promoting the Rule of Law Abroad: In Search of Knowledge* (Washington, DC: Carnegie Endowment for International Peace, 2006), 24.

27. Ibid., 335.

28. Guillermo O'Donnell, among others, notes that parties in uncompetitive systems tend to maintain the legally arbitrary power systems they represent. See O'Donnell, "Polyarchies and the (Un)Rule of Law in Latin America" (paper presented at the annual meeting of the Latin American Studies Association, Chicago, Illinois, September 24–26, 1998), 17.

29. Barry R. Weingast argues that elites in democratic systems also serve their own interests by observing the rule of law. See Weingast, "The Political Foundations of Democracy and the Rule of Law," *American Political Science Review* 91 (June 1997): 245–263, at 254.

Chapter 7

Party Systems: Data and Measures

With Jin-Young Kwak

In countries with competitive elections, political parties operate most publicly during election campaigns.[1] They are often more conspicuous in presidential elections than parliamentary elections. However, relatively few countries elect presidents, while virtually all countries have parliaments or legislatures.[2] (We use the terms synonymously.) Moreover, in some countries presidents must surrender partisan activities.[3] Parliaments, in contrast, offer a nearly universal basis for cross-national analysis of political parties. Unfortunately, votes cast in parliamentary elections often go unreported in smaller countries. Fortunately, one can almost always learn the percentage distribution of parliamentary party seats after elections. Needing to score as many polities as possible on features of their party systems, we collected data on the percentage of party seats held in lower chambers, not on the percentage of votes cast for parties in parliamentary or legislative elections.

Focusing on Parliamentary Parties

The percentage of party seats held in parliament is also theoretically more relevant to our research than the percentage of party votes. Because most electoral systems distort the conversion of votes won to seats won, party success in elections does not necessarily win party control of parliament. In presidential republics—which comprise about 25 percent of the 212 countries in our population[4]—party success in legislative elections is unrelated to heading the state. Political parties play different roles in presidential and parliamentary governments, and—as David Samuels and Matthew Shugart

105

have shown—parties' organization and behavior also differ.[5] We do not address those differences in this study. We simply assume that deputies seated by political parties are important to the legislative process in both presidential and parliamentary forms of government and that parties in parliament play a more direct role in that process than parties in elections.[6] So, both practical and theoretical considerations led to collecting data on parliamentary parties.

To assess the effect of parliamentary party systems on World Bank governance scores in 2007, we collected data on the distribution of party seats at two points: after a stimulus election prior to 2007 and after a referent election adjacent to the stimulus election.[7] "Stimulus" pertains to the election that installed the government prior to the 2007 governance scores, and "referent" indicates an earlier (or later, in some cases) election for comparison. The stimulus election captures the party system positioned to affect governance in 2007, while the referent election reflects the party system's stability over time.

We are unaware of any comprehensive statistical data on the presence of parties in parliaments in all 212 countries we are studying.[8] We collected our own data for this research from various Internet resources. By far the most important sources for the stimulus election were Adam Carr's Election Archives[9] and Wikipedia's "List of Election Results by Country."[10] Finding data for the referent election proved more difficult, forcing us to scour the Internet for information. The Inter-Parliamentary Union[11] helped considerably, as did the African Elections Database.[12] An obscure site, Travel Documents Systems, was the only source found for parliamentary seat data for the tiny polity of Réunion, an island east of Madagascar.[13]

Data in Table 7.1 on the status of parliamentary parties in 212 countries were derived mostly from the 2006 CIA *World Factbook* and apply to unicameral parliaments or to the lower chambers of bicameral parliaments.[14] Table 7.1 cross-classifies countries by two criteria: Do the deputies represent parties, and were deputies popularly elected? The second column shows that 185 of the parliaments in 2006 seated deputies by publicly identified political parties. Only 152 countries popularly elected all parliamentary seats. In another twenty-three, most seats were elected, but some were indirectly elected or appointed; in one country fewer than half were directly elected. Only 175 chose all or almost all of their deputies through popular elections—here we apply the phrase generously to direct selection by voters, regardless of the quality of the process. Macao elected less than half its assembly; five countries chose deputies in controlled elections; and four countries did not select deputies through popular elections, yet seated them by party.

Column 3 classifies nine countries with "shadowy" (unofficial or underground) parties by how deputies were selected. Seat data were obtained for only four countries (identified in boldface). Column 4 shows sixteen parliaments without party deputies, and half (mostly small island nations)

Table 7.1 Status of Parliamentary Parties in Lower Chambers in 2006[a]

Were Deputies Popularly Elected to Parliament?	Did Deputies Represent Political Parties?				
	Public Parties	Shadowy Parties	No Parties	No Parliament	Total
All deputies were popularly elected	**152**		8 *American Samoa*[b] *Marshall Islands* *Micronesia* *Nauru* *Niue* *Oman* *Palau* *Tuvalu*		160
Most were popularly elected	**23**	4 of 8 **Iran** **Jordan** **Kyrgyzstan** **Uganda** Afghanistan Bahrain Lebanon Maldives	1 Swaziland		32
Some were popularly elected	**1** **Macao**	1 Tonga	1 United Arab Emirates		3
All chosen in controlled elections	**5** **Belarus** **Cuba** **North Korea** **Laos** **Turkmenistan**				5
None chosen in elections	**4** **China** **Congo (Kinshasa)** **Eritrea**[c] **Sudan**		6 Bhutan Brunei Libya Qatar Saudi Arabia Somalia		10
No parliament existed				2 Nepal Myanmar	2
Total	**185**	9	16	2	212

Notes:

[a] Data are based on the 2006 CIA *World Factbook*. **Boldface** identifies the 189 countries for which we collected parliamentary seat data. *Italics* identify the eight countries with nonpartisan elections.

[b] American Samoa had one appointed and twenty elected deputies.

[c] Eritrea's parliament was chosen in one election, in 1994.

elected them through nonpartisan elections. Two nations in 2006 (Nepal and Myanmar) had no parliament or legislative body.

Parliamentary Party Data After Stimulus Elections

Although party seat data are more readily available than party vote data, obtaining even party seat data for 212 polities after the stimulus election was challenging and tedious. Despite the abundance of Internet resources on the world's countries, party politics are not well covered in many smaller countries. We narrowed the task by collecting data on only the three largest parliamentary parties elected in a national election held prior to 2007—the year of our Worldwide Governance Indicators. We recognized that some lag would occur between the election of a new parliament and its impact on governance, but we could only guess at the minimum lag time, which we arbitrarily chose as two years. With one exception, we fixed 2005 as the last date for a stimulus election—the parliamentary election that could affect World Bank governance scores in 2007. Table 7.2 reports the distribution of years in which stimulus elections were held. It shows that about 20 percent of the stimulus elections were held in 2005, and almost 85 percent occurred from 2002 to 2005. The earliest elections (1992 and 1994) were in Angola and Eritrea, respectively. Ten nations (Bhutan, Brunei, Libya, Myanmar, Nepal, Oman, Qatar, Saudi Arabia, Somalia, and United Arab Emirates) did not hold elections for a parliament or legislative council, although all but Nepal and Myanmar had such a body.

As Table 7.1 implies, some of the 202 elections in Table 7.2 were nonpartisan and elected no party deputies. In all, we scored 189 countries, identified in boldface in Table 7.1, for seats held by the three largest parties after the stimulus election. The remaining twenty-three countries are included in two

Table 7.2 Dates for the Stimulus Elections

Year	Frequency	Percent
1992	1	0.5
1994	1	0.5
2000	3	1.4
2001	19	9.0
2002	44	20.8
2003	37	17.5
2004	51	24.1
2005*	46	21.2
Total elections	202	95.3
No elections	10	4.7
Total countries	212	100.0

*Includes the January 25, 2006, election in the Palestinian Territories.

separate variables. Eight small countries with popular elections but nonpartisan deputies (those in italics in Table 7.1) are coded 1 (otherwise, 0) on a variable called NonPartisan, and the fifteen countries without parties are coded 1 (otherwise, 0) on a variable called NoParties. Table 7.3 reports that the three largest parties in those countries held an average of 82.5 percent of all the parliamentary seats. The median (not shown) was 89 percent, meaning that in half the countries, the three largest parties accounted for nearly 90 percent of all the seats in parliament. While we excluded some parliamentary representation by focusing on the top three parties, we did not miss much.

However, we did miss a lot of small parliamentary parties. A separate count of the total number of parties seated in parliament revealed that the average parliament seated 6.7 parties, with a high of 39 in Colombia. In few countries, however, did any parties ranking fourth or lower hold an appreciable percentage of seats. As disclosed in Table 7.3, the largest party in 189 parliaments after the stimulus election averaged almost 52 percent of the seats, compared with about 23 percent for the next largest and 8 percent for the third. In one country (Malta), the second-largest party held 49.3 percent of the seats compared with 50.7 percent for the largest party. The close division of parliamentary seats in Malta between its two largest parties implies a high degree of interparty competition. Later we rely on the percentage of seats held by the second-largest party as a prime indicator of party system competitiveness.

Parliamentary Party Data After Referent Elections

To evaluate party system stability, we compare how the three largest parties in the stimulus election performed in a referent election—an election temporally adjacent to the stimulus election. Initially, we thought that the

Table 7.3 Seats Held by Three Largest Parties After Stimulus Elections in 189 Countries

	Minimum	Mean	Maximum
Largest party percentage of seats	7.0[a]	51.7	100.0
Second-largest party percentage of seats	0.0[b]	23.2	49.3
Third-largest party percentage of seats	0.0[c]	7.6	24.0
Sum of all three parties	11.0[d]	82.5	100.0

Notes:

[a] Some countries (e.g., Belarus, Macao, and Kyrgyzstan) elected few deputies by parties, resulting in the largest party having a tiny percentage of all parliamentary seats.

[b] The second-largest party got 0 percent of seats in eleven one-party parliaments.

[c] The third-largest party held 0 percent of seats in twenty-seven two-party parliaments.

[d] Party deputies accounted for just 11 percent of all parliamentary seats in Belarus.

referent election should have occurred prior to the stimulus election. One can argue to the contrary that stability should be assessed over the lifespan of the parliament responsible for governance in 2007, not for the parliament that ends with the stimulus election. For some nations, moreover, an election after 2005 may more accurately represent its party system's maturity, as new parties become established and more familiar to voters.

Practical considerations resolved the argument in many cases. Elections prior to 2005 had often occurred many years earlier and involved defunct parties. Elections after 2005 sometimes reflected more comparable party systems. The wide range of dates in Table 7.4 hints at our difficulty in choosing referent elections. Although we favored choosing earlier elections, we chose post-2005 elections for about 35 percent of the polities. In two cases (Cuba and Pakistan), we choose 2008. Also in two cases, we were forced to choose years before 1990 (Angola, 1986; Rwanda, 1988). Eritrea's parliament, elected in 1994, has had no election since. The eleven polities that had no referent elections match the ten polities in Table 7.3 that had no stimulus elections plus Afghanistan, which had an election in 2005 but then none until 2010.

Although the Internet provided useful sources of information on parliamentary party compositions, we had to sift and analyze the data before determining how many seats each party held or even which party was which.

Table 7.4 Dates for the Referent Elections

	Frequency	Percentage
1986	1	0.5
1988	1	0.5
1993	2	0.9
1995	1	0.5
1996	4	1.9
1997	7	3.3
1998	14	6.6
1999	32	15.1
2000	28	13.2
2001	18	8.5
2002	12	5.7
2003	4	1.9
2005	1	0.5
2006	44	20.8
2007	30	14.2
2008	2	0.9
Total elections	201*	94.8
No elections	11	5.2
Total countries	212	100.0

* Eritrea had only one election, in 1994.

Different sources sometimes reported different figures. Often the sources differed on party names. Too often the parties experienced splits or mergers between elections, making them difficult to trace across elections and posing difficulties in deciding how to allocate percentages after party splits. Country experts, no doubt, will dispute some of our scoring decisions. We agonized over some calls ourselves as we rechecked our coding. We cannot verify that our data are error free, but we can link every score to a party and a source.

Table 7.5 presents our scoring results for parliamentary seats following the referent election. The scoring procedures used in Tables 7.3 and 7.5 need explanation. Whereas Table 7.3 reports on the three largest parties according to their size after the stimulus election, Table 7.5 reports on the same three parties regardless of rank after the referent election. For example, the Mexican PRI was the largest party after the 2003 stimulus election, holding 45 percent of the seats. After the 2006 referent election, the PRI won only 24 percent, making it the second-largest party. Nevertheless, we compared the PRI's seat percentages in 2003 with those in 2006. The process was reversed for the Mexican PAN, the second-largest party in 2003 with 30 percent of the seats but the largest party in 2006, with 41 percent. The PRI's percentage in Table 7.5 is included among the largest parties after the stimulus election, and the PAN's percentage is counted among the second-largest parties.

Often the largest party after the stimulus election was not always the largest after the referent election, causing the mean percentage of seats held by the largest parties to drop substantially (51.7 versus 42.4) between Tables 7.3 and 7.5. In some dramatic cases, parties holding a parliamentary majority after the stimulus election held no seats at all after the referent election.

Nevertheless, the correlation is substantial ($r = 0.60$) between the percentage of seats held by the largest party in the stimulus election and that party's performance in the referent election. Figure 7.1(a) graphs that correlation for all 189 party systems. Figure 7.1(b, c) graphs the correlations of 0.52 and 0.48, respectively, between the seats won by the second- and third-largest parties in the stimulus elections and the referent elections. Because the three seat totals cannot exceed 100 percent, the percentage of seats held after the stimulus election is logically limited to a maximum of 49.9 percent for the second-largest party and to a maximum of 33.3 percent for the third-largest

Table 7.5 Seats Held by Three Largest Parties After Referent Elections in 189 Countries

Size Status in Stimulus Year	Minimum	Mean	Maximum
Largest party percentage of seats	0.0	42.4	100.0
Second-largest party percentage of seats	0.0	23.0	100.0
Third-largest party percentage of seats	0.0	7.8	55.0
Sum of all three parties	0.0	73.2	100.0

**Figure 7.1 Correlation plots for the three largest parties in parliament
after the stimulus election and how they fared in the referent
election: (a) first-largest party and (b) second-largest party**

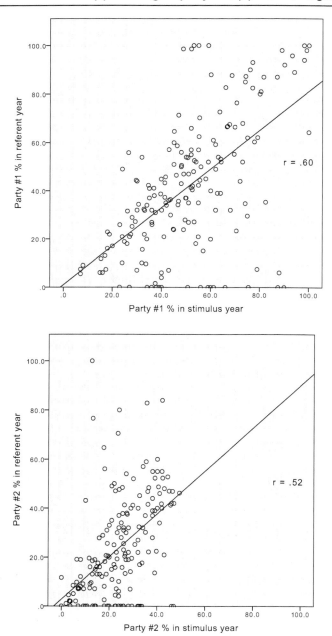

Figure 7.1 continued: (c) third-largest party

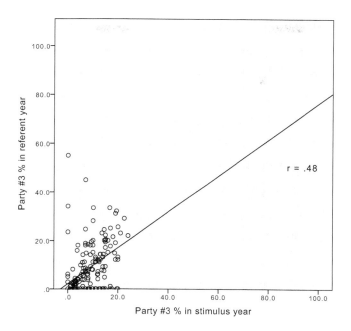

party. Note also that their seat percentages are not bounded for the referent election; that is, they can win greater seat percentages in referent elections.

We use these six items of data (the percentages of seats held by the three largest parties after two different elections) to derive various measures of parliamentary party systems as described in the next section. Appendix B lists all 212 countries and parliamentary seat data.

The Dimensions of Party Systems

The cross-national literature offers numerous measures of party-system properties.[15] Jan-Erik Lane and Svante Ersson have identified fifteen[16]:

1. *Electoral participation:* votes cast as a percentage of eligible voters
2. *Strength of largest party:* percentage of seats held by the largest party in parliament
3. *Actual number of parties in parliament:* parties holding at least one seat
4. *Number of parties reported by Thomas Mackie and Richard Rose*[17]: parties that have taken part in elections

5. *Fractionalization Index:* party number and size (created by Douglas Rae)[18]
6. *Effective number of parties:* parties weighted by their size (created by Markku Laakso and Rein Taagepera[19])
7. *Aggregation Index:* share of the largest party divided by the number of parties (created by Lawrence Mayer[20])
8. *Left-right score:* parties' scores from 0 to 10 weighted by electoral strength
9. *Polarization Index:* weighted differences in scores on a left-right scale
10. *Strength of socialist parties:* percentage of seats held by socialist parties
11. *Strength of parties to the left of socialist parties:* percentage of seats held by extreme leftist parties
12. *Strength of agrarian, ethnic, and religious parties:* percentage of seats held by parties representing these groups
13. *Strength of class-based parties:* #10 plus #11
14. *Strength of nonstructural parties:* 100 (#12 plus #13)
15. *Volatility:* changes in party strength over time (created by Mogens Pedersen[21])

The Lane and Ersson study is just part of a huge literature on conceptualizing and measuring party systems.[22] These writings reflect vastly different perspectives. Some are devoted to classifying party systems according to parties' relative strength and size.[23] At least one entire book focuses on conceptualizing competition in just two-party systems.[24] More recently, scholars have pushed for more extensive "assessment of the different arenas—distinguished vertically, horizontally, and functionally—in which parties interact with one another."[25] The point is that conceptualizing and measuring party systems is an extensive and complex enterprise. Moreover, most writings that propose different concepts and measures of party systems simply describe and analyze how their measures differ technically from others. Few proceed to determine what the measures explain about government and governance—assuming they explain anything at all.[26] Lane and Ersson say, "There are a number of relevant party-system properties and little justification for the use of one or two of these to the exclusion of the others. The study of party systems faces a conceptual problem about what the semantically relevant properties of a party system are."[27]

Although we do not expect to achieve definitive results in our study of party system effects on country governance, we hope to contribute to understanding party system properties by analyzing the measures laid out by Lane and Ersson and applying them in empirical research. We skip their measure #1, electoral participation, which pertains to voters not to parties. The next six measures (#2 through #7) deal in some way with the number and strength of parties. Four items (#8 through #11) involve estimating party ideology and issue positions, and three (#12 through #14) rely on estimating parties' social bases of support. All of the first fourteen measures assess party systems at just one point in time. Only #15, volatility, measures changes in party strength over two or more elections, making it truly different from the others.

After computing intercorrelations among all fifteen indicators for 201 elections from 1945 to 1989 in sixteen countries, Lane and Ersson found that the six strength and competition measures co-varied among themselves, as did most of the policy and social support measures.[28] They said, however, that "volatility does not co-vary with any of the other party system dimensions, which reflects the circumstance that volatility stands for party system instability in general."[29] We build on these findings in identifying attributes of party systems likely to affect the governance scores for the 212 countries in our study.

Measuring Party Systems

We did not compute all fifteen Lane-Ersson measures of party systems for our countries. We deemed their #1 on electoral participation and the number of parties competing in elections (#4) irrelevant. Lack of sufficient cross-national data precluded calculating their measures #8 to #14 involving party ideology and social support. Given Russell Dalton's evidence of the importance of party system polarization, this omission is unfortunate.[30] We are, however, able to generate measures that match Lane and Ersson's other six measures, and we generated four measures of our own, as reported in Table 7.6.

The formulas in Table 7.6 reveal that their measures #5, #6, and #7 are affected by #2, the strength of the largest party, p_1, and by #3, the number of parties in parliament, N. In all three measures, the proportion of seats held by the largest party affects the formula more than the share held by any other party. More subtly, increases in the number of parties in a system also affect the value's magnitude. In essence, items #2, #3, #4, #5, and #7 measure what might be called party system fragmentation (sometimes called fractionalization) or its opposite condition, aggregation. For example, the larger the actual number of parliamentary parties, the greater Rae's Fractionalization Index; and the greater the effective number of parties, the more fragmented the system. Conversely, the greater the strength of the largest party and the greater Mayer's Aggregation Index, the more aggregative the system.

The formula for volatility, however, is entirely different. As Pedersen wrote after evaluating the family of fragmentation indicators, "Fragmentation is a locational concept. The indicators of that concept, accordingly, are locational indicators that measure *states* of systems, not *change* in systems."[31] Pedersen's volatility measure, moreover, accords no special weight to the strength of the

Table 7.6 Ten Measures of Party Systems

Measure	Terms and Formulae	Source
#2 Strength of largest party	p_1, the proportion of seats held by the largest party	Anonymous
#3 Number of parties in parliament (count)	NPP, number of parties with at least one seat	Anonymous
#5 Fractionalization Index, F	$1-\sum_i^N p_i^2$, where p = proportion of seats held by party i	Rae[a]
#6 Effective number of parliamentary parties, $ENPP$ (formula)	$\dfrac{1}{\sum_i p_i^2}$, where p = proportion of seats held by party i	Laakso and Taagepera[b]
#7 Aggregation Index	$\dfrac{p_1}{N}$, where p_1 = percentage of seats held by the largest party; N = all seated parties	Mayer[c]
#15 Seat volatility	$\dfrac{\sum_{i=1}^{N} p_{i,t} - p_{i,t-1}}{2}$, where $p_{i,t}$ = percentage of seats held by party i at election t	Pedersen[d]
Repeat party representation	Which parties (#1, #2, and #3) won seats after both elections?	Janda, Kwak, and Suarez-Cao[e]
Strength of second-largest party	p_2, proportion of seats held by the second-largest party	"
Margin largest over second largest	Proportion of seats held by party #1 minus proportion held by party #2	"
Strength of third-largest party	p_3, proportion of seats held by the third-largest party	"

Notes:

[a] Douglas Rae, "A Note on the Fractionalization of Some European Party Systems," *Comparative Political Studies* 1 (October 1968): 413–418.

[b] Markku Laakso and Rein Taagepera, "'Effective' Number of Parties: A Measure with Applications to West Europe," *Comparative Political Studies* 12 (1979): 3–27.

[c] Lawrence C. Mayer, "A Note on the Aggregation of Party Systems," in *Western European Party Systems*, ed. Peter H. Merkl (New York: The Free Press, 1980), 515–520.

[d] Mogens N. Pedersen, "The Dynamics of European Party Systems: Changing Patterns of Electoral Volatility," *European Journal of Political Research* 7 (1979): 1–26.

[e] Kenneth Janda, Jin-Young Kwak, and Julieta Suarez-Cao, "Party System Effects on Country Governance, I" (paper presented at the annual meeting of the Midwest Political Science Association, Chicago, Illinois, April 22–25, 2010).

largest party. That is also true of the strength of the second- and third-largest parties, but their values are, to some extent, a function of the seats held by the largest one: the greater its share, the less that is available for them. Not surprisingly, all measures in Table 7.6 based on the strength of the largest party tend to intercorrelate at about 0.60 or higher. The actual number of parties in parliament and the strength of the third-largest party tend to relate moderately to all those measures. The strength of the second-largest party and the volatility score tend to be unrelated to any of the other six indicators. To avoid confusion, we avoid showing the one hundred intercorrelations among these indicators in a 10 × 10 matrix. Instead, we report a factor analysis of the one hundred correlations, which is a more powerful and precise way of determining what a set of incorrelated variables has in common.

The mathematics of factor analysis evaluates all the correlations in a matrix, then assesses the amount of variance (called communality) that each variable shares with the others and determines whether subsets of variables differ from one another. The factor analysis identifies any underlying factors that variables have in common and generates a matrix of coefficients showing how much each variable correlates with each factor. The number of factors identified depends on the pattern of intercorrelations among the variables and various criteria specified in the analysis. Our analysis, summarized in Table 7.7, extracts three factors that explained 80 percent of the total variance among the ten indicators.[32] In practice, this means that some indicators overlap, being alternative, imperfect measures of one of three distinct properties. The meaning of each property (factor), however, is left to interpretation.

Table 7.7 Factor Analysis of Ten Party System Measures

	Factor 1: System Aggregation	Factor 2: System Competition	Factor 3: System Stability
Party#1% stimulus year	0.87		
Mayer (log)	0.97		
Rae	−0.90		
Laakso-Taagepera (log)	−0.88		
Number of all parties (log)	−0.84		
Party#3% stimulus year			
Party#2% stimulus year		0.94	
Margin Party#1–#2		−0.75	
Pedersen (log)			0.78
Repeat party representation			−0.85

Notes: Extraction method: principal component analysis; rotation method: varimax with Kaiser normalization.

The decimal values in Table 7.7 are the correlations of each variable with the unobserved, underlying factors detected by the analysis.[33] These correlations are called factor loadings. Standard practice drops loadings below a certain level to prevent distracting statistical noise from obscuring the factor structure. We dropped all loadings below 0.70. The factor analysis reveals that five measures loaded on Factor 1, two on Factor 2, and two on Factor 3. One measure, the percentage of seats held by the third-largest party, had nothing much in common with the other nine measures. Again according to standard procedure, these three factors were calculated so that they all uncorrelated with one another. By inference, the ten measures tap three uncorrelated dimensions of party systems.

As mentioned above, analysts must interpret the meaning of each underlying factor. After observing which variables correlate (and how much) with each factor, analysts try to embrace the pattern under a conceptual umbrella, which amounts to naming the factor. The five variables that loaded highly on Factor 1 are often described in the literature as measuring party system fragmentation. Unfortunately, the literature often employs measures of fragmentation in confusing and contradictory ways.[34] Hoping to write on a cleaner slate, we name the factor "party system aggregation," a label with the advantage of describing the party system factor positively rather than negatively. (We discuss the labeling issue further in Chapter 10.)

We label Factor 2 "party system competitiveness" because it attracted a common measure of party competition (percentage margin between the largest and next-largest parties in parliament) and our preferred measure of system competition (percentage of seats held by the second-largest party). We name Factor 3 "party system stability" because of its high positive correlation with Pedersen's well-known measure of volatility and its high loading of a variable that indicated whether the three largest parties in the stimulus election won seats (in some order) in the referent election. (They did in only 45 percent of the countries.)

We consider the effects of each of these party system dimensions on country governance in Chapters 9 to 11.

Summary and Conclusion

To assess the effects of party systems on Worldwide Governance Indicators in 2007, we collected data on parliamentary party composition in all 212 countries at two time points: after a stimulus election held prior to 2006 and after an adjacent referent election. The stimulus election captures the party system that was positioned to affect governance in 2007, while the referent election reflects the party system's stability over time.

All but 2 of the 212 countries had a parliament, legislature, or legislative council. We identified 189 countries that had parliamentary political parties and 23 that did not. For those with parties, we determined the percentages of seats held by the three largest parliamentary parties after the stimulus election and the percentages held by the same three parties following the referent election.

Guided by previous research on party system traits, we used our data to create ten measures of party systems. Factor analysis of the ten measures disclosed three underlying and uncorrelated factors, or dimensions, of party systems: aggregation, competitiveness, and stability. In later chapters, we study the effects of party system competitiveness, aggregation, and stability on country governance. In the next chapter, however, we consider how the twenty-three countries that lack political parties fared on the Worldwide Governance Indicators in 2007.

Notes

1. Here, a political party is defined as an organization that seeks to place its avowed representatives in government positions. "To place" means through competitive elections or political appointments, which occurs in authoritarian governments. "Avowed representatives" means that candidates must compete under the party's name or publicly identify with the party when in office. "Government positions," for our purposes, means seats in a parliament or legislature. See Kenneth Janda, *Political Parties: A Cross-National Survey* (New York: The Free Press, 1980), 5.

2. For discussion of presidentialism and parliamentarism, see José Antonio Cheibub, Zachary Elkins, and Tom Ginsburg, "Beyond Presidentialism and Parliamentarism: On the Hybridization of Constitutional Form" (prepared for the Comparative Constitutional Law Roundtable, George Washington University Law School, Washington, DC, March 6, 2009). For discussions of their effects on party government, see George Tsebelis, "Veto Players and Institutional Analysis," *Governance* 13 (October 2000): 441–474; Paul Webb, "'Presidential' Rule and the Erosion of Party Government in Parliamentary Systems: The Case of the United Kingdom" ["La 'presidenzializzazione' e l'erosione del governo di partito nei sistemi parlamentari: il caso del Regno Unito"], *Rivista Italiana di Scienza Politica* 34 (December 2004): 347–377.

3. National constitutions in some twenty countries prohibit presidents from affiliating with political parties. See Kenneth Janda, *Adopting Party Law* (Washington, DC: National Democratic Institute, 2005), 21.

4. TypeExec is a variable in Pippa Norris 191 nation cross-sectional dataset 2009 release, at "Pippa Norris Data," John F. Kennedy School of Government, Harvard University, March 1, 2009, www.hks.harvard.edu/fs/pnorris/Data/Data.htm.

5. David J. Samuels and Matthew S. Shugart, *Presidents, Parties, and Prime Ministers: How the Separation of Powers Affects Party Organization and Behavior* (New York: Cambridge University Press, 2010).

6. Hans Keman summarizes the assumptions of the theory of parliamentary party government in "Party Government Formation and Policy Preferences: An Encompassing Approach," in *Democratic Politics and Party Competition: Essays in Honor of Ian Budge*, ed. Judith Bara and Albert Weale (London: Routledge, 2006), 33–55, at 36.

7. The first report of our project appeared in Kenneth Janda and Jin-Young Kwak, "Competition and Volatility in Parliamentary Party Systems for 212 Polities" (paper presented at the annual meeting of the Midwest Political Science Association, Chicago, Illinois, April 2–4, 2009).

8. Michael Gallagher maintains an important website with information on various party system measures, including the effective number of parties, at "Electoral Systems," Trinity College Dublin, www.tcd.ie/Political_Science/staff/michael_gallagher/ElSystems/index.php.

9. "Psephos: Adam Carr's Election Archive," http://psephos.adam-carr.net.

10. "List of Election Results by Country," Wikipedia, http://en.wikipedia.org/wiki/List_of_election_results_by_country.

11. Inter-Parliamentary Union, www.ipu.org/english/home.htm.

12. African Elections Database, http://africanelections.tripod.com.

13. Travel Document Systems, http://traveldocs.com.

14. The CIA provides access to the most recent *World Factbook* on its own website at https://www.cia.gov/library/publications/the-world-factbook/index.html. Earlier editions, including the 2006 edition, are available through the private site at www.theodora.com/wfb.

15. In summary form, Steven D. Wolinetz says that party system properties "include the number of parties contesting elections and winning legislative seats, their relative size and strength, the number of dimensions on which they compete, the distance which separates them on key issues, and their willingness to work with each other in government formation and the process of governing." See Wolinetz, "Party Systems and Party System Types," in *Handbook of Party Politics*, ed. Richard S. Katz and William Crotty (London: Sage Publications, 2006), 51–62, at 53.

16. Jan-Erik Lane and Svante Ersson, *Politics and Society in Western Europe*, 3rd ed. (London: Sage Publications, 1994), 180. Their list was edited somewhat to improve communication.

17. Thomas T. Mackie and Richard Rose, eds., *The International Almanac of Electoral History*, 3rd ed. (Washington, DC: Congressional Quarterly, 1991).

18. Douglas Rae, "A Note on the Fractionalization of Some European Party Systems," *Comparative Political Studies* 1 (October 1968): 413–418.

19. Markku Laakso and Rein Taagepera, "'Effective' Number of Parties: A Measure with Applications to West Europe," *Comparative Political Studies* 12 (1979): 3–27.

20. Lawrence C. Mayer, "A Note on the Aggregation of Party Systems," in *Western European Party Systems*, ed. Peter H. Merkl (New York: The Free Press, 1980), 515–520. Mayer's original formula used the "largest party in the government coalition," and he multiplied the index by 100.

21. Mogens N. Pedersen, "The Dynamics of European Party Systems: Changing Patterns of Electoral Volatility," *European Journal of Political Research* 7 (1979): 1–26.

22. Wolinetz summaries that literature in "Party Systems and Party System Types." Whole books have been devoted to measuring party system change; see Peter Mair,

Party System Change: Approaches and Interpretations (Oxford: Clarendon Press, 1997); Paul Pennings and Jan-Erik Lane, eds., *Comparing Party System Change* (London: Routledge, 1998).

23. Alan Siaroff, *Comparative European Party Systems: An Analysis of Parliamentary Elections Since 1945* (New York: Garland, 2000).

24. Alan Ware, *The Dynamics of Two-Party Politics: Party Structures and the Management of Competition* (London: Oxford University Press, 2009).

25. Luciano Bardi and Peter Mair, "The Parameters of Party Systems," *Party Politics* 14 (March 2008): 147–166, at 161.

26. A few scholars have addressed relationships between party system traits and political performance. G. Bingham Powell Jr. has done the most notable work in "Party Systems and Political System Performance: Voting Participation, Government Stability and Mass Violence in Contemporary Democracies," *American Political Science Review* 75 (December 1981): 861–879, and G. Bingham Powell Jr., "Party System Change, Election Rules and Ideological Congruence" (paper presented at the annual meeting of the Midwest Political Science Association, Chicago, Illinois, April 3–6, 2008), as well as with others in HeeMin Kim, G. Bingham Powell Jr., and Richard C. Fording, "Party Systems and Substantive Representation: Static and Dynamic Performance" (paper presented at the annual meeting of the Midwest Political Science Association, Chicago, Illinois, April 20–23, 2006). Studying fewer countries, Powell usually included polarization among party system traits. (Unfortunately, we could not obtain adequate data on polarization for this study.) His research used difference dependent variables: government stability, voting participation, and policy representation. He also used more specific indicators of domestic violence.

27. Lane and Ersson, *Politics and Society in Western Europe*, 175.

28. Ibid., 180. However, the left-right scores and polarization index correlated only –0.42.

29. Ibid., 181.

30. Russell J. Dalton, "The Quantity and the Quality of Party Systems: Party System Polarization, Its Measurement, and Its Consequences," *Comparative Political Studies* 41 (July 2008): 899–920.

31. Mogens N. Pedersen, "On Measuring Party System Change: A Methodological Critique and a Suggestion," *Comparative Political Studies* 12 (January 1980): 398. Emphasis in the original.

32. The first edition of Lane and Ersson, *Politics and Society in Western Europe* (1987), reported a factor analysis of fourteen party system measures, many—but not all—identical to the fifteen in their third edition. They uncovered five factors (p. 161) that correspond closely to the patterns discussed here. Four fragmentation measures loaded on Factor 1; three socioeconomic measures on Factor 2; three ideological measures on Factor 3; two other ideological measures on Factor 4; and two measures of change on Factor 5. The analysis did not include strength of the parties.

33. These are rotated factors.

34. See Benjamin Nyblade and Angela O'Mahony, "Counting Parties: Different Measures for Different Purposes" (paper presented at the annual meeting of the Midwest Political Science Association, Chicago, Illinois, April 22–25, 2010).

Chapter 8

Governance Without Party Systems

Why do countries have party systems? In his well-known book *Why Parties?* John Aldrich asks that simple question.[1] He concludes that politicians form political parties to solve three fundamental problems: how to regulate the number of people seeking public office, how to mobilize voters, and how to achieve and maintain the majorities needed to accomplish goals once in office. By joining together in organized political parties, those with political ambitions solve these problems of collective action.

The overwhelming majority (about 90 percent) of the 212 countries covered by the Worldwide Governance Indicators have political parties. According to the data in Table 7.1, 189 countries around 2005 had parliamentary deputies seated by political parties, while only 23 did not. Of those without parliamentary parties, eight chose deputies via popular elections while fifteen had no elections for parliament. We will see how the few countries without party systems rate on country governance compared with the many countries with parties, but first we study the two groups of countries without parties. How do they differ from each other?

Features of NoParties Versus NonPartisan Countries

Many of the fifteen countries without party systems have familiar names, such as Afghanistan, Lebanon, Libya, Nepal, Saudi Arabia, and Somalia—the last being of the five countries we are tracking. As Table 8.1 shows, countries in this group vary widely in land area, population, and wealth (gross domestic

123

Table 8.1 Fifteen Countries Without Elections and Parliamentary Parties

Country	Land Area Only (1,000 km²)[a]	Population, 2005[b]	GDP per Capita, 2004[c]
Afghanistan	652.1	27,145,300	800
Bahrain	0.7	726,617	18,817
Bhutan	47.0	637,013	3,095
Brunei Darussalam	5.3	373,819	24,143
Lebanon	10.2	4,010,740	5,930
Libya	1,759.5	5,853,452	10,769
Maldives	0.3	329,198	7,327
Myanmar (Burma)	657.6	50,519,492	1,364
Nepal	143.0	27,132,629	1,402
Qatar	11.0	812,842	28,919
Saudi Arabia	2,149.7	23,118,994	13,955
Somalia	627.3	8,227,826	600
Swaziland	17.2	1,131,000	4,995
Tonga	0.7	102,311	7,415
United Arab Emirates	83.6	4,533,145	23,818
Fifteen-country median	47.0	4,010,740	7,327
World median	95.7	5,470,728	6,324

[a] From United Nations GEO-3 Data Compendium (geocompendium.grid.unep.ch/data_sets/land/nat_land_ds.htm) and CIA Factbooks (www.cia.gov/library/publications/the-world-factbook/index.html).

[b] Population from the World Bank "Data Catalog" (data.worldbank.org/data-catalog).

[c] GDP per capita calculated as purchasing power from Wikipedia's "List of Countries by GDP (PPP) per Capita" (en.wikipedia.org/wiki/List_of_countries_by_GDP_(PPP)_per_capita).

product per capita). Table 8.1 expresses their "average" values as medians (rather than means) to eliminate the skewing effects of extreme scores (e.g., reducing the impact of Myanmar's population of 50 million). About half the countries in the mid-2000s had less than 47,000 square kilometers in area, 4 million inhabitants or less, and a GDP per capita of less than $7,500. Only the three island nations of Bahrain (off the coast of Saudi Arabia), Maldives (in the Indian Ocean), and Tonga (in the South Pacific) are "tiny" in area—less than 1,000 square kilometers. All except Bhutan, Myanmar, Nepal, Swaziland, and Tonga have Muslim majorities.

Table 8.2 lists the eight countries with elections but without parties. Few names are familiar, except perhaps for American Samoa. All but Oman are tiny island countries in the Pacific Ocean with small populations and low incomes. Oman differs from the others in several ways: It shares a land border with Saudi Arabia, has more people and territory than the seven other countries combined, and has a Muslim majority. Oman is also the only one not classified as an electoral democracy in 2005 by the Washington organization

Table 8.2 Eight Countries with Elections but Without Parliamentary Parties

Country	Land Area Only (1,000 km²)[a]	Population, 2005[b]	GDP per Capita, 2004[c]
American Samoa	0.2	57,663	8,000
Marshall Islands	0.2	63,266	1,600
Micronesia	0.7	110,487	2,000
Nauru	0.0	10,200	5,000
Niue	0.2	1,800	5,800
Oman	309.5	2,566,981	15,649
Palau	0.5	20,100	9,000
Tuvalu	0.0	11,992	1,100
Eight-country median	0.2	38,882	5,400
Worldwide median	95.7	5,470,728	6,324

[a] From United Nations GEO-3 Data Compendium (geocompendium.grid.unep.ch/data_sets/land/nat_land_ds.htm) and CIA Factbooks (www.cia.gov/library/publications/the-world-factbook/index.html).

[b] Population from the World Bank "Data Catalog" (http://data.worldbank.org/data-catalog).

[c] GDP per capita calculated as purchasing power from Wikipedia's "List of Countries by GDP (PPP) per Capita" (en.wikipedia.org/wiki/List_of_countries_by_GDP_(PPP)_per_capita).

Freedom House, which concluded that Oman's election for its legislature (which had limited powers) was not free and fair.[2] The other seven countries chose nonpartisan parliamentary deputies in free elections.

The seven countries with free elections (excluding Oman) are also tiny, averaging about 200 square kilometers in land area (slightly larger than Washington, DC) and having fewer people than Casper, Wyoming. They are close to the city-states that the Greeks thought necessary to sustaining democracy.[3] Of course, the Greeks viewed democracy more like a giant town meeting. The modern view of democracy allows for government through popularly elected parliaments chosen to represent millions of citizens. In almost all large countries today, deputies elected to parliament are organized into political parties to deal with the problems of collective action noted above. It appears that only tiny countries can sustain free, nonpartisan elections to parliament.[4] Micronesia, with just over 100,000 people living on just under 1,000 square kilometers of land, is the largest electoral democracy governed without political parties.

Effects of NoParties and NonPartisan Countries on Governance

Figure 8.1 plots the distribution of Rule of Law governance scores for all countries along with the names of countries without parties. The names in boldface identify NoParties countries, those lacking both elections and

Figure 8.1 Rule of Law scores for countries without parties

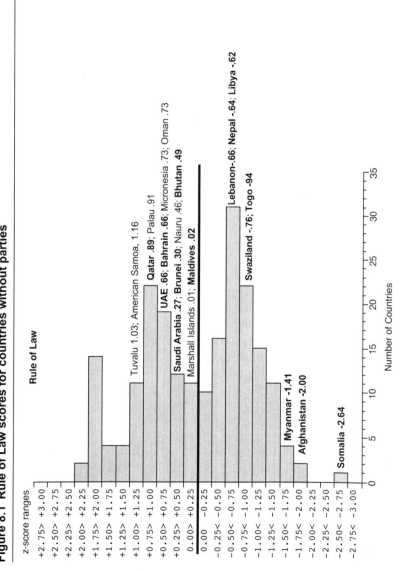

Boldface marks countries with no elections and no political parties.
Normal type marks countries with nonpartisan elections but no parties. (Niue was not rated on Rule of Law.)

parliamentary parties. The names in normal type identify NonPartisan countries, those holding elections but lacking parliamentary parties. Three observations stand out. First, no country without political parties stands near the top of the Rule of Law distribution. Second, an equal number of NoParties and NonPartisan countries are above the mean of all countries on Rule of Law. Third, the remaining NoParties countries (six) rate below the mean of all countries. Somalia, which rates at the bottom, has a parliament filled by members appointed by four major clans in 2004. Figure 8.1 shows that it is possible for countries without parties to rank above average on Rule of Law, but not having parties seems associated with lower scores on this indicator.

A problem with drawing conclusions from Figure 8.1 is that it does not provide for the effects of country size and wealth. As Chapters 4 and 5 show, country size and wealth have substantial independent effects on country governance. Figure 8.1 demonstrates that small countries without parties stand above the mean on Rule of Law, but small countries *should* rate higher on Rule of Law according to the analysis in Chapter 4. Without political parties, do they rate higher or lower than they should? A similar argument applies for country wealth. The rich oil states of Qatar, United Arab Emirates, Bahrain, and Saudi Arabia stand above the mean for Rule of Law, but wealthy states should rate higher on Rule of Law according to the analysis in Chapter 5. Lacking political parties, do they rate higher or lower than expected, allowing for country size and wealth?

Chapter 6 on the theory of party system effects on country governance advanced this proposition:

P1. *Countries with popularly elected* **nonpartisan** *parliaments score higher on governance than those with unelected* **nonparty** *parliaments, which score lower on governance than those with parties in parliament.*

P1 carries the implied condition *ceteris paribus*, meaning "other conditions being equal." In our model, that means controlling for country size and wealth in regression analysis that includes the variables NoParties and NonPartisan. NoParties is scored 1 for the fifteen countries that do not hold elections to select parliamentary deputies and whose parliaments have no political parties. All other countries are scored 0. NonPartisan is scored 1 for the eight countries that hold nonpartisan elections for parliament. All other countries are scored 0. Scoring the countries this way turns NoParties and NonPartisan into "toggle switches" in the regression analysis (more on this below).[5] The respective variables are multiplied by 1 (and thus turned "on") for the fifteen NoParties and the eight NonPartisan countries and multiplied by 0 (turned "off") for the 189 countries with parliamentary parties. In effect, the NoParties and NonPartisan countries are compared against that much larger group of countries.

P1 is vague concerning the effects of NonPartisan countries. It merely says that they should score higher on governance than NoParties countries. NonPartisan countries are expected to score higher because they hold elections. Nevertheless, they still lack political parties, so the theory is unclear concerning how NonPartisan countries compare with the overwhelming majority of countries with parties. P1 only says that they should have higher governance scores than NoParties countries, but we will require that their scores also be significantly different compared with all countries.

Including the NoParties and NonPartisan variables permits testing of hypotheses H1.1.1 through H1.1.6 and H1.2.1 through H1.2.6 concerning the effects on country governance relative to countries with political parties.

One set of hypotheses tests for the negative effects of NoParties:

H1.1.1. NoParties has a negative effect on Rule of Law (RL).
H1.1.2. NoParties has a negative effect on Government Effectiveness (GE).
H1.1.3. NoParties has a negative effect on Control of Corruption (CC).
H1.1.4. NoParties has a negative effect on Regulatory Quality (RQ).
H1.1.5. NoParties has a negative effect on Voice and Accountability (VA).
H1.1.6. NoParties has a negative effect on Political Stability (PS).

The other set of hypotheses tests for the effects of NonPartisan. P1 makes no specific prediction other than that NonPartisan countries will have higher (more positive) governance scores than NoParties countries:

H1.2.1. NonPartisan has a more positive effect than NoParties on RL.
H1.2.2. NonPartisan has a more positive effect than NoParties on GE.
H1.2.3. NonPartisan has a more positive effect than NoParties on CC.
H1.2.4. NonPartisan has a more positive effect than NoParties on RQ.
H1.2.5. NonPartisan has a more positive effect than NoParties on VA.
H1.2.6. NonPartisan has a more positive effect than NoParties on PS.

At least, that is the theory.

Rule of Law

As usual, we use Rule of Law to illustrate the regression analysis before summarizing the results for all six governance indicators. This time, however, we must decide whether to present the equation using standardized or unstandardized regression coefficients for the independent variables. To this point, we have used standardized coefficients (βs), transforming the variables into z-scores so that their means equal 0 and their standard deviations equal 1. (See Box 2.2 in Chapter 2.) By "standardizing" them this way, we can directly compare their effects. Otherwise, variables with larger means and standard deviations tend to generate larger coefficients due to the sheer scale of their numbers. To illustrate, consider the vastly different values in measuring country area and GDP per capita. The raw mean for area is 613,656 square kilometers with a standard deviation of 1.771 million. The raw mean for GDP per capita is $10,490 with a standard deviation of $10,838. A one-unit change in area (1 square kilometer out of 613,656) means less than a one-unit change in wealth ($1 out of $10,490). Standardized β coefficients adjust for scaling differences in measurement. Because a one-unit change for a β coefficient is one standard deviation, however, it is harder to imagine.

Unstandardized b coefficients have an advantage in interpretation—especially for toggle switch variables like NoParties and NonPartisan for which a one-unit change simply means going from 0 to 1, from being turned off to being turned on. Consider Equation 8.1, which uses unstandardized b coefficients:

$$RL = .20SmallArea + .74Wealth - .34NoParties + .61NonPartisan \qquad R^2_{adj} = 0.67 \ (8.1)$$

When NoParties = 0, the term $-0.34 \times$ NoParties = 0. When NoParties = 1, the term $-0.34 \times$ NoParties = -0.34. Thus, controlling for country size and wealth, the fifteen NoParties countries tended to score -0.34 z-scores lower while the eight NonPartisan countries scored 0.61 z-scores higher on Rule of Law. The effects of NoParties and NonPartisan are easy to interpret when expressed in unstandardized b coefficients, but comparing their effects across variables can be misleading. The standardized effects of SmallArea (0.20) and Wealth (0.74) make the effects of NoParties (-0.34) and NonPartisan (0.61) seem roughly comparable. That is not true. Explaining why is complicated, so bear with us as we try.

The unstandardized effects of NoParties and NonPartisan cannot be compared with the effects of SmallArea and Wealth, which became standardized by being transformed into z-scores. Recall that NoParties and NonPartisan apply to only 23 countries that scored 1 on either variable, whereas many more countries (189) scored 0 on both. Consequently, the relative effects of NoParties and NonPartisan on Rule of Law on all 211 were limited, and thus smaller. Using β coefficients to standardize the effects of all independent variables adjusts for the fewer countries that scored 1 on NoParties and NonPartisan.

Equation 8.2 gives the regression equation using standardized β coefficients, which we favor and use from this point on.

$$RL = .20SmallArea + .74Wealth - .09NoParties + .11NonPartisan \qquad R^2_{adj} = 0.67 \ (8.2)$$

In Equation 8.2, the respective effects of NoParties and NonPartisan are reduced to −0.09 and 0.11. Both variables have less impact overall than SmallArea and Wealth. The difference between the standardized and unstandardized effects of NoParties and NonPartisan (controlling for country size and wealth) is detailed and discussed in Table 8.3.

Once again, the standardized β coefficients correspond to the effect on Rule of Law due to one standard deviation unit change in any of the independent variables.[6] As before, the control variables SmallArea and Wealth have significant effects on Rule of Law. The two new variables of interest, NoParties and NonPartisan, also have significant effects and—as hypothesized—in opposite directions. The Rule of Law z-scores for countries of a similar size and wealth are −0.09 lower if those countries have no elections and no parliamentary parties, and 0.11 higher if they have no parliamentary parties but choose deputies in elections. While not having either elections or parties depresses RL, having elections increases RL—even in nonpartisan parliaments.

Table 8.3 Comparing b and β Coefficients for NoParties and NonPartisan

	NoParties		NonPartisan	
	Unstandardized Coefficients, b[a]	Standardized Coefficients, β[b]	Unstandardized Coefficients, b[a]	Standardized Coefficients, β[b]
Rule of Law	−0.34	−0.09	0.61	0.11
Government Effectiveness	−0.52	−0.13	Not significant	
Control of Corruption	−0.42	−0.11	Not significant	
Regulatory Quality	−0.56	−0.15	Not significant	
Voice and Accountability	−1.19	−0.31	Not significant	
Political Stability	−0.55	−0.14	0.51	0.09

Notes:

[a] The unstandardized b coefficients express the change in Worldwide Governance Indicator z-scores for countries scored 1 for NoParties or NonPartisan compared with all other countries scored 0. In the extreme case above for Voice and Accountability, the few countries scored 1 for NoParties tended to score −1.19 points lower than the many countries scored 0. Unstandardized coefficients do not represent the relative effects of these variables on all countries.

[b] The standardized β coefficients also express the change in Worldwide Governance Indicator z-scores as a result of one unit change, but the units are measured in standard deviations. Because only eight countries are scored 1 for NonPartisan and only fifteen scored 1 for NoParties, their respective standard deviations are only 0.19 and 0.26. Consider again the b coefficient of −1.19 for NoParties on Voice and Accountability versus the β coefficient of −0.31. A change from 0 to 1 for NoParties equals a change of only 0.26 in standard deviation units. Multiplying −1.19 by 0.26 equals −0.31. A change from 0 to 1 (unstandardized) is equivalent to a change of −0.31 standard deviation units. In this way, standardized β coefficients (used throughout the rest of the chapters) adjust for the relatively small number of countries scored 1 on either NonPartisan or NoParties.

Note that only 10 percent of the 212 countries scored on the World Bank Indicators have a score of 1 on either the NoParties or NonPartisan term in Equation 8.1. The other 189 countries with parties are scored 0 on both. Because the two terms affect only a small fraction of the countries, the explained variance ($R^2 = 0.67$) barely rises above the explained variance for Equation 5.3 ($R^2 = 0.66$) for just SmallArea and Wealth value in Chapter 5.

All Six Governance Indicators

Figure 8.2 gives the regression results for all six indicators of country governance. The NoParties countries have significant negative coefficients roughly the same size for all of the indicators except Voice and Accountability, for which NoParties' effect is almost triple. Table A.5 in Appendix A suggests why. Among the sources the World Bank used to score VA was Freedom House's rating of countries for "political rights," which includes having free and fair elections, a representative legislature, free elections, and political parties.[7] Countries with no elections and no parliamentary parties were downgraded for Voice and Accountability. So the relationship is partly definitional—hence the strong relationship.

Apparently, the few countries with free nonpartisan elections for parliament were not equally downgraded, so they did not generate negative coefficients in the regression analysis.[8] In fact, the NonPartisan coefficients were not significant for four of the six indicators. The regression analysis results clearly support all six hypotheses H1.1.1 though H1.1.6, but only H1.2.1 and H1.2.6.

Summary and Conclusion

Today, party systems exist in about 90 percent of the world's countries. Politicians form political parties to solve problems of collective action in nominating candidates, winning elections, and governing the nation. As one prominent party scholar wrote, if parties did not exist in modern societies, they would be invented.[9]

Nevertheless, 23 of the 212 countries in this study do not have political parties seated in parliament. Eight countries hold nonpartisan parliamentary elections, and fifteen have neither popular elections nor parliamentary parties. How well do countries without party systems fare in country governance?

Chapter 6 advances proposition P1: *Countries with popularly elected **nonpartisan** parliaments score higher on governance than those with unelected **nonparty** parliaments, which score lower on governance than those with parties in parliament.* We derived two sets of hypotheses from this proposition and tested them with

Figure 8.2 Effects of country size, wealth, NoParties, and NonPartisan on all six governance indicators

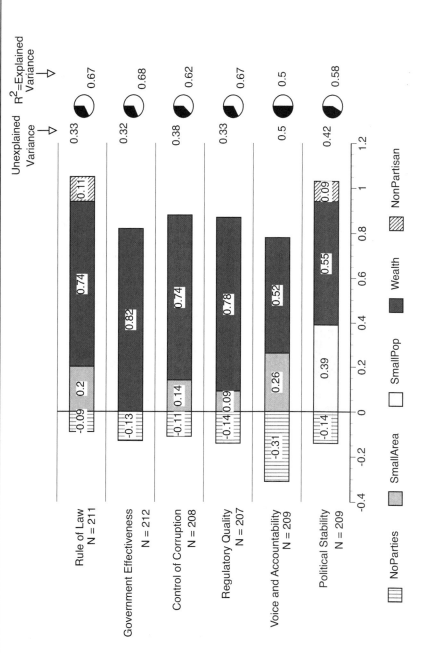

regression analysis. The results below are checked if supported and stricken through if unsupported:

H1.1.1: √ NoParties has a negative effect on RL.
H1.1.2: √ NoParties has a negative effect on GE.
H1.1.3: √ NoParties has a negative effect on CC.
H1.1.4: √ NoParties has a negative effect on RQ.
H1.1.5: √ NoParties has a negative effect on VA.
H1.1.6: √ NoParties has a negative effect on PS.

Even after controlling for country size and wealth, we found that the absence of popular elections and political parties has consistently negative effects on all six indicators of country governance. The results are not as clear for countries that have nonpartisan elections to parliament.

H1.2.1: √ NonPartisan has a more positive effect than NoParties on RL.
~~H1.2.2: NonPartisan has a more positive effect than NoParties on GE.~~
~~H1.2.3: NonPartisan has a more positive effect than NoParties on CC.~~
~~H1.2.4: NonPartisan has a more positive effect than NoParties on RQ.~~
~~H1.2.5: NonPartisan has a more positive effect than NoParties on VA.~~
H1.2.6: √ NonPartisan has a more positive effect than NoParties on PS.

These hypotheses apply to only about 10 percent of the world's countries. In Chapters 9 through 11, we consider the effects of party systems on the other 90 percent.

Notes

1. John Aldrich, *Why Parties? The Origin and Transformation of Political Parties in America* (Chicago: University of Chicago Press, 1995).

2. Freedom House also had other criteria. See "Methodology," Freedom House, www.freedomhouse.org/template.cfm?page=351&ana_page=298&year=2006.

3. Robert A. Dahl and Edward R. Tufte, *Size and Democracy* (Stanford, CA: Stanford University Press, 1973), 4.

4. For discussion of how government operates in tiny island states without political parties, see Dag Anckar, "Dominating Smallness: Big Parties in Lilliput Systems," *Party Politics* 3 (April 1997): 243–263, at 248.

5. Usually, variables scored 0 or 1 are called "dummy" variables. Referring to them as toggle switches better describes their function.

6. Because Formula 8.1 reports β coefficients, not b coefficients, the values of Non-Partisan and NoParties are no longer 0 or 1 but are the standard deviations of Non-Partisan and NoParties. Explaining this further delves too far into statistical analysis.

7. Freedom House in Washington, DC, calls itself "an independent watchdog organization that supports the expansion of freedom around the world." See http://freedomhouse.org.

8. Oman, which was included among the eight NonPartisan countries, was not classified as an electoral democracy by Freedom House for not having free elections. However, it is still included in this analysis.

9. See Paul Webb, "Conclusion: Political Parties and Democratic Control in Advanced Industrial Societies," in *Political Parties in Advanced Industrial Democracies*, ed. Paul Webb, David Farrell, and Ian Holliday (London: Oxford University Press, 2002), 438–458, at 458.

Chapter 9

The Effects of Competition

The factor analysis in Chapter 7 identified two indicators that loaded on the factor labeled "party system competitiveness." One was the point difference between the percentages of seats held by the largest and second-largest parties, which is often used as a measure of party system competitiveness.[1] The other was the percentage of seats held by the second-largest party, which has rarely been used that way.[2] After considering the concept of competitiveness and looking at the data, we conclude that the second indicator is the better measure. We also reject three other indicators used to measure competitiveness that loaded highly on the fragmentation factor. Two are the percentage of seats held by the largest party and the effective number of parties.[3] They simply do not measure competitiveness.[4] Neither does the third, Douglas Rae's fractionalization formula.

Chapter 10 describes in detail Rae's formula, which is based on the proportions of seats held by parliamentary parties. Rae proposed his measure in response to this question: "Is competitive strength concentrated in one party, or is it divided among many parties?"[5] He reasoned, "A highly fractionalized system has a great many shares of about equal magnitude so that no one of them contains a very large share of the total pool of strength."[6] Thus, he suggested that fractionalization is a measure of party system competition, and scholars have used it that way.[7] When many parties hold small proportions of seats, however, that is not party system competitiveness as it is commonly understood. Instead, the existence of a large number of equally weak parties indicates party system entropy—random disorder. If entropy is a form of competitiveness, it is a bizarre form, unstructured and stochastic, that reflects a chaotic party system. A more reasonable form envisions rival parties with substantial support alternating in government in response to popular evaluations of their policies and performance via elections. Let us begin by considering terminology.

The Concept of Competitiveness

The terms *competition* and *competitive* have been applied to very different aspects of party politics. Parties are said to compete for votes won in elections, for control of government, and even for ownership of issues.[8] According to Giovanni Sartori's formulation, competition establishes the "rules of the game" being played, while competitiveness is "a particular state of the game."[9] In election games, candidates compete to win office (decided by number of votes won). In governmental games, parties compete to win control of parliament (decided by number of seats won). In issue games, parties compete to win support for their policies (decided by public opinion).[10] In all these games, competitiveness reflects the likelihood of winning—or not losing. Sartori continues, "Competition is 'competitive' when two or more parties obtain close returns and win on thin margins."[11]

Using the most-different-systems research design,[12] we do not control for standard political factors such as type of electoral system or presidential/parliamentary government. If party system competitiveness has any significant impact on governance, it must surface through all types of political systems. We focus exclusively on contests for control of the lower chamber of the legislative body. Parties that win a majority of seats typically control that institution. Defined as "majority-bent" parties, they are "those which command an absolute majority in parliament or are likely to be able to command at some date in the normal play of institutions."[13] If no party has a majority, parties form a government coalition, receiving "payoffs" (e.g., cabinet positions) according to their proportion of seats.[14] This proportionality rule makes party control of government a function of the seats each party has won.[15] The relationship between seats held and cabinet posts acquired is strong in parliamentary systems and less strong in presidential systems.[16] Competition—from the standpoint of governing parties—comes from opposition parties that threaten to replace them after the next election. Not all opposition parties are credible threats. Threats are more serious from other majority-bent parties or from parties that can form a government coalition. Accordingly, governing parties look not only to their seat margin (as suggested by Sartori) when pondering losing office in the next election but also to the strength of their main party challengers.[17] The sheer size of the parties competing for control is important. Rival governing parties must be sufficiently large to have credible "office capacity," enabling them to adequately staff government ministries.[18]

Measuring Competitiveness

We collected data on two measures of party system competitiveness for 189 parliaments. Figure 9.1(a) graphs the point margin between the percentages of seats held by the two largest parties. It depicts a highly skewed distribution. A few parliaments tail off to the right, toward the maximum of a one-hundred-point margin difference (meaning that in a few parliaments the largest party holds all the seats), while almost forty parliaments stand toward the left, at the zero-point difference in seats between the two largest parties. Figure 9.1(b) graphs the percentage of seats held by the second-largest party after the stimulus election. It displays a more statistically desirable distribution that is symmetrical and unimodal (one category containing a plurality of the countries).

Although point margin and percentage of seats for the second party are highly correlated ($r = 0.67$), they express competitiveness very differently, as Figure 9.2 shows. As the second-largest party's percentage of seats tends toward fifty, the point margin between the two largest parties tends toward zero, whereas the point margin ranges from almost zero to almost seventy when the second-largest party holds around 20 percent of the seats.[19] Measuring competitiveness by the point margin between the two largest parties is better suited to relatively rare two-party systems, like that in the United States, than to far more common multiparty systems, like those in Europe.

For illustration, consider the following two scenarios: (1) a two-party system in which the parties split 52 to 48 in percentage of seats held, and (2) a multiparty system in which the two largest parties split 30 to 26. In both cases the margin in percentage of seats held by the two largest parties is four points. Does a four-point margin adequately reflect the competitiveness of both scenarios? The four points in seats needed to reverse the parties' positions is only an 8 percent gain for a party holding 48 percent of the seats but a 15 percent gain for one holding 26 percent. Despite facing the same point margin in seats in the two scenarios, in the second one the smaller party has to gain relatively more to replace the larger party. Does the proportion of seats held by the largest party challenger (48 percent) then provide a better measure of competitiveness between the two scenarios? Simply musing about which is better will not answer the question, but we can arrive at an answer by trying both measures in testing our theory about party system effects on country governance.

We report our statistical tests of hypotheses in the next section, but for now we can say that the percentage of seats held by the second-largest party produces consistently stronger effects on all but one of the governance indicators, for which the effects are equal. Because the more fruitful measure, which we hereafter call Party#2%, has not been used much in the literature,

Figure 9.1 Two measures of party system competitiveness: (a) margin of largest party over second-largest party and (b) percentage of seats for second-largest party

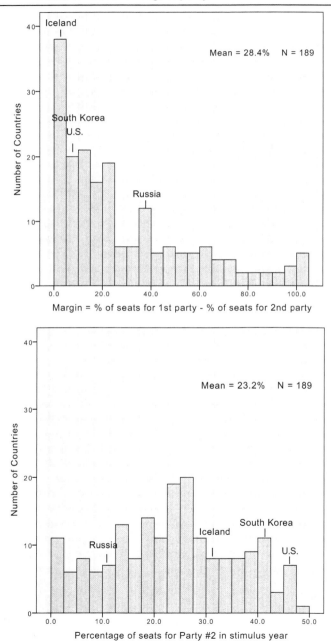

Margin = % of seats for 1st party - % of seats for 2nd party

Percentage of seats for Party #2 in stimulus year

Figure 9.2 Seat point margin by size of second party

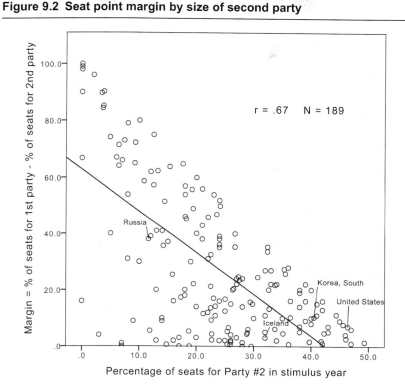

Percentage of seats for Party #2 in stimulus year

it deserves more discussion. Perhaps Party#2% is more fruitful because it conveys more information about the distribution of parliamentary seats. The point margin says nothing about the size of either parliamentary party, but Party#2% implies information about Party#1% and about Party#3%. For example, knowing that the second-largest party holds 35 percent of the seats, one also knows (because the totals cannot exceed 100) that the largest party has at least 36 percent and that the third largest has at most 29. By implying more information about the distribution of seats among the three largest parties, Party#2% may exert stronger effects in the empirical tests. Therefore, we used the size of the second party after the stimulus election (Party#2%) to operationalize "competitiveness."

Testing Hypotheses About Competitiveness

In the past, researchers have sometimes found significant party effects on political outcomes only to see them washed away with the introduction of social variables, such as population size and wealth. In his study of party systems and political system performance, G. Bingham Powell Jr. says, "Adding (log) population size greatly increases the power to explain rioting and diminishes the size of the party variable effects," and "once we control for level of economic development the party system types have little effect on deaths by violence."[20] Therefore, in testing the hypotheses in Chapters 8, 9, and 10, we routinely include both country size and country wealth as control variables, allowing in advance for their effects on country governance.

We also routinely include variables NoParties and NonPartisan introduced in Chapter 8. NoParties is scored 1 for the fifteen countries that do not hold elections to select parliamentary deputies and whose parliaments have no political parties. NonPartisan is scored 1 for the eight countries that hold nonpartisan elections for parliament. The other 189 countries with party systems are scored 0 on those two variables. Party systems are represented by converting Party#2% into z-scores. Competitive parties had high z-scores; noncompetitive parties had low scores. The mean z-score of 0 was assigned to each of the missing twenty-three countries, which fits the fact that they had no party system competitiveness.[21]

We focus on testing H2.1 through H2.6 concerning the effects of party system competition for the 189 countries with party systems. Our regression analyses include five independent variables: SmallArea (or SmallPop), Wealth, NoParties, NonPartisan, and Party#2%. We do not include any other factors—cultural or political—that may affect country governance. Concerning any omitted factors, we invoke the Latin phrase *ceteris paribus* (meaning "other conditions being equal") that economists use to ignore other factors (known and unknown) that affect the relationships under study. Because we ignore other variables with potential influence on country governance, we do not expect to reach high levels of explanation. Instead, we will be satisfied to demonstrate, after controlling for country size and wealth, whether any party system characteristics are significantly related to country governance, as operationalized by the 2007 Worldwide Governance Indicators.

Here are our hypotheses derived from P2 in Chapter 6: *The more competitive the party system, the better the country governance.*

H2.1. The larger Party#2%, the greater Rule of Law (RL).
H2.2. The larger Party#2%, the greater Government Effectiveness (GE)
H2.3. The larger Party#2%, the greater Control of Corruption (CC).
H2.4. The larger Party#2%, the greater Regulatory Quality (RQ).
H2.5. The larger Party#2%, the greater Voice and Accountability (VA).
H2.6. The larger Party#2%, the greater Political Stability (PS).

Although scholars often measure party system competition differently in the literature, most recognize the concept's theoretical importance. Albert Weale says, "Party competition in open elections is the principal institutional device used in modern political systems to implement the ideals of democracy and to secure representative government."[22] Anna Grzymala-Busse argues more forcefully for robust competition through "opposition parties that offer a clear, plausible, and critical governing alternative that threatens the governing coalition with replacement."[23] In addition, she says that "the availability of multiple and competing political options increases representation, both by encompassing wider constituencies and by providing all voters with alternatives to the government program"; further, "competition provides multiple policy and governance alternatives, and therefore it can potentially contribute to better institutional design through more extensive debates over the options, the inclusion of more viewpoints, and policy compromise."[24] Coming close to our definition of governance as producing benefits to citizens, Sarah Leary suggests that "more competitive elections lead to more provision of goods and services to voters and to longer lasting Regimes."[25] One could cite other sources making essentially the theoretical argument in P2: *The more competitive the party system, the better the country governance.* That is the theory. Does the evidence support H2.1 through H2.6 implied by the theory?

Rule of Law

Employing the statistical analysis in Chapter 4 and 5, we will focus first on the Rule of Law. As described in Chapter 8, NoParties and NonPartisan represent the missing countries. For the current regression analysis, we can interpret these two variables, along with size and wealth, as control variables, allowing us to assess the impact of party system competitiveness on Rule of Law.

Equation 9.1 reports the multiple regression analysis for all 211 countries scored for RL. All the β coefficients are at or beyond the 0.05 level.

$$RL = -.09\text{NoParties} + .18\text{SmallArea} + .72\text{Wealth} + .11\text{NonPartisan} + .10\text{Party\#2\%} \qquad R^2_{adj} = 0.68 \ (9.1)$$

Of the five independent variables in Equation 9.1, country wealth has by far the strongest effect on Rule of Law, and small country size has a somewhat larger effect than party system competitiveness. Nevertheless, the β coefficient of 0.10 states that the Rule of Law increases 10 points for each full-point increase in the z-score of Party#2%. This increase occurs after we control for country wealth and size. In other words, for equally wealthy countries of equal size, an increase of one standard deviation in Party#2% results in an estimated 0.10 increase in the Rule of Law. The lack of political parties has a comparable effect in the opposite direction, lowering RL. For the few small countries electing nonpartisan deputies, the effect is comparably positive, raising RL. The linear combination of these five variables explains more than two-thirds of the variation in RL.

Have we really improved our explanation of RL by adding the three party variables to Equation 9.1? Recall Equation 5.3 from Chapter 5, in which only two variables explained 0.66 of the variance in Rule of Law:

$$\text{Rule of Law} = .23\text{SmallArea} + .73\text{Wealth} \qquad R^2 = 0.66 \text{ (5.3)}$$

Although all five variables in Equation 9.1 increase the explained variance only slightly over that explained by Equation 5.3 (from 0.66 to 0.68), Equation 9.1 is better specified in the sense that it includes more relevant explanatory variables.[26] Figure 9.3 illustrates the relevance of the three party variables (especially competitiveness). The figure shows the regression plots for both equations—with and without competitiveness, which affects only the 189 countries with parliamentary parties. In the plot for Equation 9.1, both the United States and Russia edge closer to the regression line after we include party system competitiveness. In the United States, the second-largest party held 46.4 percent of the seats after its 2004 congressional election. In Russia, the second-largest party held 11.6 percent after its 2003 parliamentary election. Because the United States scored above average in party system competitiveness (the mean was 23.2 for Party#2%) and Russia scored below, the United States moved up in RL while Russia moved down. That is, both countries edged closer to the regression line. In South Korea and Iceland, respectively, the second-largest parties held 40.5 and 32 percent of the seats. While both party systems were more competitive than Russia's, their plot positions remained the same. Somalia, as noted previously, had no political parties, so it also edged closer to the regression line.

Although its effect is small, the percentage of seats held by the second-largest party in parliament is significantly related to the quality of governance across the world's countries. That supports H2.1: The larger Party#2%, the greater Rule of Law, which means the more competitive the party system, the greater the Rule of Law.

All Six Indicators

Having considered in some detail the regression analysis concerning the Rule of Law, we can summarize the analysis for all six indicators of country governance. Figure 9.4 gives the results for all the countries scored on five independent variables: country size (both SmallArea and SmallPop), country wealth, NoParties, NonPartisan, and party system competitiveness. Consider first the effects of our control variables, country wealth and country size.

Country Wealth. Country wealth retained its significant and strong effect on all governance indicators. We should comment, however, on its much weaker effect for Voice and Accountability and Political Stability and the Absence of

Figure 9.3 Regression plots of Equations 5.3 and 9.1

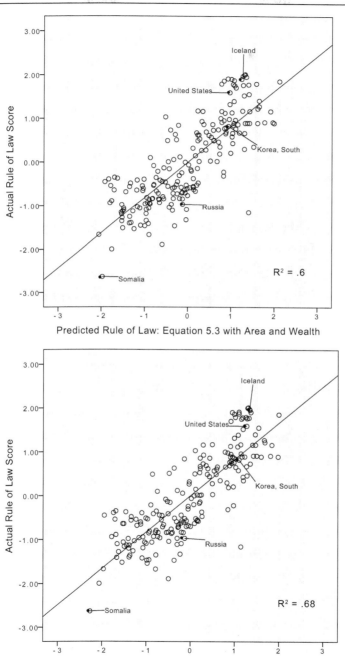

Figure 9.4 Effects of country size, wealth, NoParties, NonPartisan, and Party#2% on all six governance indicators for all countries

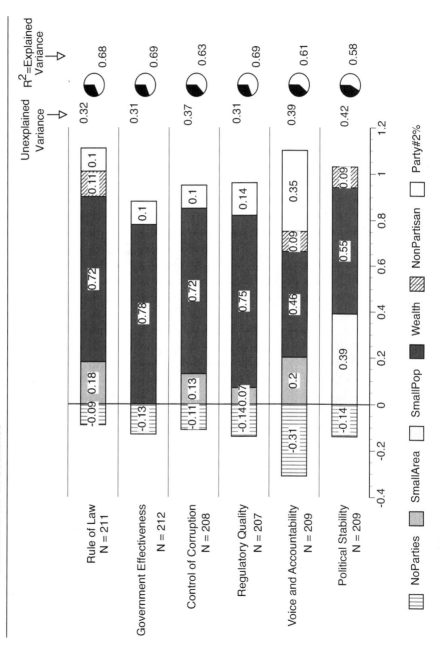

Violence. Recall from Chapter 2 that VA and PS averaged lower correlations (0.78 and 0.72, respectively) with the first four variables (RL, GE, CC, and RQ) than the four averaged among themselves (0.92). Obviously, these four variables—Rule of Law, Government Effectiveness, Control of Corruption, and Regulatory Quality—reflect different aspects of country governance than the other two. Country wealth, it appears, affects administrative indicators of country governance (RL, GE, CC, and RQ) more strongly than political indicators (VA and PS). We will repeatedly find different effects of party system traits on administrative and political aspects of country governance.

Country Size. Adding party system competitiveness to the equation had notable consequences for the importance of country size. Country size retained its significant effects on five of the six indicators, but lost significance for GE. Evidently, the slight correlation between small country size and party system competitiveness ($r = -0.19$) allowed party system competitiveness to pick up the variation that country size had previously explained. Why that occurred for GE but not for the other variables is unclear. For help, we can look to Table A.2 in Appendix A to learn what information entered the scoring of this variable. Government Effectiveness was based on such factors as turnover of government personnel, quality of the bureaucracy, satisfaction with transportation, debt management, public debt management, and use of resources. Apparently, this aspect of country governance is not especially affected by country size. Large countries as well as small can enjoy similar levels of Government Effectiveness.[27]

NoParties and NonPartisan. The coefficients are identical to those reported in Table 8.2. The consistent negative effects of NoParties and the two positive effects of NonPartisan are unchanged by adding Party#2%.

Party System Competitiveness. The percentage of seats held by the second-largest party also had significantly similar effects ($\beta \approx 0.10$) on all four administrative indicators of country governance. Its effects on the two political indicators were dramatically different, however. Its effect on Voice and Accountability reflected the same definitional problem as with the NoParties variable. That is, countries with parties, especially competitive parties, earn high VA ratings. Nevertheless, party system competitiveness still affects Voice and Accountability, for Party#2% was scored quite independently of the World Bank scoring for VA. Of more interest is the finding that party system competitiveness has no significant effect on Political Stability and the Absence of Violence—measured (according to Table A.6) using information on political terrorism and assassination, armed conflict, ethnic tensions, civil unrest, and so on. All these negative acts occur regardless of party system competitiveness.

Summary and Conclusion

Although the literature typically measures party system competition by the percentage-point difference in seats held (or votes won) between the two largest parties, we contend that the percentage of seats held (or votes won) by the second-largest party is a more fruitful measure. Operationalizing party system competitiveness by the variable Party#2% and country governance by the six Worldwide Governance Indicators, we tested these hypotheses, with the results checked if supported and stricken through if unsupported:

H2.1.   √ The larger Party#2%, the greater the RL.
H2.2.   √ The larger Party#2%, the greater the GE.
H2.3.   √ The larger Party#2%, the greater the CC.
H2.4.   √ The larger Party#2%, the greater the RQ.
H2.5.   √ The larger Party#2%, the greater the VA.
H2.6.   ~~The larger Party#2%, the greater the PS.~~

After we controlled for country wealth and country size through regression analysis, one standard deviation in party system competitiveness produced about a 10 point increase in the Rule of Law, Government Effectiveness, Control of Corruption, and Regulatory Quality. Party system competitiveness had a much larger effect on Voice and Accountability, but its effect was clouded by the way Voice and Accountability was measured. Party system competitiveness had no effect on Political Stability and the Absence of Violence. Otherwise, these findings should provide some reassurance for those working to develop competitive party systems in emerging democracies.

Notes

1. For example, see Alicia Adsera, "Are You Being Served? Political Accountability and Quality of Government," *Journal of Law Economics & Organization* 19 (October 2003): 445–490; Conor O'Dwyer, *Runaway State-Building: Patronage Politics and Democratic Development* (Baltimore: Johns Hopkins University Press, 2006), 40.

2. For works that do use the strength of the parliamentary opposition in assessing competitiveness, see Jonathan van Eerd, "Dominance and Fluidity: Conceptualizing and Explaining Party System Characteristics in Sub-Saharan Africa" (paper presented at the annual meeting of the Midwest Political Science Association, Chicago, Illinois, April 22–25, 2010); Anna Grzymala-Busse, *Rebuilding Leviathan: Party Competition and State Exploitation in Post-Communist Democracies* (New York: Cambridge University Press, 2007).

3. The size of the largest party was used to measure competitiveness by Tatu Vanhanen, *Prospects of Democracy: A Study of 172 Countries* (New York: Routledge, 1997).

The "effective number of parties" was used by Michelle Kuenzi and Gina Lambright, "Party Systems and Democratic Consolidation in Africa's Electoral Regimes," *Party Politics* 11 (July 2005): 423–446. Other scholars have used these measures too.

4. Anna Grzymala-Busse says, "Fragmentation and its mathematical analogue—the effective number of parties—have an indeterminate impact by themselves. Indicators such as 'effective number of parties' measure neither the viability of alternative governments nor the fragility of existing ones." See Anna Grzymala-Busse "Encouraging Effective Democratic Competition," *East European Politics and Societies* 21, no. 1 (2007): 91–110, at 95.

5. Douglas W. Rae, *The Political Consequence of Electoral Laws* (New Haven, CT: Yale University Press, 1971), 53.

6. Ibid.

7. Kuenzi and Lambright, "Party Systems and Democratic Consolidation in Africa's Electoral Regimes." See also Mark Kesselman, "French Local Politics: A Statistical Examination of Grass Roots Consensus," *American Political Science Review* 60 (December 1966): 963–973, at 968–969.

8. Steven B. Wolinetz, "Party Systems and Party System Types," in *Handbook of Party Politics*, ed. Richard S. Katz and William Crotty (London: Sage Publications, 2006), 51–62, at 53.

9. Giovanni Sartori, *Parties and Party Systems: A Framework for Analysis* (London: Cambridge University Press, 1976), 218.

10. See Jeremy J. Albright, "The Multidimensional Nature of Party Competition," *Party Politics* 16 (November 2010): 699–719.

11. Ibid.

12. Adam Przeworski and Henry Teune, *The Logic of Comparative Social Inquiry* (New York: Wiley Interscience, 1970), 32.

13. Maurice Duverger, *Political Parties* (New York: John Wiley, 1951), 283.

14. This has been confirmed in research for parliamentary governments. See Eric C. Browne and Mark N. Franklin, "Aspects of Coalition Payoffs in European Parliamentary Democracies," *American Political Science Review* 67 (1973): 453–469. Their finding was supported nearly three decades later by Paul V. Warwick and James N. Druckman, "Portfolio Salience and the Proportionality of Payoffs in Coalition Governments," *British Journal of Political Science* 31 (October 2001): 627–649.

15. The term comes from Lieven de Winter and Patrick Dumont, "Parties into Government: Still Many Puzzles," in *Handbook of Party Politics*, ed. Richard S. Katz and William Crotty (London: Sage Publications, 2006), 175–188, at 181.

16. In presidential systems, awarding of cabinet seats may deviate from proportionality. See Octavio Amorim Neto, "Presidential Cabinets, Electoral Cycles, and Coalition Discipline in Brazil," in *Legislative Politics in Latin America*, ed. Scott Morgenstern and Benito Nacif (New York: Cambridge University Press, 2002), 48–78. More cabinet posts may also be nonpartisan. See Octavio Amorim Neto and Kaare Strøm, "Breaking the Parliamentary Chain of Delegation: Presidents and Non-Partisan Cabinet Members in European Democracies," *British Journal of Political Science* 36 (2006): 619–643.

17. Anna Grzymala-Busse looks to share of parliamentary seats by "plausible" governing parties as an indicator of competitiveness. See Grzymala-Busse, *Rebuilding Leviathan*, 12.

18. See Asbjørn Skjœveland, "Modeling Government Formation in Denmark and Beyond," *Party Politics* 15 (November 2009): 715–735.

19. In statistical terms, this relationship is not homoscedastic, which requires that the relationship hold across the whole range of both variables.

20. G. Bingham Powell Jr., "Party Systems and Political System Performance: Voting Participation, Government Stability and Mass Violence in Contemporary Democracies," *American Political Science Review* 75 (December 1981): 861–879, at 873, 874.

21. Using all the cases preserved the original variance in RL scores, but it introduced error associated with using means to estimate missing data for Party#2%.

22. Albert Weale, "Party Competition and Deliberative Democracy," in *Democratic Politics and Party Competition: Essays in Honour of Ian Budge*, ed. Judith Bara and Albert Weale (New York: Routledge, 2006), 271–286, at 271.

23. Grzymala-Busse, *Rebuilding Leviathan*, 1.

24. Grzymala-Busse, "Encouraging Effective Democratic Competition," 92–93.

25. Sarah Leary, "Electoral Authoritarianism: A Cross-National Study of the Influence of Elections on Responsiveness to the People and Regime Longevity" (paper presented at the annual meeting of the Midwest Political Science Association, Chicago, Illinois, April 22–25, 2010), 3.

26. See the regression assumptions in Michael S. Lewis-Beck, *Applied Regression: An Introduction*, Sage University Paper Series on Quantitative Applications in the Social Sciences 07-22 (Beverly Hills, CA: Sage Publications, 1980), 26. The correlation between Party#2 and Wealth is 0.27 and between SmallArea and Party#2 is 0.19. Therefore, Wealth and SmallArea may exert indirect effects on RL. No path analysis has been conducted.

27. Interestingly, scholars have used the Worldwide Governance Indicator Government Effectiveness as an independent variable to explain "happiness." See Marcus Samanni and Sören Holmberg, "Quality of Government Makes People Happy" (Quality of Government Institute Working Paper Series 2010: 1, University of Gothenburg, Sweden, March 2010).

Chapter 10

The Effects of Aggregation

The concepts of interest aggregation and articulation are usually associated with individual parties, not party systems. Political parties vary in the extent to which they aggregate (gather) and articulate (express) political interests.[1] Green parties, for example, typically articulate policies that protect the environment, which override all other interests. Leftist parties tend to favor green policies too, but they also balance environmental issues against job losses in fossil fuel industries, aggregating conflicting interests in the process of converting them into policy alternatives.[2] Large parties usually aggregate broad interests; small parties articulate narrow interests. Party systems too can vary in articulation and aggregation according to the number and size of their parties. Arend Lijphart contends, "The best aggregators are parties in two-party systems like the Anglo-American democracies, but the larger the number and the smaller the size of the parties in a system, the less effectively the aggregation function will be performed; in the Continental European multi-party systems only a minimum of aggregation takes place."[3] Lawrence Mayer says, "Aggregation becomes a meaningful concept only when its converse, fragmentation, is a possible alternative"; he adds that "a party system with many parties fits with what is commonly understood by the term fragmented than a system with fewer parties."[4] In the view of prominent scholars then, we can consider the number and strength of parties as indicative of party system aggregation or its converse, party system fragmentation.

A contrary view, however, holds that a multiparty system can be more aggregative than a two-party system as a result of legislative bargaining among the multiple parties.[5] In the process of articulating the interests of their own voters, multiple parties can reach a consensus that effectively aggregates the interests of most voters.[6] This proposition, which runs counter to the standard argument in party theory and will be considered further below, deserves to be studied on its own. We will adopt the standard view that the more political parties in a party system, the less aggregative it is.

Party system aggregation (or its antonyms "fragmentation" and "fractionalization") is distinct from the concept of party system competitiveness. The extent to which the two concepts correlate empirically, however, depends on how aggregation is measured—which is a disputed issue. The inventory of party system measures by Jan-Erik Lane and Svante Ersson in Chapter 7 identifies no less than five variously named indicators (all involving the number or strength of parties in the system) that have been used to measure party system fragmentation or aggregation. Terminological confusion attends the concepts as well as the measures.

The Concept of Aggregation

Decades ago, scholars stressed aggregation as an important property of party systems. In 1960, Gabriel Almond wrote, "It is the party system which is the distinctively modern structure of political aggregation," which is "crucial to the performance of the political system as a whole."[7] In a famous article a few years later, Otto Kirchheimer said that European party systems had been "transformed" by the rise of "catchall" parties that aggregated broad rather than narrow interests.[8] In 1980, Mayer devised a method for measuring party system aggregation, which has been largely neglected.[9] Today, democracy assistance groups still value the aggregative function of party systems, particularly in conflict-prone societies.[10] Most scholars, however, have shifted attention from party system aggregation to party system fragmentation.

The definition of fragmentation varies across writers, but all would agree that it deals with the extent to which numerous parties in a system have relatively equal political power. Writers claim or imply various consequences of high party system fragmentation. Ruben Enikolopov and Ekaterina Zhuravskaya think that fragmentation produces weak governing parties with each having little influence over governing policies.[11] Lane and Ersson summarize standard theory: "A high degree of fractionalization—too many parties—hinders a multi-party system from delivering durable and effective government, or so established party system theory suggests."[12] Nevertheless, Lane and Ersson believe that some degree of fragmentation increases "the chances for voters to send signals to politicians/political parties and show they are monitoring their behaviour."[13]

Other scholars reflect Lane and Ersson's theoretical ambivalence. Christopher Anderson says that high fragmentation, with different parties targeting different parts of the electorate, is positively related to satisfaction with democracy.[14] Scott Mainwaring, in contrast, believes that high fragmentation reduces a president's capacity to introduce political reforms.[15] Anna Grzymala-Busse contends that high fragmentation of east-central European party systems caused electoral uncertainty, constraining the extraction of state resources by one-party dominant governments.[16] Again in contrast, Ivan Doherty holds that high fragmentation prevents the emergence of adequate political opposition.[17] Gabor Toka and Andrija Henjak worry about the destabilizing effects of both very high and very low party fragmentation.[18] Finally, Omar Sanchez says that variations in fragmentation are unimportant when party systems vary in institutionalization.[19]

We drop the "fragmentation/fractionalization" terminology and frame our study using the concept of party system aggregation. Several benefits flow from returning to the earlier emphasis in the literature. One is that doing so skirts terminological confusion attending fragmentation. Another is that aggregation refers to a desirable trait of party systems from the standpoint of country governance while fragmentation is a negative trait. Finally, and most importantly, using aggregation recaptures the older theoretical argument. We define party system aggregation as the extent to which the political parties in the system represent broad political interests. This concept is not easy to measure—as witnessed by the many efforts to do so. A systematic and semihistorical explication of five efforts is in order.

Measuring Aggregation

Scholars have historically classified party systems by the number of parties that regularly contest elections (one party, two party, or multiparty) and have recently created more elaborate classifications.[20] These categorical schemes have usually sought to reflect competitiveness rather than either aggregation or fragmentation. Two-party systems were thought more competitive than one-party systems, and multiparty systems more competitive than two-party ones. Partly in an effort to distinguish among party systems within a classification, scholars devised formulae involving the strength and number of parties to score systems by continuous values instead of categories. In creating these formulae, scholars also attempted to capture properties of party systems (e.g., fragmentation and aggregation) instead of competitiveness.

Reviewing the Measures and Formulae

Readers need some understanding of the various approaches used to operationalize the concepts of fragmentation and its converse, aggregation. We briefly review five measures, their components, and their formulae.

Strength of the Largest Party, Party#1%. The strength of the largest party, measured by percentage of the electoral vote received or by parliamentary seats held, offers the simplest operationalization of fragmentation and aggregation. The greater the number of votes or seats won by the largest party, the fewer of either available to others—so the less the fragmentation. Conversely, the larger the party, the greater the assumed interest aggregation. For our 189 countries with parliamentary seat data, the largest party averaged 52 percent of the seats (about half), and the distribution was unimodal and satisfactorily symmetrical. The fact that this simple measure says nothing about the other parties in the system, however, overshadows these statistical virtues. Its information content is low.

Number of Parties in Parliament, NPP. The number of parties that compete in parliamentary elections in any country is very difficult to determine because results often go unreported for the many parties with few votes. Fortunately, data usually are available (but tedious to collect) for parties that win seats and gain representation in parliament. Clearly, the more parties represented in parliament, the greater the fragmentation. By implication, the fewer the parties, the greater the aggregation. Our count of the total number of parties seated in 189 parliaments found that the average parliament represented 6.7 parties. The distribution was highly skewed, however, with a high of thirty-nine parties seated in Colombia. Taking the logarithm of the number of parliamentary parties reduced the skew and produced an acceptable statistical distribution. Nevertheless, the number of parties (or its log) says nothing about the percentages of seats held by each party.

Fractionalization Index, F. More than four decades ago, Douglas Rae adapted an economic index of industrial concentration to the study of party systems.[21] Combining the number and strength of the parties, Rae called it the Fractionalization Index[22]:

$$F = 1 - \sum_{i}^{N} p_i^2 \qquad (10.1)$$

where p = proportion of parliamentary seats held by party I.

F approaches 1.0 as larger numbers of parties hold equally small proportions of seats; it is equal to 0 when one party holds all the seats. Thus, it measures fragmentation rather than aggregation. (As noted on page 135, Rae viewed fractionalization in terms of competitiveness.) Computing Rae's F for our 189 parliaments produces a somewhat asymmetrical but acceptable distribution suitable for statistical analysis with a mean value of 0.61.

Effective Number of Parliamentary Parties, ENPP. Approximately a decade after Rae published his index, Markku Laakso and Rein Taagepera published a similar formula involving the same components.[23] They said it measured the effective number of parties (ENP) in the sense that it reflected the "effective access" to power by parties of different sizes.[24] ENP has been applied to both electoral and parliamentary parties. We calculate the effective number of parliamentary parties (ENPP):

$$\text{ENPP} = \frac{1}{\sum_i^N p_i^2} \qquad (10.2)$$

where p = proportion of parliamentary seats held by party I.

Whereas Rae subtracted $\sum_i^N p_i^2$ from 1 (producing decimal values ranging between 0 and 1), Laakso and Taagepera divided $\sum_i^N p_i^2$ into 1 (producing numbers ranging from 1 to N). ENPP's scoring has more intuitive appeal. An ENPP of 3.2 conjures the appropriate imagery of three relatively equal parties; the equivalent F of 0.69 is only an index score.[25] Unfortunately, ENPP requires complete data for all individual parties, but we only have data for the top three parties.[26] We adjusted the formula by replacing 1 in the numerator with the total proportion of seats held by the three parties after the stimulus election (note that p_i in the numerator is not squared):

$$\text{ENPP}_{3\,\text{parties}} = \frac{\sum_1^3 p_i}{\sum_i^3 p_i^2} \qquad (10.3)$$

Computed for our data on 189 parliaments, ENPP generates a highly skewed distribution with a mean ENPP score of 2.9. Taking its logarithm produces an acceptable distribution for analysis.[27]

Aggregation Index, A. In 1980, Mayer criticized Rae's F because it "did not distinguish between the fragmentation of the government and the opposition."[28] Mayer proposed instead an index based on the strength of the largest party (the governmental party) and the number of parties in parliament (fragmentation of the opposition). His formula divided the percentage of the largest party by the number of parties:

$$A = \frac{Party\#1\%}{NPP} \qquad (10.4)$$

where Party#1% and NPP are defined above.[29]

Applied to our data for 189 parliaments, the formula generates a mean of 16.5. Because in a few countries one party held all seats, the distribution is skewed toward 100. Taking the log of Mayer's A results in a relatively symmetrical, unimodal distribution.

Measurement Issues and Controversies

When multiple indicators vie for attention in any field, controversy arises. Scholars framed the debate over which formula above best measures party system fragmentation. In his 1980 review of alternative measures in this literature, Mogens Pedersen concludes,

> None of these have led to significant improvements on Rae's F. Several of the new indices are merely complicating and redundant reformulations of F. It might be a good idea, therefore, if students of party systems would decide to stick to one measure—namely, F. Instead of inventing new indices of fragmentation, one could instead concentrate on the task of delimiting the contexts in which F can legitimately be used.[30]

Pedersen's advice went unheeded. Scholars persisted in writing about mathematical deficiencies in the various indices and proposing alternatives. After considering existing measures, Juan Monilar proposed a new index that "behaves better in relation to the size of the largest party and to the gap between the two largest parties."[31] Nevertheless, Patrick Dunleavy and Françoise Boucek critiqued Monilar's index, dismissed it, and proposed a formula that "yields more stable and readily interpretable results" than the leading alternative—Laakso's and Taagepera's effective number of parties.[32] However, Grigorii Golosov's own review of alternative indicators said that Dunleavy and Boucek's "proposed solution is insufficient." He thought that Laakso and Taagepera created "a very good measure" but found that it "tends to produce unrealistically high scores for very concentrated party systems"—a problem that Golosov claimed he had solved.[33] These brief exchanges illustrate the extensive debate in the literature over measuring party system fragmentation.[34]

Testing Hypotheses About Aggregation

Party scholars devoted far more attention to tweaking fragmentation formulas than to clarifying the underlying concept they were trying to measure.[35] Unfortunately, they neglected to place their proposed measures in the context of party theory.[36] Instead of testing alternative measures in parallel hypotheses predicting some political process or governmental outcome, they simply tended to judge how well the measures fit their images of a fragmented party system. Some empirical tests of party theory may have helped more.

According to proposition P3 in Chapter 6, *the more **aggregative** the party system, the better the country governance.* Contemporary party theorists disagree over this proposition. One group accepts it, believing that aggregative parties compress political differences, resulting in compromises that serve citizenry generally.[37] Another argues the opposite, believing that government bargaining among several articulative parties better serves a country, particularly one divided into conflicting ethnic groups.[38] The latter look more favorably on a contrary proposition P3´: *The more* **articulative** *the party system, the better the country governance.* Most advocates of funding to improve political parties in foreign countries fit in the first group, representing the conventional view. They promote aggregative parties and nonfragmented party systems.[39] We devise hypotheses to test the conventional proposition, P3, that more aggregative party systems produce better country governance.

Confronted with five alternative measures of party system aggregation, which one should we use to operationalize the concept in our hypotheses? All five measures loaded on the same factor in Chapter 7, so they are highly intercorrelated. The mean intercorrelations for Party#1%, Mayer's A, Rae's F, and Laakso and Taagepera's ENPP range from 0.80 to 0.84. The mean intercorrelation is only 0.65 between NPP (the number of parliamentary parties) and the other indicators. NPP (more accurately, its logarithm) seems to be measuring a somewhat different property of party systems. Which should we use?

To decide, we ran thirty separate regression analyses, one for each of the six indicators using each of the five alternative measures.[40] Each analysis controlled for country size and wealth. The measure that consistently (and surprisingly) produced the strongest findings was NPPlog, the logarithm of the number of parliamentary parties. The measure that consistently produced the least significant findings was ENPP—despite its status in the field as having reached "a high level of acceptance"[41] as the "best-known"[42] and "most popular"[43] method and the "purest measure"[44] of counting parties. Perhaps ENPP failed in our analyses because we had to adapt the formula to data for only the top three parties. Perhaps NPPlog succeeded because it counted all the parties seated in parliament, albeit not their seat shares. On the other hand, perhaps, as Benjamin Nyblade and Angela O'Mahony contend, a simple count may be a superior measure: "It might be that the fragmentation measure (which treats a move from 1 to 2 parties as much larger than a move from 3 to 4 parties) is inferior to a count measure."[45]

We cannot tell from our data why a simple count of the number of parties seated in parliament better predicts to indicators of country governance than alternative formulae. The fruitful performance of NPPlog also defeats our desire to state hypotheses in a positive direction. NPPlog does not measure party system aggregation as much as it measures party system articulation. The more parties seated in parliament, the more particular interests are articulated as opposed to general interests being aggregated. Accordingly, the United States, with only two parties seated in the Congress, has the most aggregative party system. The Icelandic Althing, with five parties, is somewhat more aggregative than the South Korean National Assembly (Kukhoe), which has seven parties. The fourteen parties in the State Duma give Russia the least aggregative party system among the countries we are tracking. We use NPPlog to operationalize party system aggregation in generating hypotheses H3.1 through H3.6.

H3.1. The lower the NPPlog, the greater the Rule of Law (RL).
H3.2. The lower the NPPlog, the greater the Government Effectiveness (GE).
H3.3. The lower the NPPlog, the greater the Control of Corruption (CC).
H3.4. The lower the NPPlog, the greater the Regulatory Quality (RQ).
H3.5. The lower the NPPlog, the greater the Voice and Accountability (VA).
H3.6. The lower the NPPlog, the greater the Political Stability (PS).

Rule of Law

In Chapters 8 and 9, we led the regression analysis using Rule of Law to illustrate the effect of party systems on country governance. That does not work this time. Controlling for other variables (SmallArea, Wealth, NoParties, NonPartisan, and Party#2%), NPP has no significant relationship to Rule of Law. Unlike party system competitiveness and stability, party system aggregation (regardless of the measure used) exerts no significant impact on Rule of Law. The hypothesis must be rejected.

All Six Indicators

In the following analysis, we estimate the effects of both Party#2% (competitiveness) and NPPlog (aggregation) on all six indicators of country governance with the standard controls of country size, wealth, and the presence of parties. We can easily do that because there was virtually no correlation ($r = -0.09$) between Party#2% and NPPlog. Given the absence of an appreciable overlap between the variables, we can consider their joint significant effects (if any) in explaining the dependent variables. Figure 10.1 summarizes the results of the regression analyses.

As with Rule of Law, party system aggregation (as inversely measured by NPPlog) has no significant effect on Government Effectiveness and Control of Corruption.[46] However, NPPlog does have significant effects on the other three indicators of country governance, but in two instances the effects run opposite to the hypotheses! The findings contradict the hypotheses for

Figure 10.1 Effects of country size, wealth, NoParties, NonPartisan, Party#2%, and NPPlog on all six governance indicators

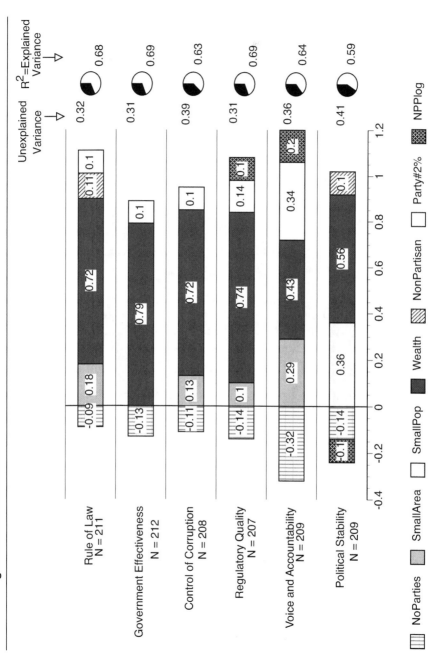

Regulatory Quality and Voice and Accountability. For each standard deviation increase in NPPlog, RQ increases 0.10 points, while a similar increase in the number of parliamentary parties results in a 0.20 increase in VA. These results suggest that—on those two dimensions—country governance increases not with party system aggregation (fewer parliamentary parties) but with party system articulation (more parliamentary parties). One possible interpretation for Voice and Accountability is that citizens react positively to having more parties represented in parliament, resulting in higher VA scores. Presumably, citizens like having many parties in parliament articulating their particular interests rather than having fewer parties aggregating them into a compromising blend. On the surface, this finding seems to support the contrary view, discussed early in the chapter, concerning the aggregative capacity of multiparty parliaments. In some instances, public interests may be better aggregated through negotiations among multiple small parties than through representation by a small number (ideally two) of large parties.

The results for Political Stability and the Absence of Violence, however, move in the opposite direction, as hypothesized. For each standard deviation increase in NPPlog, the country's PS rating decreases by 0.10 points. This implies that multiple parliamentary parties provoke political instability with their squabbling, whereas troublesome issues can be settled more quietly within a parliament with a more aggregative party system. We will not try to resolve this issue here. Our conflicting findings, however, shed new light on old controversies in comparative politics.

Summary and Conclusion

The concept of interest aggregation is normally associated with individual political parties, but it also has application to party systems. Systems with few parties are more likely to aggregate (gather and balance) conflicting interests within the parties themselves, whereas those with many parties are more likely to articulate (express) uncompromised political interests. When a parliament seats many political parties, it is often said to have a fragmented party system, which is the converse of an aggregative party system.

Scholars have disagreed over the consequences of party system fragmentation, just as they have over how to measure fragmentation—which figures more prominently in the literature than its converse, aggregation. We reviewed five operational measures: (1) strength of the largest party, (2) number of parliamentary parties, (3) Rae's Fractionalization Index, (4) the Laakso-Taagepera formula for effective number of parliamentary parties, and (5) Mayer's Aggregation Index.

Our initial regression analyses found that item (2), NPPlog, produced the most fruitful relationships to measures of country governance. Scholars differ over the effect of party system fragmentation on politics and government. Most scholars endorse P3′: *The more* **aggregative** *the party system, the better the country governance.* A vocal minority, however, argues P3′: *The more* **articulative** *the party system, the better the country governance.* We formulated six hypotheses derived from P3, with results checked, if supported, and stricken through, if unsupported:

H3.1. ~~The lower the NPPlog, the greater the RL.~~
H3.2. ~~The lower the NPPlog, the greater the GE.~~
H3.3. ~~The lower the NPPlog, the greater the CC.~~
H3.4. ~~The lower the NPPlog, the greater the RQ.~~
H3.5. ~~The lower the NPP log,, the greater the VA.~~
H3.6. √ The lower the NPPlog, the greater the PS.

The boldfacing of H3.4 and H3.5 indicates that NPP had significant effects that were contrary to those hypothesized. Both the contrary and the hypothesized finding can be interpreted within the context of party theory.

Notes

1. This discussion draws extensively from Kenneth Janda, "Interest Articulation and Interest Aggregation," in *The Encyclopedia of Political Science*, ed. George Thomas Kurian (Washington, DC: CQ Press, 2011), 3:798–799.

2. Gabriel A. Almond and G. Bingham Powell Jr., *Comparative Politics: A Developmental Approach* (Boston: Little, Brown, 1966), chap. 4, "Interest Articulation," 73–97, and chap. 5, "Interest Aggregation and Political Parties," 98–127.

3. Arend Lijphart, "Consociational Democracy," *World Politics* 21 (January 1969): 207–225, at 210.

4. Lawrence C. Mayer, "A Note on the Aggregation of Party Systems," in *Western European Party Systems*, ed. Peter H. Merkl (New York: The Free Press, 1980), 515–520, at 516.

5. Julieta Suarez-Cao effectively argued this view in commenting on a draft of this chapter.

6. This is a variant of the argument inherent in Arend Lijphart, *Democracies: Patterns of Majoritarian and Consensus Government in Twenty-One Countries* (New Haven, CT: Yale University Press, 1984), 22–23.

7. Gabriel A. Almond, "Introduction: A Functional Approach to Comparative Politics," in *The Politics of the Developing Areas*, ed. Gabriel A. Almond and James S. Coleman (Princeton, NJ: Princeton University Press, 1960), 3–64, at 40, 44.

8. Otto Kirchheimer, "The Transformation of the Western European Party Systems," in *Political Parties and Political Development*, ed. Joseph LaPalombara and Myron Weiner (Princeton, NJ: Princeton University Press, 1966), 177–200.

9. Mayer, "A Note on the Aggregation of Party Systems."

10. Benjamin Reilly and Per Nordlund, eds., *Political Parties in Conflict-Prone Societies: Regulation, Engineering and Democratic Development* (Tokyo: United Nations University Press, 2008); Democratic Governance Group, *A Handbook on Working with Political Parties* (New York: United Nations Bureau for Development Policy, United Nations Development Programme, 2006).

11. Ruben Enikolopov and Ekaterina Zhuravskaya, "Decentralization and Political Institutions," *Journal of Public Economics* 91, no. 11–12 (December 2007): 2261–2290.

12. Jan-Erik Lane, with Svante Ersson, "Party System Instability in Europe: Persistent Differences in Volatility Between West and East?" *Democratization* 14 (February 2007): 92–110, at 94.

13. Ibid., 95.

14. Christopher J. Anderson, "Parties, Party Systems, and Satisfaction with Democratic Performance in the New Europe," *Political Studies* 46 (1998): 572–588.

15. Scott Mainwaring, *Rethinking Party Systems in the Third Wave of Democratization: The Case of Brazil* (Stanford, CA: Stanford University Press, 1999), 285.

16. Anna Grzymala-Busse, "Political Competition and the Politicization of the State in East Central Europe," *Comparative Political Studies* 36 (December 2003): 1123–1147.

17. Ivan Doherty, "Democracy Out of Balance: Civil Society Can't Replace Political Parties," *Policy Review* (April–May 2001): 25–35.

18. Gabor Toka and Andrija Henjak, "Institutional Design and Voting Behavior in East Central Europe: A Cross-National Comparison of the Impact of Leaders, Partisanship, Performance Evaluation and Ideology on the Vote" (paper presented at the 21st World Congress of the International Political Science Association, Santiago, Chile, July 12–16, 2009).

19. Omar Sanchez, "Party Non-Systems: A Conceptual Innovation," *Party Politics* 15 (July 2009): 487–520.

20. See Alan Siaroff, *Comparative European Party Systems: An Analysis of Parliamentary Elections Since 1945* (New York: Garland, 2000).

21. It was the 1940s Herfindahl-Hirschman index. See Grigorii V. Golosov, "The Effective Number of Parties," *Party Politics* 16 (March 2010): 171–192.

22. Douglas Rae, "A Note on the Fractionalization of Some European Party Systems," *Comparative Political Studies* 1 (October 1968): 413–418.

23. Markku Laakso and Rein Taagepera, "'Effective' Number of Parties: A Measure with Application to West Europe," *Comparative Political Studies* 12 (April 1979): 3–27.

24. Ibid., 3.

25. Golosov, "The Effective Number of Parties," 174.

26. Rein Taagepera suggests a work-around that we use for both F and ENP. See Taagepera, "Effective Number of Parties for Incomplete Data," *Electoral Studies* 16 (1997): 145–151. He suggests using this formula: ENP = $P^2/\sum P_i^2$, where P_i^2 stands for the number (rather than fractional share) of seats or votes for the i-th party, and P is the total number of seats or valid votes. That is essentially our formula, but Taagepera proceeds to put all "other" seats into a remainder term, R, which does not fit with our situation.

27. Our attempt to adapt the Laakso-Taagepera formula for ENPP produced some odd scores. The most extreme case concerned Belarus, where the top three parties (holding 0.07, 0.03, and 0.01, respectively) filled only 0.11 of the parliamentary seats

after the 2004 election. Applying the adjusted formula to those data generated an ENPP score of 18.6. While Belarus obviously does not have "effectively" 18.6 parties, it does have an extremely fragmented party system, which the number shows.

28. Mayer, "A Note on the Aggregation of Party Systems," 517.

29. Mayer's original formula, A = 100 (*Largest party seats/Seats in parliament*) / *Number of parties*, was for raw data, not seat percentages.

30. Mogens N. Pedersen, "On Measuring Party System Change: A Methodological Critique and a Suggestion," *Comparative Political Studies* 12 (January 1980): 387–403, at 397.

31. Juan Molinar, "Counting the Number of Parties: An Alternative Index," *American Political Science Review* 85 (December 1991): 1383–1391, at 1390.

32. Patrick Dunleavy and Françoise Boucek, "Constructing the Number of Parties," *Party Politics* 9 (May 2003): 291–315, at 302, 307.

33. Golosov, "The Effective Number of Parties," 172, 188.

34. See Benjamin Nyblade and Angela O'Mahony, "Counting Parties: Different Measures for Different Purposes" (paper presented at the annual meeting of the Midwest Political Science Association, Chicago, Illinois, April 22–25, 2010).

35. Indeed, scholarship on this topic smacks of scholasticism, as described by Lawrence M. Mead, "Scholasticism in Political Science," *Perspectives on Politics* 8 (June 2010): 453–464.

36. Dunleavy and Boucek say, "The root of these problems is primarily that the political scientists who devised or advocated the index never gave a systematic *experimental* account of how its results were patterned across the full range of possible empirical outcomes" ("Constructing the Number of Parties," 292).

37. Donald L. Horowitz, "Making Moderation Pay: The Comparative Politics of Ethnic Conflict Management," in *Conflict and Peacemaking in Multiethnic Societies*, ed. J. V. Montville (New York: Lexington Books, 1991), 451–475.

38. Arend Lijphart, "The Power-Sharing Approach," in *Conflict and Peacemaking in Multiethnic Societies*, 491–509.

39. Thomas Carothers, *Confronting the Weakest Link: Aiding Political Parties in New Democracies* (Washington, DC: Carnegie Endowment for International Peace, 2006), 98; Democratic Governance Group, *A Handbook on Working with Political Parties*, 9; National Democratic Institute, *Minimum Standards for the Democratic Function of Political Parties* (Washington, DC: National Democratic Institute, 2008), ii.

40. We actually ran another set of six regressions using as independent variables the factor scores from the rotated "aggregation" factor identified in Chapter 7. These results, which readers unfamiliar with factor analysis are unlikely to understand easily, were largely insignificant. We do not report them.

41. Dunleavy and Boucek, "Constructing the Number of Parties."

42. Blau, Adrian, "The Effective Number of Parties at Four Scales: Votes, Seats, Legislative Power and Cabinet Power," *Party Politics* 14 (March 2008): 167–187, at 170.

43. Pippa Norris, *Electoral Engineering: Voting Rules and Political Behavior* (New York: Cambridge University Press, 2004), 83.

44. Arend Lijphart, *Electoral Systems and Party Systems: A Study of Twenty-Seven Democracies, 1945–1990* (Oxford: Oxford University Press, 1994), 70.

45. Nyblade and O'Mahony, "Counting Parties."

46. A comparison of Figure 10.1 and Figure 9.4 shows that adding NPP to the analysis with Party#2% retains identical effects for NoParties and NonPartisan on all six indicators. The effects of NoParties and NonPartisan for the twenty-three countries that lack parliamentary parties are effectively unchanged as party system variables are added for the other 189 countries with parliamentary parties.

Chapter 11

The Effects of Stability

The previous chapter notes that party system competitiveness and aggregation are distinct and unrelated concepts. Party system stability—meaning little change across elections—too is distinct from the concept of competitiveness. A party system can be relatively competitive and relatively stable (as in the United States) or very uncompetitive yet very stable (as in China). Although party system aggregation and stability are also distinct concepts, they are somewhat related empirically. We return to this relationship later.

Two indicators loaded highly on the factor labeled "party system stability" in Chapter 7's factor analysis. One was Mogens Pedersen's well-known and commonly used measure of volatility.[1] The other was a new variable stating whether the three largest parties in the stimulus election won seats in the referent election. Scored to measure stability, its highest score went to the 45 percent of countries in which the same three parties won seats (regardless of order) in both elections. Because the Pedersen index measured volatility while the new one measured stability, they were negatively correlated ($r = -0.36$). Our preliminary analyses showed that the Pedersen measure consistently explained more variation in country governance, so we used it throughout this analysis.[2] Although our measure of stability is based on the Pedersen index, we reverse its scoring and relabel it to align our measure with the concept of stability.

The Concept of Stability

In ordinary discourse, the term *volatile* means "inconstant," "fleeting," "capable of quick change." Applied separately to party votes and seats, the term has the same meaning in describing party systems. Electoral volatility, as popularized by Pedersen, assesses changes in percentages of votes cast for all parties in adjacent elections.[3] Seat volatility refers to changes in percentages of parliamentary seats for all parties in adjacent elections.[4] Naturally, measures of electoral and seat volatility tend to be highly correlated. Svante Ersson and Jan-Erik Lane find they correlate at 0.77 for measures for eighteen European countries.[5]

Unfortunately, volatility has negative connotations for party politics. The term implies party system instability rather than stability, which leads to confusing statements in the literature. Consider the contradiction in this sentence by Noam Lupu: "Scholars of Latin America have largely focused on electoral volatility as a broad measure of the stability of voter choices over time."[6] Similarly, Joseph Robbins says, "The first measure of party institutionalization is electoral volatility."[7] Surely volatility measures *instability* (Lupu) and implies a *lack* of institutionalization (Robbins). To avoid such terminological mismatch, we prefer the physics term *viscosity*, which refers to a fluid's resistance to flow or movement.[8] While not quite an antonym for volatility, viscosity invites talk of party system stability rather than instability.

Measuring Stability

Pedersen's original volatility formula calculated the percentage-point differences in votes cast for all parties in two adjacent elections. Our formula differs in a minor way by calculating the differences in percentages of seats won by parties in two adjacent elections. More importantly, we calculate the percentage-point differences only for the three largest parties at the stimulus election. Accordingly, the formula adjusts for the share of seats won by k parties in adjacent elections when not all parties are included in calculating changes in seat shares.[9] It replaces "2" in the divisor in Pedersen's formula with the sum of the seats won in each election by the set of parties (k) included in the calculation.[10] The modified formula no longer ranges from 0 to 100 but from 0 to 1 and expresses the proportion of change in seat percentages held by k parties in two adjacent elections.

$$\text{Volatility}_{\text{seats}} = \sum_{i=1}^{k} \left| p_{i(t)} - p_{i(t-1)} \right| \Big/ \left(\sum_{i=1}^{k} p_{i(t)} + \sum_{i=1}^{k} p_{i(t-1)} \right) \tag{11.1}$$

where $p_{i(t)}$ = percentage of seats in the stimulus year; $p_{i(t-1)}$ = percentage of seats in the reference year; $k = 3$, the number of parties for which we collected data.

Because we favor talking about party system stability instead of instability, we prefer to measure viscosity not volatility. To accomplish this, Formula 11.2 multiplies Pedersen's measure by −1.

$$\text{Viscosity}_{\text{seats}} = \text{Volatility}_{\text{seats}} \times -1 \tag{11.2}$$

High Viscosity values indicate little seat change and high party system stability.

For example, after the 2004 election, the Republican Party held 53.3 percent of the seats in the U.S. House of Representatives, which was slightly more than the 52.6 percent it had won in 2002. The Democrats dropped slightly from 46.9 to 46.4 percent. (One of the 435 House members was an independent.) The U.S. volatility score computed to 0.01, and the Viscosity score was 0.99. The United States had a very stable system compared against the mean Viscosity score of 0.75 for all 189 countries with parliamentary data. The Icelandic Viscosity score at 0.94 also indicated a stable party system. Russia, at 0.72, was almost average. South Korea at 0.57 ranked below the mean on Viscosity because the governing YUD (Yeollin Uri-dang, meaning "Our Open Party") won 50.8 percent of the seats in 2004 as a new party that had not competed in the previous election. Although China is not one of the countries we have been tracking, note that China had a perfect Viscosity score of 1.00, indicating no change between elections in the party composition of the National People's Congress. We return later to this fact.

Testing Hypotheses About Stability

According to proposition P4 in Chapter 6, *the more **stable** the party system, the better the country governance.* This accords with standard party theory, which holds that favorable governmental consequences flow from party system stability—usually measured by Pedersen's Volatility Index. Sarah Birch cites four negative consequences of high party system volatility: less accountability to voters, slower party institutionalization, more political uncertainty, and higher stakes in elections.[11] In keeping with the standard view, Robbins contends that party system volatility corresponds negatively with public goods spending levels, presumably an ingredient of governance.[12]

However, some scholars dissent from standard theory. Lane and Ersson say, "In contrast [we argue] that electoral volatility bolsters the position of the principal [the electorate] and makes the agents [elected officials] more inclined to work more for the interests of the principal relative to their own interests."[13] Shaheen Mozaffar and James Scarritt also hold that "high electoral volatility can be viewed as a system-clearing device that eliminates inefficient parties, leaving a small number of parties to compete for votes and form governments."[14] Michelle Kuenzi and Gina Lambright add that legislative volatility, particularly in new democracies, "might help invigorate formerly stagnant systems."[15] Finally, Gabor Toka and Andrija Henjak contend that "particularly low and particularly high levels of party system stabilization are both usually detrimental for instilling strong electoral accountability of governments."[16]

Despite some scholarly dissent about the consequences of party system volatility, we propose the standard view: The more stable the party system, the better the country governance. As usual, we use the Worldwide Governance Indicators for 2007 to operationalize country governance. We use our measure of party system Viscosity to operationalize stability in generating hypotheses H4.1 through H4.6.

H4.1. The more viscous the party system, the greater the Rule of Law (RL).

H4.2. The more viscous the party system, the greater the Government Effectiveness (GE).

H4.3. The more viscous the party system, the greater the Control of Corruption (CC).

H4.4. The more viscous the party system, the greater the Regulatory Quality (RQ).

H4.5. The more viscous the party system, the greater the Voice and Accountability (VA).

H4.6. The more viscous the party system, the greater the Political Stability (PS).

Rule of Law

Once again, we look first at the Rule of Law and test H4.1: The more viscous the party system, the greater the Rule of Law. This time, we find no support for the hypothesis. After controlling for the country variables SmallArea and Wealth and the party system variables (NoParties, NonPartisan, Party#2%, and NPPlog), we find no significant effect of Viscosity (Pedersen's volatility × –1) on Rule of Law for all countries. Nor does Viscosity have independent effects on the other administrative indicators of country governance: Government Effectiveness, Control of Corruption, and Regulatory Quality. However, Viscosity does have a significant effect on Political Stability. For each one-point increase in the Viscosity z-score, PS increases by 0.13.

Recalling that China has a highly stable party system (like all other one-party countries), we rethought the theory and formulated a revised proposition P4′: **In democratic countries, the more *viscous* the party system, the better the country governance.** Perhaps party system stability functions differently where elections actually decide who controls the government (i.e., in democracies) as opposed to where they do not (i.e., in nondemocracies). To test the revised proposition P4′, we separated the countries into two groups using Freedom House's classification of a country as an electoral democracy if its last nationwide election for the national legislature was free and fair.[17] For 2005, Freedom House classified 123 of 192 countries (64 percent) as electoral democracies. We applied Freedom House's criteria to the twenty countries in our study that it did not score and arrived at 137 electoral democracies. China was excluded, as was Russia, which did not qualify "because of the flawed nature of the country's parliamentary elections in December 2003 and presidential elections in 2004."[18] The criteria also automatically excluded all fifteen countries that scored 1 on NoParties. We also excluded the eight countries with nonpartisan elections, which could not be scored for party system stability. That left for analysis 130 countries or fewer, depending on the indicators used.

Dropping from the analysis all countries that were not electoral democracies clearly required dropping the two variables NoParties and NonPartisan, but it also resulted in dropping Party#2% measuring competitiveness. Party#2% was so highly correlated with electoral democracy ($r = 0.53$) that selecting only electoral democracies for analysis yielded countries that generally rated high on Party#2%. Because countries did not vary much on party system competitiveness, a variable that once had a wide range of values became one that varied over a narrow range and failed to discriminate among the remaining countries in the analysis.

Whereas Viscosity had no significant effect on Rule of Law for all 189 countries, it did have a significant effect on RL using only the 130 electoral democracies, as Equation 11.3 specifies:

$$RL = .75\text{Wealth} + .13\text{SmallArea} + .13\text{Viscosity} \qquad R^2_{adj} = 0.70 \ (11.3)$$

For each one-point increase in Viscosity's z-score, RL increased by 0.13, and the explanation of variance in RL scores increased to 70 percent. The significant effect of Viscosity in predicting to RL for electoral democracies invited extending the analysis to the other five governance indicators.

All Six Indicators

Based on our rewarding analysis for Rule of Law, we generated the following six hypotheses from a revised proposition P4´: ***In democratic countries***, *the more* ***viscous*** *the party system, the better the country governance.*

> H4.1′. In democratic countries, the more viscous the party system, the greater the RL.
>
> H4.2′. In democratic countries, the more viscous the party system, the greater the GE.
>
> H4.3′. In democratic countries, the more viscous the party system, the greater the CC.
>
> H4.4′. In democratic countries, the more viscous the party system, the greater the RQ.

H4.5′. In democratic countries, the more viscous the party system, the greater the VA.

H4.6′. In democratic countries, the more viscous the party system, the greater the PS.

Results of the regression analyses designed to test H4.1′ to H4.6′ are reported in Figure 11.1, which covers only 130 electoral democracies. As measured by Viscosity, party system stability has significant and approximately equal effects on every indicator except Regulatory Quality. Why Regulatory Quality deviated from the pattern is curious, given that party competitiveness previously demonstrated a relatively strong effect on RQ. Given that country wealth alone explains almost 75 percent of the variation in RQ, perhaps the Worldwide Governance Indicator Regulatory Quality, does reflect the "business-elite" bias claimed by Marcus Kurtz and Andrew Schrank, who say that the indicator "is premised on the notion that minimal regulation and minimal barriers to trade and investment flows are optimal and is thus conflated with (controversial) policy prescriptions."[19] Better Regulatory Quality (designed to aid business) in country governance appears to be driven by country wealth, not country size or party system stability, at least in electoral democracies.

Except for the deviation with RQ, the effects of Viscosity are significant and consistent for RL, GE, CC, VA, and PS. For each one-unit increase in the parliamentary seat Viscosity z-score, those governance indicators increase from 0.11 to 0.13 units for 130 electoral democracies. It appears that party system stability contributes to country governance only in countries where elections are substantively meaningful—that is, only in electoral democracies. Also, once the analysis is restricted to only electoral democracies, NPPlog (fragmentation) has no effect on any governance indicator except Political Stability. There it seems that party system fragmentation decreases PS. Or conversely, party system aggregation increases stability, even when the analysis is restricted to electoral democracies.

In retrospect, our findings give some credence to the standard theory: The more stable the party system, the better the country governance.

Summary and Conclusion

Party system stability and party system competitiveness are unrelated concepts. A stable party system is not necessarily a competitive one. We modify Pedersen's measure of party system volatility, reversing its scoring and calling it Viscosity so that it indicates stability, not instability.

In keeping with standard party theory, which holds that party system stability improves governmental performance, we began by testing a series of

Figure 11.1 Effects of country size, wealth, and party system stability on all six governance indicators for only electoral democracies

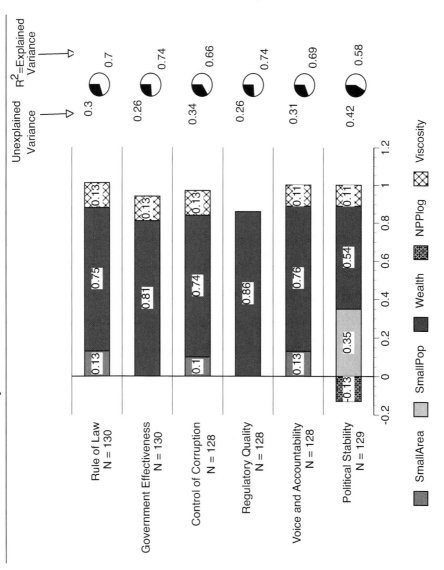

propositions derived from P4 in Chapter 6: *The more stable the party system, the better the country governance.* Finding no consistent significant effects of party system Viscosity on all six indicators of country governance, we formulated the revised proposition P4´: ***In democratic countries, the more stable the party system, the better the country governance.***

We restricted a new analysis to some 130 countries that qualified as electoral democracies according to Freedom House criteria. Operationalizing party system competitiveness by Viscosity and country governance by the six World Bank indicators, we tested these revised hypotheses, with the results checked if supported and stricken through if unsupported:

H4.1′. √ In democratic countries, the more viscous the party system, the greater the RL.

H4.2′. √ In democratic countries, the more viscous the party system, the greater the GE.

H4.3′. √ In democratic countries, the more viscous the party system, the greater the CC.

H4.4′. ~~In democratic countries, the more viscous the party system, the greater the RQ.~~

H4.5′. √ In democratic countries, the more viscous the party system, the greater the VA.

H4.6′. √ In democratic countries, the more viscous the party system, the greater the PS.

Notes

1. Mogens N. Pedersen, "The Dynamics of European Party Systems: Changing Patterns of Electoral Volatility," *European Journal of Political Research* 7 (1979): 1–26.

2. The independence of party system stability and competitiveness is demonstrated by the insignificant correlation ($r = -0.09$) between the Pedersen Volatility Index and the percentage of seats held by the second-largest party (our measure of competitiveness). A relationship between stability and fragmentation is confirmed by the significant correlation ($r = 0.30$) between Volatility and NPPlog.

3. Pedersen, "The Dynamics of European Party Systems." Jan-Erik Lane and Svante Ersson also refer to electoral volatility as "net" volatility; see Lane with Ersson, "Party System Instability in Europe: Persistent Differences in Volatility Between West and East?" *Democratization* 14 (February 2007): 92–110. Eleanor Neff Powell and Joshua A. Tucker dissect Pedersen's formula to measure two types of volatility: type A captures volatility from party entry and exit, and type B captures volatility among stable parties. See Powell and Tucker, "New Approaches to Electoral Volatility: Evidence from Postcommunist Countries" (paper presented at the annual meeting of the American Political Science Association, Toronto, Canada, September 3–9, 2009). We do not distinguish between their types for we count both types of volatility.

4. See Svante Ersson and Jan-Erik Lane, "Electoral Instability and Party System Change in Western Europe," in *Comparing Party System Change*, ed. Paul Pennings and Jan-Erik Lane (London: Routledge, 1998), 23–39.

5. Ibid., 29.

6. Noam Lupu, "Nationalization and Realignment in Twentieth-Century Argentina" (paper presented at the annual meeting of the Midwest Political Science Association, Chicago, Illinois, April 3–5, 2008), 6.

7. Joseph W. Robbins, "Party System Institutionalization and Government Spending" (paper presented at the annual meeting of the Midwest Political Science Association, Chicago, Illinois, April 3–5, 2008, 10).

8. "Viscosity," *Encyclopedia Britannica*, www.britannica.com/EBchecked/topic/630428/viscosity.

9. We learned that Sarah Birch used the same formula in *Electoral Systems and Political Transformation in Post-Communist Europe* (Basingstoke, UK: Palgrave-Macmillan, 2003), chap. 6, "Party System Stability and Change," 119–135.

10. Not accounting for all parliamentary parties at both time points raises some unresolved methodological issues. A similar, but not identical, problem is discussed in articles concerning calculating the effective number of parties (the Laakos-Taagepera formula) when all the parties are not included in the analysis. See Rein Taagepera, "Supplementing the Effective Number of Parties," *Electoral Studies* 18 (1999): 497–504; Patrick Dunleavy and Françoise Boucek, "Constructing the Number of Parties," *Party Politics* 9 (May 2003): 291–315.

11. Birch, *Electoral Systems and Political Transformation in Post-Communist Europe*, chap. 6, "Party System Stability and Change."

12. Robbins, "Party System Institutionalization and Government Spending," 24.

13. Lane and Ersson, "Party System Instability in Europe," 97.

14. Shaheen Mozaffar and James R. Scarritt, "The Puzzle of African Party Systems," *Party Politics* 11 (July 2005): 399–421.

15. Michelle Kuenzi and Gina Lambright, "Party Systems and Democratic Consolidation in Africa's Electoral Regimes," *Party Politics* 11 (July 2005): 426.

16. Gabor Toka and Andrija Henjak, "Institutional Design and Voting Behavior in East Central Europe: A Cross-National Comparison of the Impact of Leaders, Partisanship, Performance Evaluation and Ideology on the Vote" (paper presented at the 21st World Congress of the International Political Science Association, Santiago, Chile, July 12–16, 2009), 6.

17. Freedom House also had other criteria. See "Methodology," Freedom House, www.freedomhouse.org/template.cfm?page=351&ana_page=298&year=2006.

18. See "Russia Downgraded to 'Not Free,'" Freedom House, December 20, 2004, www.freedomhouse.org/template.cfm?page=70&release=242.

19. Marcus J. Kurtz and Andrew Schrank, "Growth and Governance: Models, Measures, and Mechanisms," *The Journal of Politics* 69, no. 2 (May 2007): 538–554, at 542–543.

Chapter 12

Reviewing the Theory and Research

Party Systems and Country Governance is mainly about party systems—their variations across the world and their effects on country governance. It is also about the conceptualization and measurement of country governance. In the language of research, party system traits are the independent variables, and country governance scores are the dependent variables. According to the normative values of democratic theory, the presence of competitive, aggregative, stable systems of political parties contributes to better country governance. International aid agencies have embraced the normative theory, assuming its truth. As a result, they have spent millions of dollars to develop competitive, aggregative, stable party systems. This study translates the assumed normative theory into testable empirical theory. In the introductory chapter, we raised the question, Does the nature of a country's political party system affect the quality of its governance? Our research provides evidence that largely supports the tacit assumptions of aid agencies. The nature of a country's party system does indeed positively affect the quality of its governance.

The Nature of Country Governance

The book focuses initially on the concept of country governance in the belief that one must understand a dependent variable before trying to explain it. Chapter 1 shows that over the past three decades, *governance* has evolved from a quaint term to a hot topic. Increasingly, the term has been applied to business firms, labor unions, and social clubs—as well as to government corporations and international organizations. Relatively quickly, the term lost its special political meaning, even lapsing into popular usage as synonymous with "government." For example, the *Wall Street Journal* reported that the 2010 referendum in Kyrgyzstan would "usher in a parliamentary system of governance."[1]

We return to the term's political usage, regarding governance as a quality of governmental performance by nation-states rather than institutional structure. We define country governance as the extent to which a state delivers to its citizens the desired benefits of government at acceptable costs.[2] Including the adjective "country" to modify "governance" should help distinguish the term from its other uses.

Defining a concept of country governance is one thing; measuring it adequately across countries is something else. It is a huge empirical challenge. Chapter 2 describes efforts by scholars at the World Bank to develop and apply governance indicators to virtually all countries of the world.[3] They identified six abstract metavalues that should appeal to citizens in every country and, using scores of reports from thirty-five different international sources, scored over two hundred countries on six Worldwide Governance Indicators: Rule of Law (RL), Government Effectiveness (GE), Control of Corruption (CC), Regulatory Quality (RQ), Voice and Accountability (VA), and Political Stability and the Absence of Violence (PS). The first four (RL, GE, CC, and RQ) intercorrelate more highly (mean $r = 0.92$) than VA and PS ($r = 0.68$). We regard the first four as administrative indicators and the last two as political indicators. Although the Worldwide Governance Indicators have their critics, they are widely recognized as the best data set available on country governance.[4] We use the 2007 scores for all six indicators for 212 countries to operationalize the concept of country governance. They constitute six dependent variables in our hypothesis tests.

Country governance is undoubtedly affected by party politics, but it is also affected by many other factors. The vision, integrity, and competence of country leaders are important factors not considered in this study. Nor do we consider most environmental conditions, such as ethnic and religious divisions or educational levels. Chapter 3 inquires about the logical status of country governance—whether it is a cause or a consequence of environmental conditions. We study effects of only two such conditions. One is country size, for established theory suggests that large countries are harder to govern than small ones. The other is country wealth, for strong theory implies that poor countries are harder to govern than rich countries.

Environmental Effects on Country Governance

Two chapters assess the effects of country size and wealth on governance. Chapter 4 uses country size, a pure exogenous variable, as the sole variable in regression analyses predicting to each of the six country governance indicators. Country size—measured usually by area but also by population—had a statistically significant effect on every indicator of country governance, explaining from 5 to 27 percent of the variance. Chapter 5 adds country wealth to the regression analyses along with country size. In all six cases, the effects of country wealth were greater, usually considerably greater, than the effects of country size, but the reduced effects of size remained statistically significant. Together, the two variables explained from 41 to 67 percent of the variance for each of the country indicators. Commonly in cross-national analysis, explaining so much of the existing variance with nonpolitical factors leaves relatively little room for political variables to exert any influence. That did not happen with the party system factors.

Party System Effects on Country Governance

Chapter 6 elaborates a theory of party system effects on country governance in a set of assumptions and propositions. Four major propositions guided the empirical research:

P1. *Countries with popularly elected **nonpartisan** parliaments score higher on governance than those with unelected **nonparty** parliaments, which score lower on governance than those with parties in parliament.*

P2. *The more **competitive** the party system, the better the country governance.*

P3. *The more **aggregative** the party system, the better the country governance.*

P4. *The more **stable** the party system, the better the country governance.*

We used the existing Worldwide Governance Indicators for 2007 as our six dependent variables but collected our own data on party systems. Chapter 7 describes our efforts at collecting matching data on party systems for the same 212 countries. Using Internet sources, we collected data on the percentage of parliamentary seats held by the three largest parties in 189 countries after two elections: a stimulus election in the mid-2000s and an adjacent referent election usually held prior to the stimulus election. We identified fifteen additional countries that did not hold elections for parliamentary parties and eight countries that held elections but nonpartisan ones, seating no deputies by party. Together these 212 countries account for virtually all the variations in party systems across the world. Chapter 7 reviews previous efforts at measuring party systems, arriving at the three major dimensions of party system competitiveness, aggregation, and stability. We developed measures of each dimension, using parliamentary seat data for 189 countries over two elections and scoring the twenty-three countries without parties as either NoParties or NonPartisan.

Chapter 8 is designed as an empirical test of the hypotheses derived from proposition P1: *Countries with popularly elected* **nonpartisan** *parliaments score higher on governance than those with unelected* **nonparty** *parliaments, which score lower on governance than those with parties in parliament.* The variable NoParties was created with a value of 1 (otherwise 0) for the fifteen countries lacking elections and parties. The variable NonPartisan was created with a value of 1 (otherwise 0) for the eight countries with elections but nonpartisan parliaments. Controlling for country size and wealth, the regression analyses showed significant negative effects of NoParties on country governance, supporting all six hypotheses. In general, the mean Worldwide Governance Indicators scores were significantly higher for the 189 countries with parties than for the fifteen countries lacking elections and parties. Controlling for country size and wealth, the regression analyses showed significant positive effects of NonPartisan only on Rule of Law and Political Stability, supporting only two of the six hypotheses. Including NoParties and NonPartisan with country size and wealth in the regression equations explained from 50 to 68 percent of the variance, marginally more than country size and wealth alone.

Chapter 9 tests the hypotheses derived from proposition P2: *The more* **competitive** *the party system, the better the country governance.* It rejected the more common measures of party competitiveness in favor of the percentage of seats held by the second-largest party, represented by the variable Party#2%. That variable was included in six regression analyses along with four other variables: country size, wealth, NoParties, and NonPartisan. Party#2% was significant in five of the six equations, failing only in explaining Political Stability. The percentages of variance explained ranged from 0.58 to 0.69—a substantial increase in explanation compared with when Party#2% is not included.

Chapter 10 tests the hypotheses derived from proposition P3: *The more* **aggregative** *the party system, the better the country governance.* It began by clearing away some terminological and conceptual confusion concerning the concept of aggregation and its converse, fragmentation. It then reviewed five alternative measures proposed for one or the other concept and tried them in preliminary regression analyses. The logarithm of a simple count of the number of parliamentary parties (NPPlog) consistently and surprisingly produced the strongest findings. It was used with five other variables—country size, wealth, NoParties, NonPartisan, and Party#2%—in testing six hypotheses about party system aggregation and country governance. Only one hypothesis was supported: The lower the NPPlog (which means more party system aggregation), the greater the political stability. Three other hypotheses were flatly rejected. Moreover, in two analyses the coefficients were statistically significant in the opposite direction to that expected. The less aggregative the party system (that is, the more parties seated in parliament), the greater the Regulatory Quality and Voice and Accountability. The percentages of variance explained ranged from 0.59 to 0.69, slightly nudging up the explained variation.

Chapter 11 tests the hypotheses derived from P4: *The more **stable** the party system, the better the country governance.* It begins by adopting Mogens Pedersen's formula for computing party system volatility, rescored and renamed Viscosity to measure stability instead of instability. In contrast to the other regression analyses, Viscosity shows no consistent significant relationships to the country governance indicators over all 212 countries. After rethinking the theory and concluding that party system stability would have a positive effect on country governance only when elections actually determined the composition of government, we formulated the revised proposition P4´: ***In democratic countries,*** *the more **viscous** the party system, the better the country governance.* We reran the regression analyses for only the 130 countries in our study that qualified as electoral democracies.[5] Viscosity proved statistically significant for five of the six hypotheses, excluding only Regulatory Quality—for which only country wealth now had any explanatory significance. The percentages of explained variance ranged from 0.58 to 0.74.

Lessons and Limitations of the Study

This study has definite limitations. One stems from using the Worldwide Government Indicators for the dependent variable. Although highly regarded, they are usually used as independent variables in economic analyses, not as dependent variables in political analyses of governmental performance. Moreover, the indicators are highly intercorrelated, raising questions of whether they truly measure different aspects of governance. However, this study suggests that all indicators—particularly Voice and Accountability and Political Stability—have different causes. That the indicators respond differently to causal factors suggests that they do measure different qualities of governance.

A more serious limitation stems from the measures of party systems, which we essentially generated from only six items of data for each country: the percentages of seats held only by the three largest parties over only two elections. Because of the difficulty in acquiring data on parties' ideologies or issue positions in almost two hundred party systems, our study also does not examine how policy polarization affects country governance. One might not expect such shallow data on political parties to produce mostly strong and consistent effects of party systems on country governance, but they did.

As noted in the introduction, our cross-national study employs the most-different-systems design, which offers the advantage of including all varieties of existing party systems—such as competitive systems, noncompetitive systems, in-between systems—and even countries that lack political parties. Unlike the prevailing most-similar-systems designs that focus on democratic countries with relatively strong parties, we include countries in which parties are weak, shadowy, and nonexistent. By including virtually all the world's countries in our study, we can better assess the effect of different types of party systems on country governance.

But the strength of the most-different-systems design—concentrating on the possible variations in party systems—is also its weakness. It avoids considering nonparty factors that affect country governance. To some extent, we provide for other factors by including country size and country wealth in our analyses. But we neglect to include much. For example, we do not consider the effects of different types of electoral systems. Nor do we consider the difference between presidential and parliamentary forms of government, an important distinction that other scholars stress.[6] Nor do we consider the nature of individual parties in the party system. David Samuels and Matthew Shugart, who consider both factors in *Presidents, Parties, and Prime Ministers*, write,

> Most broadly, this book suggests that many of the alleged differences in governance between democratic regimes—between presidentialism and parliamentarism, for example—are not a function of regime-type per se but are a function of the ways in which political parties function under different democratic regimes. The interactions to which we have called attention are not with the *numbers* of parties, as much previous research has claimed, but with their *nature*—the ways they organize and behave.[7]

Because we neglect so many variables in our analysis, the results are all the more remarkable. Even without controlling for important variables—such as the form of government, the nature of parties, the type of electoral system, colonial history, length of time as an independent country, and so on—we find that party system factors manage to exert statistically significant effects on country governance, surfacing above the uncontrolled variables operating across more than two hundred countries.

After controlling only for country size and wealth, we find that countries without elections and political parties consistently rate lower on all six indicators of country governance. That finding may agree with normative theory, but it was not preordained. We also find that countries with competitive party systems rate higher on all six indicators except Political Stability. Moreover, electoral democracies with stable party systems rate higher on all six indicators except Regulatory Quality. The tests of these hypotheses generally support the two propositions (P2 and P4) from which they derive. The consistency of results across the six indicators also implies that party system traits are primarily a cause, not a consequence, of country governance.

Deviant results did occur, however, in testing the hypotheses derived from the proposition that party system aggregation would produce better governance (P3). That proposition was too simplistic, ignoring the scholarly debate over the majoritarian model of democracy (which favors fewer parties that aggregate interests) and the consensual model (which favors more parties that articulate interests). That debate's conflicting arguments are reflected in what Thomas Carothers describes as an international aid agency's view of "a desirable party system"—one "balanced between ideological polarization and homogeneity and between fragmentation and concentration."[8] The relationship of party system aggregation or fragmentation is much more complex than stated in P3 and should probably be studied using controls for ethnic, religious, and regional differences among countries. That is a task for future research. (Students who undertake an original research project outlined in Appendix C might consider the presence or absence of cultural differences within countries as factors in country governance.)

On the other hand, the negative findings concerning party system aggregation may flow from a major limitation of this study: that we based our measures of aggregation only on the percentages of seats held by the top three parties in parliament. The most popular measure of party system fragmentation, effective number of parties (ENP), assumes that data are available for all parties in parliament. As noted earlier, our modification of the ENP formula may have robbed it of explanatory power. Although the data limitation would not apply to our measure of party system competitiveness, it would apply to our measure of party system stability, based on changes in percentages of seats for only the top three parties at the first election. While the findings for party system stability are significant and mostly consistent theoretically, the paucity of data underlying the measure may have weakened the effects.

Despite its limitations concerning the depth of party data in each country, the study did produce mostly strong and consistent results that should comfort those who fund international programs to develop party systems abroad. This cross-national study of 212 countries could have produced no evidence of any significant relationships between party systems and country governance. Instead, it produced relatively strong evidence that party system competitiveness and stability are significantly related to country governance.

Notes

1. Kadyr Toktogulov and Richard Boudreaux, "Kyrgyz Voters Back Democratic Rule," *Wall Street Journal*, June 28, 2010, A11.

2. For a structurally similar definition applied to governance at the microlevel, see Jamus Jerome Lim, "Governance Indicators in the Social Sectors" (paper presented at the annual meeting of the Midwest Political Science Association, Chicago, Illinois,

April 2–4, 2009). He defines microlevel governance as "*the extent to which social, political, and institutional structures successfully align the incentives of actors with the overall objectives for which these structures were designed (or evolved) to accomplish*" (emphasis in original, p. 3). Mark E. Warren says, "The democratic potentials of governance reside in the potentially responsive linkages between what governments do and what citizens receive," in "The Concept of Governance-Driven Democratization" (paper presented at the annual meeting of the Midwest Political Science Association, Chicago, Illinois, April 2–4, 2009).

3. Daniel Kaufmann, Aart Kraay, and Pablo Zoido-Lobatón launched the first major cross-national set of indicators in what became the Worldwide Governance Indicators.

4. Steven Radelet, *Challenging Foreign Aid: A Policymaker's Guide to the Millennium Challenge Account* (Washington, DC: Center for Global Development, 2003). For criticism of the Worldwide Governance Indicators, see Marcus J. Kurtz and Andrew Schrank, "Growth and Governance: Models, Measures, and Mechanisms," *The Journal of Politics* 69, no. 2 (May 2007): 538–554; Sandra Botero and Katherine Schlosse, "What We Talk About When We Talk About Governance: Measurement and Conceptual Issues in the World Governance Indicators" (paper presented at the annual meeting of the Midwest Political Science Association, Chicago, Illinois, April 22–25, 2010), 34.

5. Freedom House also had other criteria. See "Methodology," Freedom House, www.freedomhouse.org/template.cfm?page=351&ana_page=298&year=2006.

6. In his early research, G. Bingham Powell Jr. found important differences between parliamentary and party systems; see Powell, "Party Systems and Political System Performance: Voting Participation, Government Stability and Mass Violence in Contemporary Democracies," *American Political Science Review* 75 (December 1981): 861–879. More recently, David J. Samuels and Matthew S. Shugart emphasized the difference in *Presidents, Parties, and Prime Ministers: How the Separation of Powers Affects Party Organization and Behavior* (New York: Cambridge University Press, 2010).

7. Samuels and Shugart, *Presidents, Parties, and Prime Ministers*, 250.

8. Thomas Carothers, *Confronting the Weakest Link: Aiding Political Parties in New Democracies* (Washington, DC: Carnegie Endowment for International Peace, 2006), 98–99.

Appendices

Measures, Data, and Student Research

Appendix A

Worldwide Governance Indicator Data Sources

The list of data sources for the 2007 Worldwide Governance Indicators comes from Daniel Kaufmann, Aart Kraay, and Massimo Mastruzzi, "Appendix A: Sources for Governance Indicators," in "Governance Matters VII: Aggregate and Individual Governance Indicators, 1996–2007" (World Bank Policy Research Working Paper 4654, Washington, DC, June 2008). The text is available at http://papers.ssrn.com/sol3/papers.cfm?abstract_id=1148386. See Table 1 on page 29. We expanded and explained some acronyms to improve understanding.

ADB	African Development Bank Country Policy and Institutional Assessments
AEO	OECD Development Center African Economic Outlook
AFR	Afrobarometer
ASD	Asian Development Bank Country Policy and Institutional Assessments
BPS	Business Enterprise Environment Survey
BRI	Business Risk Service from Business Environment Risk Intelligence
BTI	Bertelsmann Transformation Index
CCR	Countries at the Crossroads from Freedom House
CPIA	World Bank Country Policy and Institutional Assessments
DRI	Global Insight Global Risk Service
EBR	European Bank for Reconstruction and Development Transition Report

EGV   Global E-Government Index
EIU   Economist Intelligence Unit
FRH   Freedom House
GCB   Transparency International Global Corruption Barometer Survey
GCS   World Economic Forum Global Competitiveness Survey
GII   Global Integrity Index
GWP   Gallup World Poll
HER   Heritage Foundation Index of Economic Freedom
HUM   Cingranelli Richards Human Rights Database and Political Terror
        Scale
IFD   IFAD Rural Sector Performance Assessments
IJT   iJET Country Security Risk Ratings
IPD   Institutional Profile Database
LBO   Latino-Barometro
MIG   Merchant International Group Gray Area Dynamics
MSI   International Research and Exchanges Board Media Sustainability
        Index
OBI   International Budget Project Open Budget Initiative
PRC   Political Economic Risk Consultancy Corruption in Asia
QLM   Qualitative Risk Measure (from Business Environment Risk
        Intelligence)
PRS   Political Risk Services International Country Risk Guide
RSF   Reporters Without Borders Press Freedom Index
TPR   U.S. State Department's Trafficking in People Report
VAB   Vanderbilt University Americas Barometer
WCY   Institute for Management Development World Competitiveness
        Yearbook
WMO   Global Insight Business Conditions and Risk Indicators

Using these thirty-five sources from different organizations around the world, Kaufmann, Kraay, and Mastruzzi selected several hundred individual variables measuring perceptions of governance to create the six indicators. They list, by source, the type of information used to create the indicators in "Appendix D: Technical Details on the Construction of the WGI," in "Governance Matters VII." There they distinguish between two types of sources:

1. Representative sources "cover a set of countries in which the distribution of governance is likely to be similar to that in the world as a whole."
2. Nonrepresentative sources "cover either specific regions (for example the BPS survey of transition economies or the Latinobarometer survey of Latin American countries), or particular income levels (for example the World Bank CPIA ratings that cover only developing countries)."

Tables A.1 through A.6 report by source the type of information used to create the indicators. This information was extracted from Appendix D of "Governance Matters VII," but the tables are presented in different order.

Table A.1 Rule of Law

Code	Representative Sources
DRI	*Losses and Costs Associated with Crime:* A one-point increase on a scale from 0 to 10 in crime during any twelve-month period
	Kidnapping of Foreigners: An increase in scope, intensity, or frequency of kidnapping of foreigners that reduces the gross domestic product (GDP) growth rate by 1 percent during any twelve-month period
	Enforceability of Government Contracts: A one-point decline on a scale from 0 to 10 in the enforceability of contracts during any twelve-month period
	Enforceability of Private Contracts: A one-point decline on a scale from 0 to 10 in the legal enforceability of contracts during any twelve-month period
EIU	Violent crime
	Organized crime
	Fairness of judicial process
	Enforceability of contracts
	Speediness of judicial process
	Confiscation/expropriation
GCS	Common crime imposes costs on business.
	Organized crime imposes costs on business.
	Quality of police
	The judiciary is independent of political influence by members of government, citizens, or firms.
	The legal framework to challenge the legality of government actions is inefficient.
	Intellectual property protection is weak.
	Protection of financial assets is weak.
	Tax evasion
GWP	Confidence in the police force
	Confidence in the judicial system
	Have you been a victim of crime?
HER	Property rights
HUM	Independence of judiciary
IPD	Respect for law in relations between citizens and the administration
	Security of persons and goods
	Organized criminal activity (drug trafficking, arms trafficking, etc.)
	Importance of the informal economy
	Importance of tax evasion in the formal sector
	Importance of customs evasion (smuggling, underdeclaration, etc.)
	Running of the justice system

Security of traditional property rights
Security of formal property rights
Security of contracts between private agents
Government respect for contracts
Justice in settlement of economic disputes and commercial matters
Intellectual property
Arrangements for the protection of intellectual property
Security of rights and property transactions in the agricultural sector

MIG Organized crime
Legal safeguards

PRS *Law and Order:* The law subcomponent is an assessment of the strength and impartiality of the legal system, while the order subcomponent is an assessment of popular observance of the law (assessed separately).

QLM Direct financial fraud, money laundering, and organized crime

TPR Trafficking in People Report

WMO *Judicial Independence:* An assessment of how far the state and other outside actors can influence and distort the legal system, which will determine the level of legal impartiality investors can expect

Crime: An assessment of how much of a threat businesses face from crime such as kidnapping, extortion, street violence, burglary, etc.

Nonrepresentative Sources

ADB Property rights

AFR Based on your experiences, how easy or difficult is it to obtain help from the police when you need it?

ASD Rule of law

BPS What is the level of fairness, honesty, enforceability, speed, and affordability of the court system?
How adequate is property rights protection?
How problematic is organized crime for the growth of your business?
How problematic is the judiciary for the growth of your business?
How problematic is street crime for the growth of your business?

BRI Enforceability of contracts

BTI Rule of law
Private property

CCR Rule of law

CPIA Property rights

FRH *Rule of Law:* This considers judicial/constitutional matters as well as the legal and de facto status of ethnic minorities.

GII Executive accountability
Judicial accountability
Rule of law
Law enforcement

IFD Access to land
Access to water for agriculture

LBO   Trust in judiciary
Trust in police
Have you been a victim of crime?
VAB   Trust in justice
Trust in police
Trust in supreme court
Have you been a victim of crime?
WCY   Tax evasion is a common practice in your country.
Justice is not fairly administered in society.
Personal security and private property are not adequately protected.
Parallel economy impairs economic development in your country.
Patent and copyright protection is not adequately enforced in your country.

Table A.2 Government Effectiveness

Code	Representative Sources
DRI	*Government Instability:* An increase in the government personnel turnover rate at senior levels that reduces the GDP growth rate by 2 percent during any twelve-month period. *Government Ineffectiveness:* A decline in government personnel quality at any level that reduces the GDP growth rate by 1 percent during any twelve-month period. *Institutional Failure:* A deterioration of government capacity to cope with national problems as a result of institutional rigidity that reduces the GDP growth rate by 1 percent during any twelve-month period.
EGV	Global e-government
EIU	Quality of bureaucracy Excessive bureaucracy/red tape
GCS	Quality of general infrastructure Quality of public schools
GWP	Satisfaction with the public transportation system Satisfaction with roads and highways Satisfaction with the education system
IPD	Government-citizen relations Capacity of the tax administration to implement measures decided on Quality of the supply of public goods (e.g., education and basic health) Capacity of the political authorities
MIG	Quality of bureaucracy
PRS	*Bureaucratic Quality:* This measures institutional strength and quality of the civil service; it also assesses how much strength and expertise bureaucrats have and how able they are to manage political alternations without drastic interruptions in government services or policy changes.
WMO	*Policy Consistency and Forward Planning:* This assesses how confident businesses can be of the continuity of economic policy

stance—whether a change of government will entail major policy disruption and whether the current government has pursued a coherent strategy.

Bureaucracy: This assesses the quality of the country's bureaucracy. The better the bureaucracy, the quicker decisions are made, and the more easily foreign investors can go about their business.

Nonrepresentative Sources

ADB Management of public debt
Policies to improve efficiency of the public sector
Revenue mobilization
Budget management

AFR Based on your experiences, how easy or difficult is it to obtain household services (like electricity or telephone)?
Based on your experiences, how easy or difficult is it to obtain an identity document (like a birth certificate or passport)?
Government handling of health services
Government handling of education

ASD Civil service
Revenue mobilization and budget management
Management and efficiency of public expenditures

BPS How problematic are telecommunications for the growth of your business?
How problematic is electricity for the growth of your business?
How problematic is transportation for the growth of your business?

BRI Bureaucratic delays

BTI Consensus building
Governance capability
Effective use of resources

CPIA Management of external debt
Quality public administration
Revenue mobilization
Budget management

IFD Allocation and management of public resources for rural development

LBO Trust in government

WCY Government economic policies do not adapt quickly to changes in the economy.
The public service is not independent from political interference.
Government decisions are not effectively implemented.
Bureaucracy hinders business activity.
The distribution infrastructure of goods and services is generally inefficient.
Policy direction is not consistent.

Table A.3 Control of Corruption

Code	Representative Sources
DRI	*Losses and Costs Associated with Corruption:* A one-point increase on a scale from 0 to 10 in corruption during any twelve-month period
EIU	Corruption
GCS	What is the level of public trust in the financial honesty of politicians?
	Is diversion of public funds due to corruption common?
	Do firms frequently make extra payments connected to import/export permits?
	Do firms frequently make extra payments connected to public utilities?
	Do firms frequently make extra payments connected to tax payments?
	Do firms frequently make extra payments connected to awarding of public contracts?
	Do firms frequently make extra payments connected to getting favorable judicial decisions?
	To what extent do firms' illegal payments to influence government policies impose costs on other firms?
	Is there undue political influence?
GWP	Is corruption in government widespread?
IPD	Corruption
MIG	*Corruption:* An immense variety of activities may be construed as corrupt. Bribery is the most obvious. However, what constitutes a bribe is a matter of presentation and perception—much like "corruption" itself. Some of the issues that executives should consider include accounting standards; anticorruption policy credibility and enforceability; cronyism, nepotism, and vested interests; cultural differences; judicial independence; and transparency of decision making.
PRS	*Corruption:* This measures corruption within the political system, which distorts the economic and financial environment, reduces the efficiency of government and business by enabling people to assume positions of power through patronage rather than ability, and introduces an inherent instability into the political system.
QLM	Indirect diversion of funds
WMO	*Corruption:* This index assesses the intrusiveness of the country's bureaucracy. The amount of red tape likely is assessed, as is the likelihood of encountering corrupt officials and other groups.

	Nonrepresentative Sources
ADB	Transparency/corruption
AFR	How many elected leaders (parliamentarians or local councilors) do you think are involved in corruption?
	How many judges and magistrates do you think are involved in corruption?
	How many government officials do you think are involved in corruption?
	How many border/tax officials do you think are involved in corruption?

ASD	Anticorruption
BPS	How common is it for firms to have to make irregular additional payments to get things done?
	On average, what percentage of total annual sales do firms pay in unofficial payments to public officials?
	How often do firms make extra payments to influence the content of new legislation?
	To what extent do firms' payments to public officials to affect legislation impose costs on other firms?
	How problematic is corruption for the growth of your business?
	How frequent is bribery in areas dealing with utilities, permits, procurement, health, fire inspection, the environment, taxes, customs, and the judiciary?
BRI	*Internal Causes of Political Risk:* Mentality, including xenophobia, nationalism, corruption, nepotism, willingness to compromise, etc.
BTI	Corruption
CCR	Transparency/corruption
CPIA	Transparency/corruption
FRH	Corruption
GCB	Frequency of corruption
	Frequency of household bribery
GII	Anticorruption law
	Anticorruption agency
IFD	Accountability, transparency, and corruption in rural areas
LBO	Have you heard of acts of corruption?
PRC	Corruption index
VAB	Frequency of corruption among government officials
WCY	Bribery and corruption exist in the economy.

Table A.4 Regulatory Quality

Code	Representative Sources
DRI	*Regulations, Exports:* A 2 percent reduction in export volume as a result of a worsening in export regulations or restrictions (such as export limits) during any twelve-month period, with respect to the level at the time of the assessment
	Regulations, Imports: A 2 percent reduction in import volume as a result of a worsening in import regulations or restrictions (such as import quotas) during any twelve-month period, with respect to the level at the time of the assessment
	Regulations, Other Business: An increase in other regulatory burdens, with respect to the level at the time of the assessment, that reduces total aggregate investment in real LCU terms by 10 percent
	Ownership of Business by Nonresidents: A one-point increase on a scale from 0 to 10 in legal restrictions on ownership of business by nonresidents during any twelve-month period

Ownership of Equities by Nonresidents: A one-point increase on a scale from 0 to 10 in legal restrictions on ownership of equities by nonresidents during any twelve-month period

EIU Unfair competitive practices
Price controls
Discriminatory tariffs
Excessive protections

GCS Administrative regulations are burdensome.
The tax system is distortionary.
Import barriers are obstacles to growth.
Competition in the local market is limited.
Antimonopoly policy is lax and ineffective.
Environmental regulations hurt competitiveness.
The tax system is complex.
It is easy to start a company.

HER Foreign investment
Banking/finance
Wages/prices

IPD Administrative business start-up formalities
Administered prices and market prices
Ease of market entry for new firms
Competition regulation arrangements

MIG Unfair competition
Unfair trade

PRS Investment profile

WMO *Tax Effectiveness:* How efficient the country's tax-collection system is
Legislation: An assessment of whether the necessary business laws are in place

---

Nonrepresentative Sources

ADB Trade policy
Competitive environment
Labor market policies

ASD Trade policy and foreign exchange regime
Enabling environment for private-sector development

BPS Is information on the laws and regulations easy to obtain?
How problematic are anticompetitive practices for the growth of your business?
How problematic are unpredictable regulations for the growth of your business?
How problematic are labor regulations for the growth of your business?
How problematic are tax regulations for the growth of your business?
How problematic are custom and trade regulations for the growth of your business?

BTI Competition
Price stability

CPIA	Competitive environment
	Trade policy
EBR	Price liberalization
	Trade and foreign exchange system
	Competition policy
IFD	Enabling conditions for rural financial services development
	Investment climate for rural businesses
	Access to agricultural input and produce markets
WCY	Access to capital markets (foreign and domestic) is easy.
	Ease of doing business
	Banking regulation does not hinder competitiveness.
	Competition legislation in your country does not prevent unfair competition.
	Customs' authorities do not facilitate the efficient transit of goods.
	Financial institutions' transparency is not widely developed in your country.
	It is easy to start a company.
	Foreign investors are free to acquire control in domestic companies.
	Price controls affect pricing of products in most industries.
	Public-sector contracts are sufficiently open to foreign bidders.
	Real corporate taxes are nondistortionary.
	Real personal taxes are nondistortionary.
	The legal framework is detrimental to your country's competitiveness.
	Protectionism in your country negatively affects the conduct of business in your country.
	Labor regulations hinder business activities.
	Subsidies impair economic development.

Table A.5 Voice and Accountability

Code	Representative Sources
EIU	Orderly transfers
	Vested interests
	Accountability of public officials
	Human rights
	Freedom of association
FRH	*Civil Liberties*: Freedom of speech, assembly, demonstration, religion, and equal opportunity, as well as freedom from excessive governmental intervention
	Political Rights: Free and fair elections, representative legislative, free vote, political parties, no dominant group, respect for minorities
FRP	Freedom of the press
GCS	Newspapers can publish stories of their choosing without fear of censorship or retaliation.
	When deciding upon policies and contracts, government officials favor well-connected firms.

The national parliament/congress is effective as a law-making and oversight institution.

Passive voice

GWP   Confidence in honesty of elections

HUM   Domestic and foreign travel restrictions

Freedom of political participation

Imprisonment of people due to ethnicity, race, or political or religious beliefs

Government censorship

IPD   Political rights and functioning of political institutions

Freedom of the press

Freedom of association

Freedom of assembly and demonstration

Respect for minorities (ethnic, religious, linguistic, etc.)

Transparency of public action in the economic field

Transparency of economic policy (fiscal, taxation, monetary, exchange rate, etc.)

Award of public procurement contracts and delegation of public service

Free movement of persons, information, etc.

PRS   *Military in Politics:* The military are not elected by anyone, so their participation in government, either direct or indirect, reduces accountability and therefore represents a risk. The threat of military intervention might lead as well to an anticipated potentially inefficient change in policy or even in government.

Democratic Accountability: This quantifies how responsive government is to its people—the less response there is, the more likely it is that the government will fall, peacefully or violently. This includes not only whether free and fair elections are in place but also how likely the government is to remain in power.

RSF   Press freedom index

WMO   *Institutional Permanence:* An assessment of how mature and well established the political system is

Representativeness: How well the population and organized interests can make their voices heard in the political system

---

Nonrepresentative Sources

AEO   Hardening of the regime

AFR   Free and fair elections

BTI   Stateness

Political participation

Institutional stability

Political and social integration

CCR   Civil liberties

Accountability and public voice

GII   Civil society organizations

Media

	Public access to information
	Voting and citizen participation
	Election integrity
	Political financing
IFD	Policy and legal framework for rural organizations
	Dialogue between government and rural organizations
LBO	Satisfaction with democracy
	Trust in parliament
MSI	Media sustainability index
OBI	Open budget index
VAB	Trust in parliament
	Satisfaction with democracy
WCY	Transparency of government policy

Table A.6 Political Stability and Absence of Violence/Terrorism

Code	Representative Sources
DRI	*Military Coup Risk:* A military coup d'état (or a series of such events) that reduces the GDP growth rate by 2 percent during any twelve-month period
	Major Insurgency/Rebellion: An increase in scope or intensity of one or more insurgencies/rebellions that reduces the GDP growth rate by 3 percent during any twelve-month period
	Political Terrorism: An increase in scope or intensity of terrorism that reduces the GDP growth rate by 1 percent during any twelve-month period
	Political Assassination: A political assassination (or a series of such events) that reduces the GDP growth rate by 1 percent during any twelve-month period
	Civil War: An increase in scope or intensity of one or more civil wars that reduces the GDP growth rate by 4 percent during any twelve-month period
	Major Urban Riot: An increase in scope, intensity, or frequency of rioting that reduces the GDP growth rate by 1 percent during any twelve-month period
EIU	Armed conflict
	Violent demonstrations
	Social unrest
	International tensions
GCS	*Country Terrorist Threat:* Does the threat of terrorism in the country impose significant costs on firms?
HUM	Frequency of political killings
	Frequency of disappearances
	Frequency of torture
IJT	Security risk rating
IPD	Conflicts of an ethnic, religious, or regional nature

Violent actions by underground political organizations
Violent social conflicts
External public security

MIG *Extremism:* The term *extremism* covers the threat posed by any individuals or organizations holding a narrow set of fanatical beliefs.
Extremists are likely to believe that any and all means are justified
to eradicate the target of hostility, and they are not afraid to destroy
themselves in the process. This ideological aspect of extremism
makes it highly unpredictable, and its close association with violence
makes it highly dangerous. The extent to which extremism should be
judged a threat to a particular business in a particular market can be
assessed along the following lines: integration issues, religious tensions, pressure groups, terrorist activity, and xenophobia.

PRS *Internal Conflict:* Assesses political violence and its influence on governance
External Conflict: Assesses both the risk to the incumbent government
and to inward investment
Government Stability: Measures the government's ability to carry out its
declared programs and its ability to stay in office
Ethnic Tensions: Measures the degree of tension within a country at-
tributable to racial, nationality, or language divisions

PTS Political terror scale

WMO *Civil Unrest:* How widespread is political unrest, and how great a threat
does it pose to investors? Demonstrations themselves may not be
cause for concern, but they will cause major disruption if they esca-
late into severe violence. At the extreme, this factor would amount to
civil war.
Terrorism: Does the country suffer from a sustained terrorist threat,
and if so, from how many sources? The degree of localization of the
threat is assessed, as is whether the active groups are likely to target
or affect businesses.

Nonrepresentative Sources

AEO Political troubles

BRI Fractionalization of the political spectrum and the power of these fac-
tions
Fractionalization by language, ethnic, and/or religious groups and the
power of these factions
Restrictive (coercive) measures required to retain power
Organization and strength of forces for a radical government
Societal conflict involving demonstrations, strikes, and street violence
Instability as perceived by nonconstitutional changes, assassinations,
and guerrilla wars

WCY Risk of political instability

Appendix B

Countries with Party System Data

		Stimulus Election							Referent Election			
Country	Year	Party#1	Seats (%)	Party#2	Seats (%)	Party#3	Seats (%)	Number of Parties in Parliament*	Year	Party #1% Seats	Party #2% Seats	Party #3% Seats
Afghanistan	2005							xx				
Albania	2005	PD	40	PSS	30	PR	13	9	2001	4	52	0
Algeria	2002	FLN	51	RND	12	MSP	10	23	2007	35	16	18
American Samoa	2004							x	2006			
Andorra	2005	PLA	50	PSD	43	CDA	7	3	2001	54	21	18
Angola	1992	MPLA	59	UNITA	32	PRS	3	12	1986	100	0	0
Anguilla	2005	ANF/ANA	36	ASA	18	AUP	9	4	2000	27	0	18
Antigua and Barbuda	2004	UPP	71	ALP	24	BPM	0	2	1999	24	71	6
Argentina	2005	FV	39	UCR	8	PJ	7	15	2003	0	19	45
Armenia	2003	RPA	24	OE	14	JA	11	5	2007	49	7	0
Aruba	2005	MEP	52	AVP	38	MPA	5	4	2001	57	28	0
Australia	2004	Liberal	50	Labor	40	National	8	4	2007	37	55	7
Austria	2002	OVP	43	SPO	38	FPO	10	4	2006	36	37	11
Azerbaijan	2005	NAP	45	APF/F	5	CSP	2	10	2001	60	5	2
Bahamas	2002	PLP	72	FNM	18			2	2007	44	56	
Bahrain	2002							xx	2006			
Bangladesh	2001	BJD	64	BAL	21	JIB	6	8	1996	39	49	1
Barbados	2003	BLP	77	DLP	23			2	1999	93	7	
Belarus	2004	KPB	7	APB	3	LDPB	1	3	2000	6	5	1
Belgium	2003	PS	17	VLD	17	MR	16	10	2007	13	12	15
Belize	2003	PUP	76	UDP	24			2	1998	90	10	
Benin	2003	UBF	38	PRB	18	PRD	13	4	2007	0	0	12
Bermuda	2003	PLP	61	UBT	39			2	2007	61	39	
Bhutan								xx				
Bolivia	2005	MAS	55	PDS	33	FUN	6	4	2002	21	0	0

continues

Country		Stimulus Election							Referent Election			
	Year	Party#1	Seats (%)	Party#2	Seats (%)	Party#3	Seats (%)	Number of Parties in Parliament*	Year	Party #1% Seats	Party #2% Seats	Party #3% Seats
Bosnia and Herzegovina	2002	SDA	24	SBiH	14	SDS	12	13	2006	21	19	7
Botswana	2004	BDP	77	BNF	21	BCP	2	3	1999	83	15	3
Brazil	2002	PT	18	PFL	16	PMDB	15	19	2006	16	13	17
Brunei Darussalam								xx				
Bulgaria	2005	KzB	34	NDSV	22	DPS	14	7	2001	20	50	9
Burkina Faso	2002	CDP	52	ADF/RDA	15	PDP/PS	9	10	2007	66	13	2
Burundi	2005	CNDD-FDD	59	FRODEBU	24	UPEONA	10	5	1993	0	80	20
Cambodia	2003	KPK	59	FUNCINPE	21	PSR	20	3	1993	52	35	12
Cameroon	2002	RPDC	74	SDF	12	UDC	3	4	2007	85	9	2
Canada	2004	Liberal	43	CP	32	BQ	17	4	2002	57	22	18
Cape Verde	2001	PAICV	55	MPD	42	ADM	3	3	2006	57	40	0
Cayman Islands	2005	PPM	60	UDP	33			2	2000	0	0	
Central African Republic	2005	KNK	40	MLPC	10	RDC	8	7	1998	0	43	18
Chad	2002	MPS	73	RDP	6	FAR	6	15	1997	52	2	1
Chile	2005	CPcD	54	Alliance	45	FRI	1	3	2001	52	47	0
China	2003	CCP	100					1	1998	100		
Colombia	2002	PLC	33	PCC	13	Coalition	7	39	2006	22	19	0
Comoros	2004	CIA	36	CRC	18			2	1996	0	0	0
Congo (Brazzaville)	2002	PCT	34	FDU	20	UPRM	4	4	2007	34	0	0
Congo (Kinshasa)	2003	PPRD	19	MLC	19	PLU	7	8	2006	22	13	19
Cook Islands	2004	DP	50	CIP	46			2	2006	54	42	
Costa Rica	2002	LN	30	AC	26	ML	11	5	2006	44	32	11
Cote D'Ivoire	2000	FPI	43	PDCI	42	RDR	2	6	1996	7	84	8
Croatia	2003	HDZ	44	SDPiHSLS	23	HSS	7	12	2000	30	47	11
Cuba	2003	PCC	98					1	2008	100		

continues

Country	Year	Party#1	Seats (%)	Party#2	Seats (%)	Party#3	Seats (%)	Number of Parties in Parliament*	Year	Party #1% Seats	Party #2% Seats	Party #3% Seats
										Referent Election		
Cyprus	2001	AKEL	36	DSISI	34	DIKO	16	6	2006	32	32	20
Czech Republic	2002	CSSD	35	ODS	29	KSCM	20	4	2006	37	40	13
Denmark	2005	VDLP	30	SD	27	DF	14	7	2001	32	30	13
Djibouti	2003	RPP	100					1	1997	100		
Dominica	2005	PLP	38	UWP	25	DFP	0	2	2000	31	28	34
Dominican Republic	2002	PRD	49	PLD	27	PRSC	24	3	2006	24	54	22
Ecuador	2002	PRE	15	ID-RED	13	PRIAN	10	24	2006	6	13	28
Egypt	2005	NDP	69	MuslimBr	19	NWP	1	5	2000	88	0	2
El Salvador	2003	FMLN	37	ARENA	32	PCN	19	5	2006	38	40	12
Equatorial Guinea	2004	PDGE	98	CPDS	2	UP	0	2	1999	94	1	5
Eritrea	1994	PFDJ	100					1	1997	100		
Estonia	2003	K	28	IPL/RP	28	RE	19	6	2007	29	19	31
Ethiopia	2005	EPRDF	60	CUD	20	UEDF	10	11	2000	88	0	0
Fiji	2001	SDL	45	FLP	38	MV	8	7	2006	51	44	0
Finland	2003	Kesk	28	SD	26	Kok	20	8	1999	25	23	26
France	2002	UMP	63	PS	24	UDF	5	8	2007	54	32	0
French Guiana	2004	PSG	55	UMP	23	DFG	23	3	1998	35	0	29
Gabon	2001	PDG	73	RNB	7	ADR	3	9	2006	68	7	3
Gambia	2002	APRC	94	PDOISRNC	4	NRC	2	9	2007	89	2	0
Georgia	2004	NMO	90	RO	10	SMK	0	2	1999	0	0	55
Germany	2005	CDU/CSU	37	SPD	36	FDP	10	6	2002	41	42	8
Ghana	2004	NPP	56	NDC	41	CPP	1	3	2000	50	46	0
Greece	2004	ND	55	PASOK	39	KKE	4	4	2002	42	52	4
Grenada	2003	NNP	53	NDC	47			2	1999	100	0	
Guam	2004	Republic	60	Democrat	40			2	2002	40	60	
Guatemala	2003	FRG	27	GANA	26	UNE	20	12	1999	56	0	0
Guinea	2002	PUP	75	UPR	18	UPG	3	6	1995	62	8	2

continues

Country	Year	Party#1	Seats (%)	Party#2	Seats (%)	Party#3	Seats (%)	Number of Parties in Parliament*	Year	Party #1% Seats	Party #2% Seats	Party #3% Seats
										Referent Election		
Guinea-Bissau	2004	PAIGC	45	PRS	35	PUSD	17	5	1999	24	37	0
Guyana	2001	PPC-C	52	PNC-R	41	Action	3	4	2006	55	34	2
Haiti	2000	Lavalas	88	Mochrena	4	OpenGate	2	18	2006	6	2	0
Honduras	2005	PLH	48	PNH	43	PUD	4	5	2001	43	48	4
Hong Kong	2004	DABHK	20	LP	17	DP	15	10	2000	17	12	20
Hungary	2002	MSzP	48	FIDESz	47	SzDSz	5	3	2006	50	42	5
Iceland	2003	SSF	35	SF	32	FSF	19	5	1999	41	27	19
India	2004	INC	27	BJP	25	CPI(M)	8	31	1999	21	34	6
Indonesia	2004	Golkar	23	PDI-P	20	PPP	11	17	1999	26	33	13
Iran	2004	Conserv	54	Reform	13			2	2000	18	77	0
Iraq	2005	UIA	51	DPAK	27	IL–NIL	15	12	2005	47	19	9
Ireland	2002	FF	49	FG	19	Labour	12	6	2007	47	31	12
Israel	2003	Likud	32	Labour	16	Shinui	13	12	2006	10	16	0
Italy	2001	CDL	58	L'Ulivo	38	PRC	4	3	2006	45	55	0
Jamaica	2002	PNP	58	JLP	42			2	2007	45	55	
Japan	2005	LDP	62	DP	24	Komeito	6	7	2003	49	37	7
Jordan	2003	IAF	16					1	2007	6		
Kazakhstan	2004	Otan	55	Agrarian	14	Asar	5	4	2007	100	0	0
Kenya	2002	KANU	30	LDP	26	DP	17	9	2007	7	0	1
Kiribati	2003	MTM	57	BK	38			2	2007	15	39	
Korea, North	1998	WPK	87	KSDP	8	CCP	3	3	1998	87	8	3
Korea, South	2004	YUD	51	HD	41	MND	3	7	2000	0	49	0
Kosovo	2004	LDK	41	PDK	26	AAK	8	9	2007	21	31	8
Kuwait	2003	Islamic	42	GOVT	28	Liberals	6	3	2006	34	32	14
Kyrgyzstan	2000	Communist	8	UDF	7	War Vets	3	6	2007	9	0	0
Laos	2002	LPRP	99					1	2006	98		
Latvia	2002	JL	26	PCTVL	24	TP	21	6	2006	18	6	23

continues

Country	Year	Party#1	Seats (%)	Party#2	Seats (%)	Party#3	Seats (%)	Number of Parties in Parliament*	Year	Party #1% Seats	Party #2% Seats	Party #3% Seats
								Stimulus Election		Referent Election		
Lebanon	2005							xx	2000			
Lesotho	2002	LCD	64	BNP	18	NIP	4	8	2007	52	3	18
Liberia	2005	CDC	23	LP	14	UP	13	11	1997	0	0	11
Libya								xx				
Liechtenstein	2005	FBPL	48	VU	40	FL	12	3	2001	56	40	4
Lithuania	2004	DP	27	UDL	23	TS	18	10	2000	0	0	0
Luxembourg	2004	ADR	40	LSAP	23	DP	17	5	1999	32	22	25
Macao	2005	ANMD	7	UCUM	7	UD	7	8	2001	7	7	7
Macedonia	2002	ZMZ	51	VMRO-DPM	28	DUI	13	6	2006	27	38	14
Madagascar	2002	TIM	66	FP	14	RPSD	3	8	2007	83	0	0
Malawi	2004	MCP	31	UDF	25	MC	14	11	1999	34	48	0
Malaysia	2004	PKMB	50	PCM	14	PGRM	5	9	1999	37	15	3
Maldives	2005							xx	1999			
Mali	2002	ADEMA	33	RPM	29	CNID	8	10	2007	32	7	4
Malta	2003	PN	51	MLP	49			2	1998	54	46	
Marshall Islands	2003							x	1999			
Martinique	2004	MIM	68	PPM	22	UDF	10	3	1998	32	17	15
Mauritania	2001	PRDS	79	UFP	5	RFD	4	7	2006	7	8	16
Mauritius	2005	AS	61	MSM-MMM	36	OPR	3	3	2000	0	83	3
Mexico	2003	PRI	45	PAN	30	PRD	19	7	2006	24	41	32
Micronesia	2005							x	2003			
Moldova	2005	PCRM	55	BMD	34	PPCD	11	3	2001	70	0	11
Monaco	2003	UPM	88	UND	13			2	1998	0	100	
Mongolia	2004	MPRP	49	EON-MAN	46	BNM	1	6	2000	99	0	0
Montenegro	2002	PCG	48	ZzY	39	LSCG	7	6	2006	51	14	4
Morocco	2002	USFP	15	PI	15	PJD	13	22	2007	12	16	14
Mozambique	2004	FRELIMO	64	RENAMO	36			2	1999	53	47	

continues

		Stimulus Election							Referent Election			
Country	Year	Party#1	Seats (%)	Party#2	Seats (%)	Party#3	Seats (%)	Number of Parties in Parliament*	Year	Party #1% Seats	Party #2% Seats	Party #3% Seats
Myanmar								xx				
Namibia	2004	SWAPO	71	CoD	6	DTA	5	7	1999	76	10	10
Nauru	2004							x	2003			
Nepal								xx				
Netherlands	2003	CDA	29	PvdA	28	VVD	19	10	2006	27	22	15
Netherlands Antilles	2002	PRA	18	PNP	9	MAN	9	11	2006	23	9	14
New Caledonia	2004	RPCR	30	FT	30	FLNKS	15	8	1999	44	0	22
New Zealand	2005	Lab	41	Nat	40	NZF	6	8	2002	43	23	11
Nicaragua	2001	PLC	53	FSLN	46	PCN	1	3	2006	27	41	0
Niger	2004	MNSD	42	CDS	20	PNDS	15	10	1999	46	21	19
Nigeria	2003	PDP	62	ANPP	27	AD	9	7	1999	59	21	20
Niue								x	2002			
Norway	2005	AP	36	FrP	23	H	14	7	2001	26	16	23
Oman								x	2007			
Pakistan	2002	PPP	26	PML(Q)	25	PML(N)	7	15	2008	32	16	25
Palau								x	2000			
Panama Canal Zone	2004	PRD	53	AP	22	SP	12	7	1999	48	25	6
Papua New Guinea	2002	NAP	17	PDM	12	PPP	7	24	1997	7	7	15
Paraguay	2003	ANR-PC	46	PLRA	26	MPQ	13	5	1998	59	41	0
Peru	2001	PP	38	PAP	23	UN	14	11	2006	2	30	14
Philippines	2004	LCMD	32	NPC	23	LP	15	29	1998	54	4	7
Poland	2005	PiS	34	PO	29	SRP	12	7	2001	10	14	12
Portugal	2005	PS	53	PSD	33	PCP	6	5	2002	42	45	5
Puerto Rico	2004	PNP	63	PPD	35	PIP	2	3	2000	39	59	2
Qatar								xx				
Reunion	2004	PCR	60	UMP	24	PS-G	16	3	1998	20	0	20
Romania	2004	PSD+PUR	40	JTA	34	GRP	15	26	2000	45	18	24

continues

Country	Stimulus Election								Referent Election			
	Year	Party#1	Seats (%)	Party#2	Seats (%)	Party#3	Seats (%)	Number of Parties in Parliament*	Year	Party #1 Seats	Party #2 Seats	Party #3 Seats
Russia	2003	UR	50	CP	12	LDPR	8	14	1999	28	20	4
Rwanda	2003	FRP	76	PSD	13	PL	11	3	1988	0	0	0
Saint Kitts and Nevis	2004	SKNLP	64	CCM	18	NRP	9	4	2000	73	18	9
Saint Lucia	2001	SLLP	82	UWP	18			2	2006	35	65	
Saint Vincent and Grenadine	2005	ULP	80	NDP	20			2	2001	80	20	
Samoa	2001	HRPP	47	SNDP	27	IUP	14	3	2006	71	20	0
San Marino	2001	PDCS	42	PSS	25	PD	20	6	2006	35	0	0
Sao Tome and Principe	2002	MLSTP/PSD	44	MDFM-PCD	42	ADI	15	3	2006	36	42	20
Saudi Arabia								xx				
Senegal	2001	SOPI	74	AFP	9	PSS	8	7	2007	87	0	0
Serbia	2003	SRS	33	DSS	21	G17PLUS	14	6	2007	32	11	8
Seychelles	2002	SPPF	68	SNP	32			2	2007	68	32	
Sierra Leone	2002	SLPP	74	APC	24	PLP	2	3	2007	35	48	0
Singapore	2001	PAP	93	SDA	3	WP	3	3	2006	96	2	2
Slovakia	2002	HZDS	24	SDKU	19	Smer	17	7	2006	10	21	33
Slovenia	2004	SDS	32	LDS	26	ZLSD	11	7	2000	16	38	12
Solomon Islands	2001	PAP	40	SIAC	24	PPP	6	4	2006	6	4	0
Somalia								xx				
South Africa	2004	ANC	70	DA	13	IFP	7	12	1999	67	10	7
Spain	2004	PSOE	47	PP	42	CiU	3	11	2000	36	52	4
Sri Lanka	2004	UPFA	47	EJP	36	ITAK	10	5	2001	34	48	0
Sudan	2005	NC	52	SPLM	28	NOP	14	3	2000	99	0	0
Suriname	2005	NFD	45	NDP	29	VVV	12	5	2000	65	20	6
Swaziland	2003							xx	1998			
Sweden	2002	S	41	M	16	C	6	7	2006	37	28	8
Switzerland	2003	SVP	28	SDP	26	FDP	18	14	1999	22	26	22
Syria	2003	NPF	67					1	1998	67		
Taiwan	2004	MJD	40	GMT	35	QMD	15	8	2001	39	30	20

continues

		Stimulus Election						Number of Parties in Parliament*	Referent Election			
Country	Year	Party#1	Seats (%)	Party#2	Seats (%)	Party#3	Seats (%)		Year	Party #1% Seats	Party #2% Seats	Party #3% Seats
Tajikistan	2005	PDPT	78	CPT	6	IRPT	3	3	2000	60	19	3
Tanzania	2005	CCM	82	CCW	9	Chadema	3	5	2000	87	7	2
Thailand	2005	TRT	75	PP	19	PCT	5	4	2001	30	26	6
Timor-Leste	2001	FRTLI	62	PD	8	PSD	7	12	2007	32	12	9
Togo	2002	RPT	89	RSDD	4	UDSP	3	5	1999	98	0	0
Tonga	2005							xx	2002			
Trinidad and Tobago	2002	PNM	56	UNC	44			2	2000	44	53	
Tunisia	2004	RCD	80	MDS	7	PUP	6	6	1999	81	7	4
Turkey	2002	AKP	66	CHP	32	MHP	0	2	1999	0	0	24
Turkmenistan	2004	DPT	100					1	1999	100		
Tuvalu	2002							x	1998			
Uganda	2001	NRM	100	FDC	0	UPC	0	1	2006	64	12	3
Ukraine	2002	NU	25	ZEU	23	KPU	15	8	2006	19	0	5
United Arab Emirates								xx				
United Kingdom	2005	LAB	55	CON	31	LIB	10	12	2001	63	25	8
United States	2004	REP	53	DEM	46			2	2002	53	47	
Uruguay	2004	FA-EP-NM	53	PN-B	36	PC	10	10	1999	40	22	33
Uzbekistan	2005	ULDP	34	UPDP	23	SNDP	15	5	1999	0	19	0
Vanuatu	2004	VP-VNUP	35	UMP	17	VRP	8	5	2002	42	29	6
Venezuela	2005	MVR	70	PDS	11	PPT	6	12	2000	55	0	0
Vietnam	2002	FF	90		0		0	1	1997	92	0	0
Virgin Islands	2004	DP	67	ICM	27			2	2002	67	13	
West Bank/Gaza	2006	Hamas	56	Fatah	34	MAAM	3	3	1996	0	57	0
Yemen	2003	MSA	79	TYI	15	HIY	3	5	1997	62	18	0
Zambia	2001	MMD	46	UPND	33	UNIP	9	6	2006	47	17	0
Zimbabwe	2005	ZANU-PF	52	MDC	27			2	2000	41	38	

* x = nonpartisan elections, no parties in parliament

xx = no elections and no parties in parliament

Appendix C

Student Research Projects

Our regression analyses found that the size of a country, its wealth, and characteristics of its party system explained over one-half to more than two-thirds of the variation in 2007 Worldwide Governance Indicators (WGI) for 212 countries. That still left unexplained from one-third to one-half of country differences in governance. Moreover, individual countries sometimes deviated greatly from their predicted governance scores according to the regression equation. Some countries scored much higher than predicted, while others scored much lower.

This project asks you to probe beyond the statistical formulas in the book to explain why some countries govern better (or poorer) than expected on the major WGI measure of governance Rule of Law. The discussion below is based on Equation 9.1, which uses SmallArea, Wealth, NoParties, NonPartisan, and Party#2% as independent variables. The extent to which countries deviated from their predictions on Rule of Law is shown graphically at our Internet site, www.partypolitics.org/governance. The site breaks down all the countries by twenty-one regions of world as determined by the Statistics Division of the United Nations.[1]

Here is the challenge: Select two countries in the same region of the world. One country should be an overachiever and one an underachiever. Consider a +25 deviation from the predicted score as indicative of an overachiever and a −25 deviation signaling an underachiever. Conduct original research to explain why one country did much better than expected and the other did much worse than expected. Following the length and style specifications of your instructor, write a paper explaining your results.

In accounting for country differences between governance overachievers and underachievers, you might consider these factors:

- Do sharp ideological differences exist among the parties in one party system but not the other?
- Do contentious ethnic, religious, or regional differences exist between the countries?
- Do both countries have the same governmental structure (e.g., presidential and parliamentary), or are they profoundly different?
- Do both countries have the same electoral system (e.g., proportional representation or majority representation), or are they profoundly different?
- Do the countries differ critically in their history concerning war, foreign intervention, economic collapse, or length of independence?
- Do they differ in their source of wealth? In particular, does their wealth come from oil or other exploited natural resources in one country but not the other?
- Are the differences in governance due to their history of exceptionally good or bad political leadership?

We ask you to compare two countries within the same region to avoid the tendency to employ "national character" explanations of differences in country governance. For example, one might be tempted to say that an eastern European country underachieved on Rule of Law because eastern Europeans favor "strong leaders," while a western European country overachieved because western Europeans trust their legal systems.

Region is also important because, as Figure C.1 shows, countries in different regions of the world differ substantially on their predicted and actual Rule of Law scores. Consider the African countries first. As a group, the fifteen countries in western Africa average –0.94 for their predicted scores on Rule of Law, but on average they perform 0.21 points better than predicted. Eastern African countries also perform somewhat better than predicted, but that is not true in the rest of Africa.

The Asian countries tell a mostly similar story. The nine countries in southern Asia average –0.68 on predicted scores on Rule of Law but perform 0.18 points better than predicted. Countries in the other Asian regions perform somewhat worse than predicted. Australia, New Zealand, and island countries in the Pacific Ocean score, on average, above predictions.

In the Americas, only countries in North America (Canada, the United States, and Bermuda) show positive deviations. European countries are divided. Those in the East and South perform below predictions while those in the North and West perform above predictions.

We make these broad generalizations about the major regions of the world only to illustrate how to read the twenty-one graphs at http://partypolitics .org/goverance, given for specific regions and individual countries. Go there to view the graphs and to choose your pair of countries for this project.

Figure C.1 Mean scores for Rule of Law for countries in twenty-one world regions

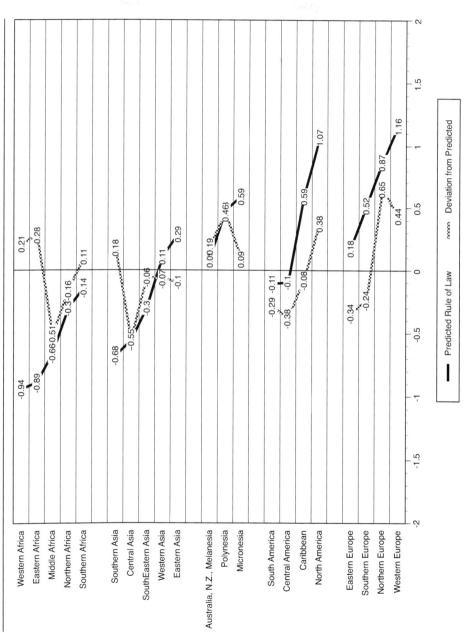

Note

1. "Composition of Macro Geographical (Continental) Regions, Geographical Sub-Regions, and Selected Economic and Other Groupings," United Nations Statistics Division, April 1, 2010, http://unstats.un.org/unsd/methods/m49/m49regin.htm.

Index

Note: Italicized b's, f's, and t's refer to boxes, figures, and tables

Competitiveness, 136–145; *See also* Party systems; country size and, 145; country wealth and, 142–145; hypothesis testing, 139–145; measuring, 137–139; political stability/absence of violence, 145; rule of law, 141–142; voice and accountability, 145

Congo-Brazzaville, 82–84; GDP per capita, 85*f*; stimulus/referent elections data, 199*t*

Congo-Kinshasa, stimulus/referent elections data, 199*t*

Control of Corruption (CC), 21; aggregation and, 156; correlation with other governance indicators, 25*f*, 27–28; effects of country size, wealth and party system on, 169*f*; governance scores, 36*f*; nonrepresentative sources, 189–190*t*; party system competitiveness and, 140; regulatory quality and, 26–27; representative sources, 189*t*

Cook Islands, stimulus/referent elections data, 199*t*

Correlation coefficient, 26*f*, 74*b*

Costa Rica: governance score, 30, 30*f*, 31; stimulus/referent elections data, 199*t*

Cote D'Ivore, stimulus/referent elections data, 199*t*

Country governance, 51–57; causality, 52–54; country politics and, 55–56; country size and, 54; country wealth and, 55; definition of, 4–5; endogenous variables, 53*f*; environmental effects on, 174–175; exogenous variables, 53*f*, 54–56; measurement of, 19–45; model, 53*f*; nature of, 173–174; no parties vs. nonpartisan countries, 123–133; party system effects on, 175–177; party system variables, 53*f*; viscosity of party systems and, 167–168; without party systems, 123–133

Country politics, 55–56

Country size, 54, 59–77; absolute size, 60; country wealth and, 85–90; effect on governance indicators, 53–54, 75*f*, 175; effects of, 66–75; electoral democracies and, 169*f*; measuring, 60–66; party system competitiveness and, 145

Country wealth, 55, 81–91; country size and, 85–90; effects of, 85–90; electoral democracies and, 169*f*; governance and, 53–54, 175; measuring, 82–85; party system competitiveness and, 142–145

Crime, 185–186*t*

Croatia, stimulus/referent elections data, 199*t*

Cross-sectional design, 52

Cuba: referent elections, 110; stimulus/referent elections data, 199*t*

Cyprus, stimulus/referent elections data, 200*t*

Czech Republic, stimulus/referent elections data, 200*t*

D

Dahl, Robert, 59

Dalton, Russell, 115

Democracy: *See also* Party systems; electoral, 166–167; governance and, 11–13, 55–56; stability and, 166–168

Democratic accountability, 193*t*

Democratic governance concept, 12

Democratic People's Republic of Korea. *See* North Korea

Denmark, stimulus/referent elections data, 200*t*

Dictatorships, 29–30

Djibouti, stimulus/referent elections data, 200*t*

Doherty, Ivan, 151

Dominica, stimulus/referent elections data, 200*t*

Dominican Republic, stimulus/referent elections data, 200*t*

Dunleavy, Patrick, 154

Duverger, Maurice, 95

country wealth and, 53–54; definition of, 3–5; democracy and, 11–13, 55–56; domain of application, 5–6; European, 6–7; measuring, 33; no parties vs. nonpartisan countries, 123–133; outputs/outcomes, 7; party systems and, 53–54, 56; process, 6–7; qualitative dimensions, 10–11; quantitative measurement, 8–10; structure, 6; without party systems, 123–133

Governance scores: control of corruption, 36*f*; government effectiveness, 35*f*; margin of errors, 32*b*; political stability, 39*f*; rule of law, 34*f*; voice and accountability, 38*f*

Governing parties, 98

Government: contracts, 185*t*; party government, 98; popularly elected, 98; public opinion and, 98

Government Effectiveness (GE), 21; aggregation and, 156; correlation with other governance indicators, 25*f*, 27–28; effects of country size, wealth and party system on, 169*f*; governance scores, 35*f*; nonrepresentative sources, 188*t*; party system competitiveness and, 140; representative sources, 187–188*t*; variable distributions, 41*f*

Greece, stimulus/referent elections data, 200*t*

Green parties, 149

Greenland, 68*b*

Grenada, stimulus/referent elections data, 200*t*

Gross domestic product (GDP). *See* GDP (Gross domestic product)

Gross domestic variable, 55

Gryzmala-Busse, Anna, 141, 151

Guam, stimulus/referent elections data, 200*t*

Guatemala, stimulus/referent elections data, 200*t*

Guinea, stimulus/referent elections data, 200*t*

Guinea-Bissau, stimulus/referent elections data, 201*t*

Guyana, stimulus/referent elections data, 201*t*

H

Haiti, stimulus/referent elections data, 201*t*

Handbook of Political Science, 3

Henjak, Andrija, 151, 165

Hobbes, Thomas, 12*b*

Honduras, stimulus/referent elections data, 201*t*

Hong Kong: rule of law, 68; stimulus/referent elections data, 201*t*

Hungary, stimulus/referent elections data, 201*t*

I

Iceland: area, 73*t*; control of corruption, 36*f*, 41*f*; GDP per capita, 83, 84*f*; governance scores, 30, 32, 35–36; government effectiveness, 35*f*, 41*f*; number of parties, 23*b*; party system competitiveness, 138*f*; political stability, 39*f*, 45*f*; regulatory quality, 37*f*, 43*f*; rule of law scores, 34*f*, 40*f*, 73*t*; stimulus/referent elections data, 201*t*; viscosity score, 165; voice and accountability, 38*f*, 44*f*

Icelandic Althing, 156

Impact of Parties, The (book), 96

Import regulation, 190*t*

Income, 63

India: country size, 60; population, 61*f*, 68*b*; stimulus/referent elections data, 201*t*

Indonesia: area, 68*b*; population, 61*f*, 68*b*; stimulus/referent elections data, 201*t*

Institutional failure, 187*t*

Institutional permanence, 193*t*

Insurgency, 194*t*

Internal conflict, 195*t*

Inter-Parliamentary Union, 106

About the Authors

Kenneth Janda works in American government, political parties, elementary statistics, and computer methods. His books include *Political Parties: A Cross-National Survey, Parties and Their Environments: Limits to Reform?*, and the American government textbook *The Challenge of Democracy*. He co-founded and co-edits the international journal *Party Politics*. In 2000, he won a "Lifetime Achievement" award from the American Political Science Association for his research on political parties. In 2005, he was a co-winner of the APSA Award for Best Instructional Software, and in 2009 he received the APSA's Frank J. Goodnow Award for service to the profession.

Jin-Young Kwak is former chair and current professor in the Department of Political Science at Konkuk University in Seoul, South Korea. Her co-authored Korean books include *Governance: Diffusion and Internalization, American Governance in the 21st Century, Understanding Contemporary Party Politics*, and *The Politics of Governance*. She also publishes widely on electoral behavior, women's rights, and regional issues in Asia. She currently serves as Secretary General of the Korean Association of Party Studies.